For my parents

Contents

Acknowledgements

For helpful comments on this book, invaluable discussion of its themes, or general support and inspiration, I would like to thank the following individuals: Alan Cardew, Adrian Cunningham, David Curtis, Herbert van Erkelens, Karl Figlio, James Hall, Mike Johnson, Stephen Karcher, Shiho Main, Victor Mansfield, Jan Marlan, Renos Papadopoulos, James Plaskett, Robert Segal, Andrew Samuels and David Tacey. Thanks, too, to Kate Hawes, Helen Pritt and Dawn Harris at Brunner-Routledge for their excellent editorial support.

Grateful acknowledgement is made for permission to reprint from the following previously published material:

Jung, C.G., *Collected works*, vol. 8, *The Structure and Dynamics of the Psyche*, 2nd ed, G. Adler and R.F.C Hull (eds and trans) 1969, published by Taylor & Francis.

Jung. C.G., *Collected Works*, vol. 8, *The Structure and Dynamics of the Psyche*, 2nd ed, G. Adler and R.F.C Hull (eds and trans). Copyright © 1969 by Princeton University Press. Reprinted by permission of Princeton University Press.

Jung. C.G., *Collected Works*, vol. 10, *Civilization in Translation*, 2nd ed, G. Adler and R.F.C Hull (eds and trans) 1970, published by Taylor & Francis.

Jung. C.G., *Collected Works*, vol. 10, *Civilization in Translation*, 2nd ed, G. Adler and R.F.C Hull (eds and trans). Copyright © 1970 by Princeton University Press. Reprinted by permission of Princeton University Press.

Extracts originally appearing in *Harvest: International Journal for Jungian Studies* Volume 46 Number 2 (2000) under the title 'Religion, Science and Synchronicity', reprinted with kind permission of Karnac, London, www.karnacbooks.com

'Religion, Science, and the New Age', in J. Pearson (ed) *Belief Beyond Boundaries: Wicca, Celtic Spirituality, and the New Age*, 2002 Open University Press.

'Introduction,' in R. Main (ed) *Jung on Synchronicity and the Paranormal*, 1997 Routledge.

Religious experience is *numinous*, as Rudolf Otto calls it, and for me, as a psychologist, this experience differs from all others in the way it transcends the ordinary categories of space, time, and causality. Recently I have put a great deal of study into synchronicity (briefly, the 'rupture of time'), and I have established that it closely resembles numinous experiences where space, time, and causality are abolished.

From Jung's 1952 interview with Mircea Eliade, in W. McGuire and R. F. C. Hull, *C. G. Jung Speaking: Interviews and Encounters*

Introduction

A radical challenge

Analytical psychology, the psychological model developed by Carl Gustav Jung (1875–1961), presents a set of ideas that in many respects is radically at variance with the embedded assumptions of mainstream modern culture in the West. With its concepts of the collective unconscious, universal archetypes, the teleological process of individuation, the transpersonal self, and the epistemological priority of psychic over physical reality, Jung's model champions notions that are not easily squared with the materialistic, reductive, naturalistic, and causal emphases of modern western culture. On the one hand, this variance is one of the strengths and attractions of analytical psychology, for it provides a perspective from which the mainstream cultural assumptions can be criticised, relativised, and prevented from too readily acquiring the status of unquestioned truths. On the other hand, the variance is unfortunate, for Jung himself, later Jungians, and others interested in analytical psychological ideas have wished to make positive and acceptable contributions to mainstream western culture. Jung, for instance, was at pains to align himself with orthodox science, often wrote in a style and published in outlets that would ensure him a wide general readership, and proudly referred to his honorary doctorates from Oxford and Harvard when his scientific and academic credibility were impugned (1973: 328–9; 1976: 232). Similar aspirations have been pursued, admittedly in greatly changed intellectual circumstances, by contemporary Jungians, and, as an indication of their success, analytical psychology can now be found not just on many academic syllabuses but even, in some universities, as entire degree schemes (see Kirsch 2000: 55–6, 121–3). Strong tensions remain (see Tacey 1997a; Brooke 1997; Papadopoulos 1997b; Ulanov 1997), and questions have been raised about whether this accommodation with the mainstream may sometimes have come at a cost to the integrity of Jung's ideas (Tacey 1997b). However, it is difficult to imagine that Jung would have been displeased that his ideas are enjoying this measure of accommodation.[1]

This book is about an idea of Jung's that arguably presents his most radical challenge of all to mainstream cultural assumptions and accordingly seems the most difficult of all to integrate into mainstream thought: the idea of synchronicity. In its basic form, this idea is not difficult to understand. Life frequently presents coincidences in which a person's dream or thought is matched by something that happens in the physical world, without it being possible that either event could have caused the other. Sometimes such coincidences seem especially meaningful to their experiencers, who are therefore prompted to wonder whether something more than mere chance may be involved. For example, Jung relates the following episode:

> I walk with a woman patient in a wood. She tells me about the first dream in her life that had made an everlasting impression upon her. She had seen a spectral fox coming down the stairs in her parental home. At this moment a real fox comes out of the trees not 40 yards away and walks quietly on the path ahead of us for several minutes. The animal behaves as if it were a partner in the human situation.
>
> (Jung 1973: 395)

Properly appreciated, the existence of such 'meaningful coincidences' requires, in Jung's view, a fundamental revision of the prevalent scientific, religious, and commonsense views of the world. For reasons that will become clearer as we proceed, synchronicity suggests that there are uncaused events, that matter has a psychic aspect, that the psyche can relativise time and space, and that there may be a dimension of objective meaning accessible to but not created by humans. The implications of all or any of this are far-reaching. If there are uncaused events, particularly at the level of ordinary human experience, this means that our familiar forms of explanation in terms of later events being caused by earlier ones will have to be supplemented. If matter has an inalienable psychic aspect, then scientific descriptions of the world that aspire towards completeness can no longer be framed solely in material terms but will have to take account of psychic properties of meaning and value. If the psyche can relativise time and space, then it becomes possible for temporally and spatially distant events somehow to involve themselves in the here and now without any normal channel of causal transmission. If there is a dimension of objective meaning, this implies that the meaning we experience is not always or entirely our subjective creation, individually or as a species, but that we may be woven into an order of meaning that transcends our human perspective.

In view of the radical nature of these and related claims and implications, it is not surprising that the idea of synchronicity tends to provoke strong reactions in those who encounter it. By some it is enthusiastically embraced, by others scathingly dismissed, and by others again studiously disregarded. The enthusiasm is understandable because the idea of synchronicity gives expression – and a major psychologist's stamp of approval – to a whole range of concerns that, while currently marginalised, were formerly integral to both the popular and the official world-views of western culture. Two or three centuries of the dominance of reason and science are insufficient to repress, let alone eradicate, these millennia-old habits of thought. However, the dismissiveness is also understandable because the benefits of reason and science are real and substantial and not to be lightly compromised by the admission of what appears to be the very kind of superstition from which reason and science struggled so long and hard to free themselves. Moreover, even a sympathetic commentator on the idea of synchronicity is hard put not to find Jung's presentation of it at times seriously confused. It is understandable, too, why many who encounter it should choose to disregard the idea of synchronicity, not only because its presentation is confused but also because its proponents are often embarrassingly superficial, its implications are disturbing, and, since the current consensus world-view appears to work well enough on the whole, the introduction of such a radical idea seems quite simply unnecessary. Fortunately, at least one further kind of response to the idea of synchronicity is possible – that of respectfully sticking with it and sympathetically yet critically asking what Jung really meant by the idea and why it was so important to him.

Jung must have anticipated that his writings on synchronicity would lessen the credibility of his psychological model in the eyes of many, and it is doubtless for that reason that he refrained for almost thirty years from publishing more than a few hints of his thinking on the topic (1952b: par. 816; 1973: 378–9). Nevertheless, it is clear that he attached great importance to synchronicity, both practically and theoretically. In the Foreword to his essay 'Synchronicity: An Acausal Connecting Principle', he comments on 'how much these inner experiences meant to my patients' as well as how they 'open up a very obscure field that is philosophically of the greatest importance' (1952b: par. 816). Once he had published his ideas, he thereafter regularly referred to them at appropriate points in his subsequent works as well as in his voluminous correspondence.

Jung's most important works on synchronicity are his essay of 1952, 'Synchronicity: An Acausal Connecting Principle' (1952b), originally published alongside a paper by Wolfgang Pauli in a book entitled *The Interpretation of Nature and the Psyche* (Jung and Pauli 1955), and his shorter paper, 'On Synchronicity' (1951b), originally delivered as a lecture at the Eranos conference of 1951.[2] These were preceded by two shorter but also important expositions made in the context of discussions of the *I Ching* (1930: pars. 77–85; 1950a: pars. 966–74). Occasional but illuminating observations occur throughout other volumes of Jung's *Collected Works*, especially volumes 8, 9i, 9ii, 10, 11, 12, 14, 15, 16 and 18. Additional anecdotes and insights can be found in *Memories, Dreams, Reflections* (1961), the two volumes of Jung's general *Letters* (1973, 1976), the correspondence between Jung and Pauli (Meier 2001), seminars (especially Jung 1928–30, 1930–4, 1934–9), and interviews (McGuire and Hull 1978). All of this material has been thoroughly examined for the present work.

Among Jung's close associates, Marie-Louise von Franz is the one who took up his work on synchronicity most energetically. She published several books dealing extensively with the idea, in particular its connection to divination (1980) and its possible role in effecting a rapprochement between psychology and physics (1974, 1992). Her writings often present Jung's thinking in terms clearer than Jung's own and usefully connect the idea with recent work in science that was not available to Jung. However, she mostly confines herself to retracing the lines of inquiry marked out by Jung and in general does not achieve the critical distance needed in order to address squarely the problems in the idea of synchronicity.

Excepting Jung's own works, the three books on synchronicity that I have found most helpful are those by Robert Aziz (1990), Victor Mansfield (1995) and Paul Bishop (2000). Aziz's scholarly study, *C. G. Jung's Psychology of Religion and Synchronicity* (1990), examines the significance of synchronicity for Jung's psychology of religion, using the lens of Ninian Smart's dimensional model for the phenomenological study of world-views. Most helpfully, Aziz illuminates the role in synchronicity of the psychological processes of compensation and individuation. He also carefully analyses many of Jung's own synchronistic experiences and interpretations of them. In part, the present work takes inspiration from and builds on Aziz's study. However, there has seemed a need to range more widely and, on many points, to probe more deeply and critically than Aziz in each of the areas of theory, contexts and applications.

Mansfield's book *Synchronicity, Science, and Soul-Making* (1995) explores synchronicity in relation to Jungian psychology, modern physics, and Middle Way Buddhism. He connects these disparate perspectives by showing for each the central relevance of meaning, space–time transcendence, acausality, and unity. Like Aziz, Mansfield shows that synchronistic events draw their meaning from relationship to Jung's core psychological processes of compensation and individuation, arguing further that this is what distinguishes them from parapsychological events. The paradoxical properties now firmly established in relativity and quantum physics are invoked to lessen resistance to analogous properties in synchronicity. Meanwhile, an idealist version of the Buddhist emptiness doctrine provides a philosophical framework within which synchronicity appears both intelligible and natural, though unresolved dissonance between the Jungian and Buddhist perspectives is acknowledged. Mansfield's book is a careful, deep, and challenging study, exemplary in its cautious handling of the relationship between physics and psychology and inspiring in its exploration of connections between the three fields of psychology, science and religion (see also Mansfield 2002). However, the focus and balance of Mansfield's book, with its concern for the contemporary plausibility of synchronicity and its extensive discussions of physics and Buddhism, differ from those of the present study, which is more concerned with the importance of synchronicity for Jung and for the psychological model he bequeathed.

Bishop's *Synchronicity and Intellectual Intuition in Kant, Swedenborg, and Jung* (2000) is an erudite contextual study that elucidates important sources of the concept of synchronicity in Jung's preoccupation with the 'mind–body problem' and the notion of 'intellectual intuition' in German Idealist philosophy. The focus of the book on this one context means that it has been of limited specific use for the present study, which has broader aims. However, the thoroughness of Bishop's work stands as a paradigm of the depth of research that ideally needs be undertaken on each of the many aspects of synchronicity broached in the following pages.

In addition to these scholarly studies, there are several accessibly yet intelligently written books on synchronicity of a more general or introductory character, among which those by Jean Shinoda Bolen (1979), Allan Combs and Mark Holland (1994) and Robert Hopcke (1997) especially succeed in conveying the richness and fascination of the phenomenon. Another general study, by Ira Progoff (1973), remains more at the level of abstract discussion and meditation, as does the book by F. David Peat (1987), which seems to take its inspiration at least as much from the physics theories of David Bohm as from the psychological model of Jung.

Some of the most helpful discussions of synchronicity have appeared in articles and book chapters. Many of these discussions have a clinical emphasis, though usually with theoretical reflections added (e.g., Fordham 1957, 1962; Williams 1957, 1963b; Dieckmann 1976; Gordon 1983; Wharton 1986; Hopcke 1990). In others, the theoretical component is foremost, either clarifying Jung's thought or connecting it to other fields (e.g., Meier 1963; Gammon 1973; Jaffé 1967, 1979; Keutzer 1982, 1984; Kelly 1993). Others again explore historical aspects of synchronicity (e.g., Lindorff 1995a, 1995b; Zabriskie 1995; Main 2000).

By no means all the work on what Jung called synchronicity has been done within the framework of analytical psychology. Coincidences have also attracted the attention of psychical researchers and parapsychologists (e.g., Johnson 1899; Koestler 1972; Hardy *et al.* 1973; Beloff 1977; Grattan-Guinness 1978, 1983; Inglis 1990; Henry 1993), not to mention psychoanalysts (e.g., Freud 1919, 1921a, 1921b, 1925, 1933; Devereux 1953; Eisenbud 1983, 1990; Faber 1998). A comprehensive study of the phenomenon of meaningful coincidence would have to engage in detail with the arguments stemming from these perspectives.

Most of the studies referred to in the above review provide at least some examples of meaningful coincidences, and some of the studies include substantial collections. A final category of works that can be mentioned is those which have as their principal aim simply to present accounts of coincidences (e.g., Vaughan 1989; Anderson 1995; Cousineau 1997; Plaskett 2000). While not devoid of theoretical reflection, these works are generally more content to let the anecdotes speak for themselves. They provide a reminder of the sheer enigma that Jung and other theorists in this area are struggling to understand.

In spite of all the work that has been done on synchronicity, there remains a need for further serious explorations of the topic. In particular, there is need for a closer examination of how synchronicity fits into Jung's overall psychological model and what is the significance of its apparent inconsistencies; a wider investigation of the personal, intellectual and social contexts of Jung's thinking on synchronicity; and a more thorough consideration of how Jung himself applied the theory beyond the clinical setting. Addressing these needs, the present book aims to clarify what Jung really meant by synchronicity, why the idea was so important to him, and how it informed his thinking about modern western culture. It approaches these questions in a critical yet sympathetic manner and especially tries to avoid being deflected by the difficulties of Jung's writings into either selective interpretation or exasperated rejection of them.

The study in the following pages focuses as much as possible on the actual words Jung wrote and uttered about synchronicity. The discussion is largely textual and theoretical but adopts a variety of disciplinary perspectives – psychological, historical, philosophical, sociological and religionist. This multidisciplinary approach is largely forced upon the researcher by Jung's own diverse and eclectic handling of the topic. The multiplicity of perspectives is both a strength, in that it allows for a relatively comprehensive examination of Jung's theory, and a limitation, in that it restricts the space that can be devoted to exploration of any one perspective. Nevertheless, the present study may still go deeper into many areas than previous studies have succeeded in doing, partly because the comprehensive approach enables pertinent areas for deeper exploration to be more accurately identified.

The present study does not engage extensively with post-Jungian work. The aim has primarily been to clarify Jung's own understanding both of synchronicity and of the model of analytical psychology in relation to which the notion of synchronicity was elaborated. Accordingly, the Jungian psychology explored in this book is largely 'classical', with little discussion of how synchronicity might look from 'developmental' or 'archetypal' perspectives in which the theoretical and clinical emphases differ, sometimes quite markedly, from Jung's own (see Samuels 1985; Young-Eisendrath and Dawson 1997). Nevertheless, this book should still have value in relation to post-Jungian revisions, for those revisions will have been made based on a particular understanding of Jung's work and so could be affected by any enrichment or modification of that understanding prompted by the following study.

Similarly, because the emphasis is on clarifying Jung's thought, there has been only limited discussion of parapsychological, psychoanalytic, and other alternative theoretical models for explaining experiences of meaningful coincidence. Where such discussion occurs, as in Chapter 1, the purpose is mainly to bring out by contrast what is distinctive about Jung's model rather than to engage in comparative evaluation. The book is a focused exploration of Jung's idea of synchronicity, not of the phenomenon of meaningful coincidence *per se*. Again, the book aims not to evaluate the idea of synchronicity but simply to understand it and its role within Jung's thinking. Indeed, one of the motivations for the book is precisely that the idea has prompted too much premature evaluation, both positive and negative, and that what is needed instead is fuller clarification of the idea in its own terms and in relation to the body of work of which it is a part.

The book is in three parts, each containing two chapters. In Part 1, 'The Theory of Synchronicity',[3] I examine in detail Jung's exposition of synchronicity, presenting several perspectives and features that have not been sufficiently addressed in previous literature but are necessary for an adequate appreciation of the topic. First, in Chapter 1, 'Synchronicity and Analytical Psychology', I attempt to provide a coherent account of the definition and dynamics of the theory and its relationship to Jung's psychological model as a whole. This includes briefly expounding the principal concepts of analytical psychology as classically understood by Jung, as well as considering the role of synchronicity in Jung's late revisions of the concepts of the collective unconscious and archetypes. In this chapter I also briefly mention some alternative theoretical models that have been proposed to explain meaningful coincidences in order to indicate what is distinctive about Jung's theory.

In Chapter 2, 'Intellectual Difficulties', I take a more critical look at Jung's theory. I survey Jung's actual examples of synchronicity throughout his writings and consider to what extent his definitions of synchronicity adequately account for the phenomena he presents. From both his examples and his definitions, as well as from other characterisations he offers, I note a range of crucial points about synchronicity on which Jung appears to be uncertain or confused. Closer examination of the core concepts involved in the theory – time, acausality, meaning and probability – reveals further difficulties. I assess to what extent these difficulties with the theory might be resolvable through fuller consideration of its basis in analytical psychology, through a deeper and more up-to-date understanding of some of the disciplines and fields of knowledge on which Jung drew, or through a chronological appreciation of how his thinking on synchronicity developed. Even after such attempts at resolution, however, many aspects of Jung's theory remain problematic.

Rather than be discouraged by these intellectual difficulties, Part 2 of the study, 'Synchronicity in Context', attempts to gain deeper and broader perspectives on the theory by looking more fully at its personal, social and intellectual contexts. In Chapter 3, 'Sources and Influences', I examine the numerous acknowledged and unacknowledged sources of and influences on Jung's thinking about synchronicity. These include personal experiences, spiritualism, philosophy, astrology, the *I Ching*, analytical psychological theory and practice, psychical research and parapsychology, physics, and the history of religions and western esotericism. I consider how this multiplicity of sources and influences provided Jung with differing kinds of insight, perspective and encouragement, and how this diversity may have contributed to the lack of overall coherence of his presentation.

In Chapter 4, 'Religion, Science, and Synchronicity', I raise the question as to whether there is a perspective from which the confusions, uncertainties and other difficulties with Jung's presentation of his theory of synchronicity might be better understood. I suggest that Jung's lifelong struggle with the relationship between religion and science might provide such a perspective. After briefly discussing some historical interactions between religion and science, I examine how analytical psychology in general and the theory of synchronicity in particular constitute an attempt to integrate these two domains – or rather to articulate a third domain that inalienably participates in and connects the other two. From this perspective, I then review the intellectual difficulties noted in Chapter 2 and consider to what extent they may have been clarified.

Part 3 of the study, 'Synchronicity Applied', turns from theoretical and contextual considerations to Jung's explicit and implicit application of synchronicity as both a support for and an instance of his critique of modern western culture. Chapter 5, 'Synchronicity and Jung's Critique of Science, Religion and Society', discusses first Jung's perception of modern western culture; then his overall analytical psychological critique of that culture; and finally the specific contribution of synchronicity to that critique, focusing in turn on the three core areas of science, religion and society.

In Chapter 6, 'Synchronicity and the Spiritual Revolution', I look at some of the connections between synchronicity and religion more broadly. I focus in particular on a trend, already emergent in Jung's day and now widespread, towards the detraditionalisation and privatisation of religion, or rather the rejection of 'religion' in favour of 'spirituality'. I consider how synchronicity may support this move by providing a framework for understanding a wide range of traditional religious concepts and themes with minimal or no reference to their traditional theological and cultural settings. I then look closely at one widespread contemporary manifestation of religion that has been called variously New Age, alternative, or holistic spirituality, noting the numerous affinities between this kind of spirituality and Jung's theories of synchronicity and analytical psychology generally. A widely respected definition of this trend in contemporary spirituality as 'a popular western culture criticism expressed in terms of a secularized esotericism' (Hanegraaff 1998: 522) provides the basis for a detailed discussion of New Age spirituality in the light of the theory of synchronicity.

Finally, 'Conclusion: The Rupture of Time', summarises the findings of the study, discusses some of their broader implications as well as their limitations, and points towards possibilities for future work.

Part I

The theory of synchronicity

Chapter 1

Synchronicity and analytical psychology

The theory of synchronicity emerged within the framework of analytical psychology, and analytical psychological assumptions underpin much of what is most distinctive about the theory. It is therefore appropriate to begin this study by looking in detail at how the theory of synchronicity, as Jung presented it, is embedded within his overall psychological model. Many previous studies from a Jungian orientation have inevitably addressed this relationship, often in an illuminating way (for example, Fordham 1957; Williams 1957; Bolen 1979; Wharton 1986; Aziz 1990; von Franz 1992; Mansfield 1995; Bright 1997). However, the present chapter aims to examine a wider range of aspects of the relationship than previous studies and to do so more systematically. Indeed, it is organised so that it might serve as an introduction not only to synchronicity but also to Jung's basic understanding of analytical psychology. An additional aim is to present the theory of synchronicity in an optimally coherent and integrated form, without for the time being probing too deeply into possible difficulties with it. The justification for such an approach is that the theory touches on so many controversial issues that it is all too easy to be deflected into evaluations or interpretations of it in terms of one's prior understanding of some other field or phenomenon, with the result that the theory of synchronicity itself never comes to be adequately appreciated in its own terms. The acknowledged difficulties with the theory will not be ignored but will be reserved for discussion in Chapter 2.

The following account involves an initial presentation of the theory through defining and illustrating synchronicity. Then comes an exposition of the basic model of analytical psychology that forms both the implicit background of the theory and the explicit framework into which Jung wishes to integrate it. Partly accompanying and partly following this, the chapter looks in detail at how synchronicity works in the light of analytical psychology. It also notes the contribution of synchronicity to some significant and far-reaching modifications of analytical psychology. The chapter concludes by briefly mentioning some alternative theoretical models that have been proposed to explain experiences of meaningful coincidence, since comparison with these highlights what is distinctive about Jung's theory.

Jung's illustration and definition of synchronicity

Jung presents the following incident as 'a paradigm of the innumerable cases of meaningful coincidence that have been observed not only by me but by many others, and recorded in large collections' (1951b: par. 983). The account is from his shorter 1951 essay on synchronicity. Another version appears in the 1952 essay (1952b: pars. 843, 845), and my discussion later will also draw on that, when it includes pertinent details not mentioned here. In his 1951 essay Jung wrote:

> My example concerns a young woman patient who, in spite of efforts made on both sides, proved to be psychologically inaccessible. The difficulty lay in the fact that she always knew better about everything. Her excellent education had provided her with a weapon ideally suited to this purpose, namely a highly polished Cartesian rationalism with an impeccably 'geometrical' idea of reality. After several fruitless attempts to sweeten her rationalism with a somewhat more human understanding, I had to confine myself to the hope that something unexpected and irrational would turn up, something that would burst the intellectual retort into which she had sealed herself. Well, I was sitting opposite her one day, with my back to the window, listening to her flow of rhetoric. She had had an impressive dream the night before, in which someone had given her a golden scarab – a costly piece of jewellery. While she was still telling me this dream, I heard something behind me gently tapping on the window. I turned round and saw that it was a fairly large flying insect that was knocking against the window-pane in the obvious effort to get into the dark room. This seemed to me very strange. I opened the window immediately and caught the insect in the air as it flew in. It was a scarabaeid beetle, or common rose-chafer (*Cetonia aurata*), whose gold-green colour most nearly resembles that of a golden scarab. I handed the beetle to my patient with the words, 'Here is your scarab.' This experience punctured the desired hole in her rationalism and broke the ice of her intellectual resistance. The treatment could now be continued with satisfactory results.
>
> (Jung 1951b: par. 982)

Jung defined synchronicity in a variety of ways. Most succinctly, he defined it as 'meaningful coincidence' (1952b: par. 827), 'acausal parallelism' (1963: 342), or 'an acausal connecting principle' (1952b). More fully, he defined it as 'the simultaneous occurrence of a certain psychic state with one or more external events which appear as meaningful parallels to the momentary subjective state' (ibid.: par. 850). In the above example, the *psychic state* is indicated by the patient telling Jung her dream of being given a scarab. The *parallel external event* is the appearance and behaviour of the real scarab. The telling of the dream and the appearance of the real scarab were *simultaneous*. Neither of these events discernibly or plausibly caused the other by any normal means, so their relationship is *acausal*. Nevertheless, the events parallel each other in such unlikely detail that it is difficult to escape the impression that they are indeed *connected*, albeit acausally. Moreover, this acausal connection of events is both symbolically informative (as we shall see) and has a deeply emotive and transforming impact on the patient and in these senses is clearly *meaningful*.

The features of such coincidences that Jung most emphasises are the simultaneity of their component events, their acausality, and their meaning. He frankly acknowledged that the first of these features, simultaneity, is not straightforward. For there are other events that Jung wants to designate as synchronistic where the element of simultaneity is not so apparent, events that either cannot at the time be known to be simultaneous (as, for example, with apparently clairvoyant visions) or seemingly are not simultaneous at all (as, for example, with apparently precognitive dreams). He offers examples of both these kinds of synchronicities. His example involving events whose simultaneity could not be known at the time is the following incident that had also fascinated Kant. It concerns the Swedish mystic Emanuel Swedenborg's well-attested vision of the great fire in Stockholm in 1759. Swedenborg was at a party in Gothenburg about 200 miles from Stockholm when the vision occurred. He told his companions at six o'clock in the evening that the fire had started, then described its course over the next two hours, exclaiming in relief at eight o'clock that it had at last been extinguished, just three doors from his own house. All these details were confirmed when messengers arrived in Gothenburg from Stockholm over the next few days (1952b: pars. 912, 915).

Jung's example involving events that seemingly are not simultaneous at all concerns a student friend of his whose father had promised him a trip to Spain if he passed his final examinations satisfactorily. The friend then had a dream of seeing various things in a Spanish city: a particular square, a Gothic cathedral, and, around a certain corner, a carriage drawn by two cream-coloured horses. Shortly afterwards, having successfully passed his examinations, he actually visited Spain for the first time and encountered all the details from his dream in reality (Jung 1951b: par. 973).[1]

In order to account for these further kinds of coincidences, Jung presents, in his 1951 essay, the following three-pronged definition:

All the phenomena I have mentioned can be grouped under three categories:
1. The coincidence of a psychic state in the observer with a simultaneous, objective, external event that corresponds to the psychic state or content (e.g., the scarab), where there is no evidence of a causal connection between the psychic state and the external event, and where, considering the psychic relativity of space and time, such a connection is not even conceivable.
2. The coincidence of a psychic state with a corresponding (more or less simultaneous) external event taking place outside the observer's field of perception, i.e., at a distance, and only verifiable afterward . . .
3. The coincidence of a psychic state with a corresponding, not yet existent

future event that is distant in time and can likewise only be verified afterward.

In groups 2 and 3 the coinciding events are not yet present in the observer's field of perception, but have been anticipated in time in so far as they can only be verified afterward. For this reason I call such events *synchronistic*, which is not to be confused with *synchronous*.

(Jung 1951b: pars. 984–5)

The first prong of this definition adequately captures events such as the scarab incident. The second prong aims to capture events such as happened to Swedenborg, where the objective event (the Stockholm fire) occurs at a distance, can only be verified afterwards, but verification of which is 'anticipated in time' by a psychic image (Swedenborg's vision). The third prong aims to capture events such as happened to Jung's student friend, where the objective event (encountering the scene in the Spanish city) occurs in the future, can only be verified afterwards, but it is 'anticipated in time' by a psychic image (the student's dream).

Jung makes no such attempt to accommodate exceptions when it comes to acausality. As the first prong of his definition states, the possibility of a causal connection between the psychic state and external event of a synchronicity is 'not even conceivable'.

Regarding the factor of meaning, Jung could rest with noting that experiencers of remarkable coincidences, as a matter of record, often do attribute meaning to them. However, he goes further than this and provides, albeit largely implicitly, a sophisticated theoretical account of why people attribute this meaning. This account converts Jung's work on synchronicity from the level of phenomenological description to that of theoretical explanation. To appreciate this theoretical explanation of the meaningfulness of coincidences requires that we briefly consider Jung's overall psychological model and its principal connections to his theory of synchronicity.

Jung's psychological model and its connections to synchronicity

For Jung, the human psyche consists of consciousness and the unconscious, and his psychological work, including his work on synchronicity, was primarily concerned with elucidating and promoting the relationship between them.

Consciousness

Consciousness, for Jung, is defined in terms of the relationship of psychic contents to the ego. It both is this relationship, insofar as it is perceived by the ego, and is the function or activity that maintains the relationship (1921: par. 700). Consciousness comprises all the experiences, memories, thoughts, imaginings, intentions, and so on, of which the ego is aware, as well as the process that keeps these contents related to and perceived by the ego. Psychic contents of which the ego is not aware, even if they happen to be related to the ego, are unconscious (ibid.). Jung's psychology is much concerned with the development of consciousness; that is, becoming aware of an ever-wider range of one's psychic activity and thereby increasing one's ability to act intentionally in relation to that psychic activity.

Any synchronicity that comes to be recognised as such clearly must involve consciousness. However, synchronicities not only involve but also can enhance consciousness by disclosing its connection both to the unconscious psyche and to the outer world. For example, the scarab coincidence connected the rationalistic conscious attitude of Jung's patient with 'something unexpected and irrational' that turned up both from her unconscious, in the form of the dream about a scarab jewel, and from the outer physical world, in the form of the real scarabaeid beetle that appeared at the window.

The *ego*, or ego-complex, that is so important for consciousness Jung defines as 'a complex of ideas which constitutes the centre of my field of consciousness and appears to possess a high degree of continuity and identity' (1921: par. 706). Because psychic contents are only conscious insofar as they are related to and perceived by the ego, Jung notes that the ego is 'as much a content as a condition of consciousness' (ibid.). In other words, without the ego one could not be conscious of anything; with it, one can be conscious of, among other things, the ego itself. Jung stresses that the ego is one psychic complex among others, and therefore is not identical with the entire psyche. Nor, though it is the centre of consciousness, is it the centre of the entire psyche, for the psyche consists of the unconscious as well as consciousness (ibid.). The primary role of the ego, for Jung, is to discriminate among objects, qualities and states that originally are psychically undifferentiated. For example, it is with the development of ego consciousness that a child differentiates itself from its parents, an adolescent discriminates moral and social values, and a psychologically maturing adult distinguishes images of people from the real people onto whom those images have been projected.

The relationship between synchronicity and the ego is a delicate one. On the one hand, the discrimination and continuity of the ego are essential for the task of interpreting and integrating the meaning of synchronicities. If Jung's patient does not have a sufficiently consolidated ego either to recognise the relationship between her conscious attitude and the synchronicity or to reflect in a sustained way on its significance, any potential of the synchronicity for promoting her psychological development will be lost. On the other hand, the limited perspective of the ego can obstruct realisation of the meaning of the unconscious contents emerging in the synchronicity. In the case of Jung's patient, the extreme rationalism with which her ego was identified had already made her 'psychologically inaccessible' to all forms of treatment. There must have been a risk that the same rationalistic orientation could have been used to explain away rather than explore the implications of her synchronistic experience. However, whether as an aid or an obstruction, the ego comes into operation in synchronicities only after the actual event of the synchronicity has taken place. The synchronicity itself, being acausal, unpredictable, and altogether irrational, bypasses the ego and its mechanisms of defence and control. The ego cannot resist the occurrence of synchronicities but can only take up a position on their acknowledgement and interpretation. In the case of Jung's patient, the content that emerged from the bypassing of the ego also specifically challenged the ego. Jung's statement that, following the synchronicity, the treatment of the patient 'could now be continued with satisfactory results' suggests that in this case she managed to rise to the challenge.

The consciousness of people varies not only according to the particular contents of which it is comprised, derived from each person's individual life history, but also according to their *psychological type*. Jung recognised two basic psychological attitudes and four basic functions of consciousness. The combination of attitude and functions predominant in a person's consciousness determines that person's psychological type. A psychological attitude, for Jung, is 'a readiness of the psyche to act or react in a certain way' (1921: par. 687). The two basic such attitudes are *extraversion* and *introversion*. Those with an extraverted attitude habitually direct their energy towards objects in the external world, while those with an introverted attitude habitually direct their energy towards objects in the internal world. A psychological function, for Jung, is 'a particular form of psychic activity that remains the same in principle under different conditions' (ibid.: par. 731). He identified four such functions: *thinking, feeling, sensation* and *intuition*. Briefly, thinking tells us what something is, feeling what its value is, sensation what it is, and intuition what its possibilities are. Thinking and feeling are considered to be rational functions in that they are concerned with judging (this not that, good not bad), while sensation and intuition are considered to be irrational functions in that they are concerned with perceiving (outer facts, inner visions). Both attitudes and all four functions exist in each person, but they can stand in various relations of prominence. One's type is characterised by the combination in one's consciousness of predominant attitude, strongest function (*superior function*), and next strongest function (*secondary function*). If the superior function is a rational function, then the secondary function must be one of the irrational functions. The other rational function will then be relatively unavailable to consciousness and be designated as the *inferior function*. Thus, there are sixteen possible psychological types in Jung's model. For example, one person might be an introverted intuitive type with secondary thinking, another might be an extraverted intuitive type with secondary feeling, and a third might be an extraverted feeling type with secondary sensation. In the case of the first two examples the inferior function will be sensation (since the superior function is the other irrational function of intuition), while in the third example the inferior function will be thinking (since the superior function is the other rational function of feeling).

The particular character of synchronistic events will often depend on the conscious orientation of the experiencer, and this in turn will partly depend on the experiencer's psychological type. Jung's patient would appear to have had a highly developed thinking function. She would therefore be expected to have an inferior feeling function. Jung indicates this when he refers to the need 'to sweeten her rationalism with a somewhat more human understanding'. The synchronicity that occurs under these conditions provides an experience and image that are able to touch her at the level of feeling, breaking 'the ice of her intellectual resistance'.

The unconscious

The human psyche, in Jung's view, cannot be understood from a consideration of consciousness alone. For the psyche comprises not only consciousness but also *the unconscious*. Jung defines the unconscious as 'a psychological borderline concept, which covers all psychic contents or processes that are not conscious, i.e., not related to the ego in any perceptible way' (1921: par. 837). It is a border-line concept in the sense that it marks the limits of what we know rather than describes an area of knowledge. When previously unconscious contents and processes become known they become conscious and thereby obviously cease to be unconscious. Nevertheless, from observing the vicissitudes of conscious behaviour, feeling and thought, in others and in oneself, it is possible to infer that a large part of psychic life proceeds either unrelated to the ego or without its relation to the ego being perceived. One acts in unintended ways, succumbs to unaccountable moods, and has thoughts that do not seem to derive from one's conscious preoccupations.

The relationship between synchronicity and the unconscious has several aspects. One is that synchronicities stem from the unconscious. No conscious intention on the part of Jung's patient brought about the synchronicity that occurred to her, nor did she consciously influence that it involved the image of the scarab beetle, whose symbolic meaning she did not know (Jung 1952b: par. 845). Another aspect is that synchronicities express the perspective of the unconscious. In the case of Jung's patient, the unconscious expressed above all its perspective of greater wholeness that would not tolerate one-sided intellectualism. A third aspect is that synchronicities enrich our view of the unconscious. They do this partly by revealing specific unconscious contents, such as the symbol of the scarab, and partly by providing clues about the deeper structure of the unconscious – clues that prompted Jung to some far-reaching revisions of his model of the psyche, as we shall see towards the end of this chapter.

Jung's observations and researches led him to infer that the unconscious consists partly of contents that derive from one's personal life history and partly of contents that are inherited by all human beings. He refers to the former as the *personal unconscious*. This includes contents that previously were in consciousness but have been forgotten, either unintentionally because of their lacking the energy to remain salient or intentionally through *repression* on account of their painful nature. It also includes perceptions that, while passing through consciousness, have not received sufficient attention to be consciously apprehended (apperceived) but, as may subsequently appear, have been registered unconsciously. All these kinds of contents originate in personal life. They tend to group themselves in the unconscious into feeling-toned *complexes*: psychic fragments that interfere with conscious functioning, express themselves in dreams and symptoms, and indeed can often behave like independent personalities.

The *collective unconscious*, by contrast, includes 'unconscious psychic associations . . . which have never been the object of consciousness and must therefore be wholly the product of unconscious activity' (1952b: par. 840). Such contents 'do not originate in personal acquisitions but in the inherited possibility of psychic functioning in general, i.e., in the inherited structure of the brain' (ibid.: par. 842). Their presence in the unconscious is expressed by 'the mythological associations, the motifs and images that can spring up anew anytime anywhere independently of historical tradition or migration' (ibid.). Jung refers to these contents of the collective unconscious as *archetypes*. He distinguishes between archetypes themselves, which are irrepresentable and unknowable, and *archetypal images*, which are manifestations in consciousness deriving from the archetypes, the filling out of the empty form of the archetypes with imagery drawn from specific personal, social and cultural contexts. Archetypal images are characterised by the spontaneity of their appearance, autonomy of their development, and heightened emotional charge and sense of otherness (*numinosity*). An archetype can generate an indefinite number of archetypal images, each of which partially expresses its nature. Only the archetypes themselves, not the archetypal images, are inherited.

Jung writes little about how the personal unconscious might be involved in synchronicity. However, it is likely that the personal unconscious provides at least some of the content of synchronicities. Jung's patient dreamed of being given a golden jewel. This image of receiving a precious gift could readily be understood in personal terms as reflecting her unconscious wish to receive something valuable from her therapist Jung. This would not preclude that the same image could also have an archetypal aspect relating to the collective unconscious. For in practice the personal and collective levels of the unconscious involve each other and are often difficult to distinguish (see Williams 1963a). The personal unconscious can also be involved in synchronicity negatively through giving a personalised and dissociated bias to interpretations. Such would have been the case, for instance, if Jung's patient had interpreted the giving of the scarab, in her dream and in reality, as a prize for the excellence of her intellect.

The collective unconscious and its contents, the archetypes, are the most important Jungian concepts for understanding synchronicity. Jung writes that 'by far the greatest number of spontaneous synchronistic phenomena that I have had occasion to observe and analyse can easily be shown to have a direct connection with the archetype' (1952b: par. 912). He considers that, although archetypes do not cause synchronicities, the constellation or activation of an archetype in a situation makes the occurrence of synchronicities more likely. In the example involving the scarab beetle, he notes that 'there seems to be an archetypal foundation' (ibid.: par. 845) and suggests, more specifically, that it was the archetype of rebirth that was constellated. For, as he explains, 'Any essential change of attitude signifies a psychic renewal which is usually accompanied by symbols of rebirth in the patient's dreams and fantasies. The scarab is a classic example of a rebirth symbol' (ibid.). The accompanying emotional charge or numinosity of the incident is evident from the power with which, Jung says, it 'broke the ice of [the patient's] intellectual resistance'.

Jung considered that there are as many archetypes as there are typical human situations (1936a: par. 99). Some archetypes concern the universal processes and events of life such as birth, entry into adulthood, marriage, parenthood and death. Others concern various forms of psychic relationship and are expressed by Jung through images and personifications. Among these are the *persona*, which represents the mask one puts on to relate to the social world (1928: pars. 243–53); the *shadow*, which represents all those, in one's own eyes, negative qualities in oneself that one has no wish to acknowledge or relate to (1951a: pars. 13–19); the *anima* and *animus*, which represent a man's inner image of woman and a woman's inner image of man respectively, both images being means by which consciousness can relate to the unconscious (1928: pars. 296–340; 1951a: pars. 20–42); and the *mana personality*, which, in its various forms such as magician, wise old man or wise old woman, represents the extraordinary energy and insight released when a high degree of psychological integration is achieved (1928: pars. 374–406).

Of particular importance among the archetypes discussed by Jung is the *self*. For Jung, the self is at once the symbol of psychic totality, the central archetype of the collective unconscious, and the goal of psychic development. 'The self', he writes, 'is our life's goal, for it is the completest expression of that fateful combination we call individuality' (1928: par. 404). The self, as Jung understands it, needs to be differentiated from the ego. While the ego is the centre of consciousness, the self is the hypothetical centre of the whole psyche, consciousness and the unconscious together. The self also needs to be distinguished from the mana personality. The mana personality is one-sidedly spiritual with an emphasis on extraordinary power and wisdom, while the self epitomises psychic balance, occupying a middle position between spirit and the mundane world, indeed between all opposites. It can be expressed in consciousness by many kinds of images, including personifications such as the king, hero, prophet, or saviour, geometrical symbols such as the square and circle (especially 'mandalas'), and images of the union of opposites such as the Chinese Yin-Yang symbol, the interplay of light and shadow, or the motif of the hostile brothers (1921: par. 790). Jung finds many images of the self functionally indistinguishable from images of God, so that the self 'might equally well be called the "God within us"' (1928: par. 399). However, God images in which one side of a pair of opposites (good, spirit, masculinity) is not balanced with the other side of the pair (evil, matter, femininity) are considered by Jung to be incomplete. For Jung, therefore, archetypal images of the self take precedence over images of God.

In principle, synchronicities can involve any archetype. However, there are particularly strong connections between synchronicity and the archetype of the self. For synchronicity, as we shall see below, promotes the process of integrating opposites that leads to realisation of the self. Furthermore, Jung sometimes characterises synchronicity as already expressing the condition of unitary being (for which he uses the alchemical term *unus mundus*, 'one world') which is part of what he means by the concept of the self. 'If mandala symbolism is the psychological equivalent of the *unus mundus*,' he writes, 'then synchronicity is its parapsychological equivalent' (1955–6: par. 662).

The relationship between consciousness and the unconscious

Jung accounts for the relationship between consciousness and the unconscious largely in terms of *psychic energy*. He uses this term interchangeably with *libido* but, unlike Freud, does not consider sexuality to be its only or its most basic form. Rather, it is a kind of life energy that can take various instinctual and spiritual forms, none of which is fundamental. 'Psychic energy', Jung states, 'is the intensity of a psychic process, its psychological value' (1921: par. 778). By analogy with energy in physics, Jung conceives of psychic energy as limited in quantity and indestructible, and he was greatly concerned with studying its transformations. Both conscious and unconscious processes involve psychic energy.

Jung insists that the relationship between the component events of a synchronicity, being acausal, cannot be thought of in terms of energy (1952b: par. 836). However, the notion of psychic energy can still help account for some of the psychological dynamics associated with synchronicity. For example, the notion is implicit in Jung's accounts of the affectivity or numinosity that attends synchronistic events (ibid.: par. 859; see also 1976: 21). Furthermore, the unconscious images that form the psychic component of synchronicities are able to enter consciousness because, when an archetype is active, there is a lessening of the energy of consciousness and a corresponding heightening of the energy of the unconscious (1952b: par. 856). A gradient is established between the unconscious and consciousness, with the result that contents are able to flow more readily than usual from the one to the other.

Borrowing another notion from physics, Jung considered that psychic energy exists as the tension between two opposing forces. The notion of *opposites* therefore occupies a crucial position in his theory: 'The opposites', he writes, 'are the ineradicable and indispensable preconditions of all psychic life' (1955–6: par. 206). Many of the concepts of Jung's psychological theory are conceived as, or in terms of, opposites. Most fundamental is the opposition between consciousness and the unconscious. Notably, too, within Jung's typological theory, thinking is the opposite of feeling, sensation is the opposite of intuition, the first of these pairs (the rational functions) is the opposite of the second pair (the irrational functions), and introversion is the opposite of extraversion. Among the archetypes, the persona, which relates consciousness to the outer world, is the opposite of the anima/animus, which relates consciousness to the inner world. The archetype of the self is defined largely as a synthesis and harmony of opposites. In addition, all archetypes are considered to have opposing poles. For instance, the mother archetype can be both positive, generating images of a good, nurturing mother, and negative, generating images of a bad, devouring mother. Again, Jung distinguishes between opposite instinctual and spiritual aspects of the archetype (1947/1954: pars. 404–8). For instance, the mother archetype relates to experiences of nurturing that are literal and biological, on the one hand, and symbolic and spiritual, on the other.

We have already seen that synchronicities often manifest according to a principle of opposition. The content of a synchronicity typically expresses a point of view of the unconscious that is opposed to that of consciousness. While the consciousness of Jung's patient was dominated by an attitude of rationalism and rigid intellectuality, the synchronicity with the scarab beetle expressed the opposite values of the irrational, spontaneous and natural. The notion of opposites also plays a role in Jung's definitions and characterisations of synchronicity. He presents synchronicity not just as an alternative principle to causality but as an opposite principle, and he even presents this opposition diagrammatically (1952b: pars. 961, 963).

In Jung's model, the psyche is considered a self-regulating system that aims to maintain a balance between opposites through the mechanism of *compensation*. This means that the general attitude of consciousness, which will have various one-sided emphases, is continually being balanced, adjusted and supplemented by the unconscious (1921: pars. 693–4). For example, if a person's conscious orientation is excessively introverted and intuitive, the neglected opposite qualities of extraversion and sensation will gather energy in the unconscious. This unconscious counterposition will exercise an inhibitory effect on consciousness and, if the tension between consciousness and the unconscious becomes strong enough, may eventually break into consciousness in the form of dreams, spontaneous fantasies and symptoms. 'Normally,' however, so Jung asserts, 'compensation is an unconscious activity, i.e., an unconscious regulation of conscious activity' (ibid.: par. 695).

The notion of compensation makes explicit one of the most important dynamics of synchronicity, which has already been implicit in the discussions of psychological types and opposites: synchronistic events compensate a one-sided conscious attitude, thereby relating consciousness to the unconscious. In the case of Jung's patient, her one-sided rationalism and resulting psychological stasis were compensated by an event that both in its symbolism and in its action expressed the power of the irrational and the possibility of renewal.

The compensation of consciousness by the unconscious does not simply aim at establishing a static harmony but ultimately serves the process of personality development that Jung called *individuation*. As Jung defines it, 'Individuation means becoming an "in-dividual," and in so far as "individuality" embraces our innermost, last and incomparable uniqueness, it also implies becoming one's own self. We could therefore translate individuation as "coming to selfhood" or "self-realization"' (1928: par. 266). The drive towards individuation is inherent in the psyche, but the difficulty of the process means that only a few people take it up consciously. Individuation aims 'to divest the self of the false wrappings of the persona on the one hand and the suggestive power of primordial images [i.e., archetypes] on the other' (ibid.: par. 269). It entails a continual, arduous integration of unconscious contents into consciousness: first the contents of the personal unconscious and then those of the collective unconscious.[2]

Although he does not explicitly say so, Jung's whole presentation of synchronicity implies that it promotes individuation. Synchronicity connects consciousness and the unconscious through the principle of compensation and does so in a way that leads towards fuller realisation of that conjunction of opposites that Jung names the self. That the incident involving the scarab beetle promoted the patient's individuation is indicated by Jung's statement that, following the synchronicity, 'The treatment could now be continued with satisfactory results.'

Insofar as individuation is concerned with realisation of the self and the integration of unconscious contents into consciousness, it is also concerned with the reconciliation of opposites. At a conscious level, there often seems no way of resolving the conflict between opposite points of view – for example, between the spiritual and the sensual. However, when the tension between opposites is especially acute, the unconscious psyche can give rise spontaneously to *symbols* that, paradoxically and unexpectedly, express both sides of the opposition without giving precedence to either. Unlike a sign, which merely stands in for something else that is better known (for example, as a logo stands in for a company), a symbol, according to Jung, is 'the best possible description or formulation of a relatively unknown fact' (1921: par. 814). As such, it is 'a living thing . . . pregnant with meaning' (ibid.: par. 816); it 'compels [the observer's] unconscious participation and has a life-giving and life-enhancing effect' (ibid.: par. 819). The entire process by which apparently irreconcilable opposites are reconciled in a spontaneously arising symbol is called by Jung the *transcendent function* (ibid.: par. 828; see also 1957).

The content of synchronicities typically is symbolic and arises when there is a psychological impasse brought on by the confrontation of irreconcilable opposites. Synchronicity can therefore be viewed as a form of transcendent function. Jung is unequivocal that the content of his patient's synchronicity was symbolic: 'The scarab', he writes, 'is a classic example of a rebirth symbol' (1952b: par. 845). He is also explicit about the impasse that called forth the symbol. He recounts that his patient presented 'an extraordinarily difficult case to treat, and up to the time of the dream little or no progress had been made . . . Evidently something quite irrational was needed which was beyond my powers to produce' (ibid.). What made the case so difficult was the seemingly irreconcilable conflict between the patient's desire to learn about and change her condition, indicated by her presence in analysis, and her 'highly polished Cartesian rationalism' that led her to believe 'she always knew better about everything'.

Techniques for relating consciousness and the unconscious

A number of techniques are recommended by Jung for identifying and interpreting unconscious contents and hence promoting their integration into consciousness. Most favoured by Jung is *dream analysis*. For Jung, the dream is 'a spontaneous self-portrayal, in symbolic form, of the actual situation in the unconscious' (1916/1948: par. 505). Analysing the dream can therefore provide insight into the active complexes and constellated archetypes in the unconscious. The dream is located within its personal psychological context through examining the dreamer's *associations* to the imagery of the dream (1945/1948a: pars. 539–43). It is then sometimes also appropriate to uncover the universal archetypal pattern within the dream through the process of *amplification*, which seeks wider cultural, historical, and mythological parallels of the imagery in the dream (1935: pars. 173–4, 249).

The content of synchronicities resembles that of dreams in that it is symbolic and portrays the situation in the unconscious. It can therefore be analysed in much the same way as the content of dreams. However, since Jung considers the content of synchronicities almost invariably to be archetypal, we can suppose that amplification rather than the eliciting of personal associations is the more important process in analysing synchronicities. In the example with the scarab beetle, Jung does not mention having explored the patient's personal associations to the image of the scarab beetle but he does elaborate upon the significance of the image within ancient Egyptian mythology in order to establish its status as an archetypal image of rebirth (1952b: par. 845).

Dream analysis provides not only a model for how to analyse synchronicities but also an important context within which synchronicities are liable to be noticed. For the close attention to inner imagery that dream analysis fosters will increase the likelihood of one's registering when outer physical events have inner psychic parallels. Jung's earliest recorded discussions of synchronicity occurred in the course of a series of seminars on dream analysis (1928–30: 24–5, 35–6, 43–5, 417), and his classic synchronicity involving the scarab occurred in relation to a dream that was being reported by his patient.

A further technique developed by Jung for relating consciousness to the unconscious is *active imagination*. This involves concentrating on an image (which may be from a picture, a dream, a fantasy, or the memory of an actual event, or may take a non-pictorial form such as a mood) until the unconscious spontaneously produces a series of further images that unfold as a story (1935: par. 398). Crucial to the process is 'that the images have a life of their own and that the symbolic events develop according to their own logic' (ibid.: par. 397). Often employed towards the end of an analysis, the technique can supersede the analysis of dreams, over which it has certain advantages. For example, because active imagination is practised while awake and so with the participation of consciousness, the fantasy material obtained is often 'in a creative form' (it is often painted, written down, or otherwise creatively expressed), and this 'quickens the process of maturation' aimed at by analysis (ibid.: par. 399). The material tends to be 'more rounded out than the dreams with their precarious language'; for example, it both has feeling-values in it and is amenable to judgement by feeling in a way that is not usually the case with dreams (ibid.: par. 400).

Active imagination, like dream analysis, can lead to the registering of synchronistic events through focusing attention on patterns of inner psychic images. Insofar as active imagination helps one to home in specifically on archetypal images, it can even bring one's consciousness into psychic terrain where synchronistic events are likely to occur. Several of the personal synchronicities that Jung recounts in *Memories, Dreams, Reflections* involve imagery that emerged or was being explored in the course of active imagination (e.g., 1963: 176, 289–90). Conversely, the image that forms the content of a synchronicity, such as the scarab beetle in Jung's example, could itself provide an interesting starting point for active imagination. Further, synchronistic contents, like the fantasies of active imagination, emerge in the waking state when consciousness, though not controlling them, is in a position immediately to respond to them. Synchronicity may therefore share with active imagination the ability to provide creative, accelerated, and rounded contributions to psychological maturation.

In attempting to gain insight into the unconscious, Jung also made ample use of the techniques of *transference and countertransference*. He viewed transference as 'a specific form of the more general process of projection' (1935: par. 312), which in turn is 'a general psychological mechanism that carries over subjective contents of any kind into the object' (ibid.: par. 313). Transference 'is a projection which happens between two individuals and which, as a rule, is of an emotional and compulsory nature' (ibid.: par. 316), such that 'the emotion of the projected contents always forms a link, a sort of dynamic relationship, between the subject and the object' (ibid.: par. 317). Jung's view of transference differs from the classical psychoanalytic view in holding that the projected contents can be archetypal as well as personal (ibid.: par. 324). Clinically, Jung seems to have been ambivalent about the value of transference. On the one hand, he says he welcomed analyses in which 'there is only a mild transference or when it is practically unnoticeable' (1946: par. 359). On the other hand, he agrees with Freud that 'The main problem of medical psychotherapy is the *transference*' (1963: 203). Earlier than Freud or any other psychoanalyst, Jung also recognised the positive therapeutic importance of the countertransference – the projections of the analyst onto the patient, stemming not only from the analyst's unresolved complexes but also, crucially, from the changes brought about by the patient in the analyst's unconscious. Sensitivity to these changes, Jung notes, provides the analyst with 'a highly important organ of information' (1929: par. 163).

The intense emotional bond that occurs in the transference, especially the archetypal transference, provides another context conducive to the occurrence of synchronicities. For in this context deep structures of the unconscious are activated and the patterns of imagery and behaviour that they generate are closely observed. Such a relationship is likely to have existed between Jung and the patient who dreamed of the scarab. In that incident, Jung's immediate and seemingly effective response to the appearance of the scarab at his consulting room window – catching it and presenting it to his patient in a re-enactment of the scene from her dream – suggests that he was attuned to and was acting out of well-judged counter-transference feelings.

The concept of synchronicity also provides a way of understanding how some transference and countertransference phenomena might manifest. For example, it sometimes happens that an analyst has experiences that would make perfect sense as countertransference responses to the patient's state of mind, except that the analyst and patient are not in each other's presence. Jung describes such an incident where he experienced a series of sensations corresponding, in their nature and timing, to his patient's deepening depression and eventual suicide, including the sensation of a bullet entering his head and coming to rest at the back of the skull (1963: 136–7). It is difficult to account for such detailed correspondences simply as an extrapolation from previously achieved attunement. The notion of synchronicity, invoked by Jung in relation to the above incident, provides an alternative framework for understanding.

Some revisions to Jung's psychological model in the light of synchronicity

At around the same time as he was developing his theory of synchronicity, Jung also modified and expanded his conception of the collective unconscious and archetypes. In particular, he began to write of the '*psychoid*' character of the collective unconscious and of the relativisation of space and time within the unconscious. These modifications, stated explicitly in the essay 'On the Nature of the Psyche' (1947/1954), were postulated by Jung largely in order to account for synchronistic phenomena.

'Synchronicity', says Jung in a letter to Michael Fordham (1 July 1955), 'tells us something about the nature of what I call the *psychoid* factor, i.e., the uncon-scious archetype' (1950–5: par. 1208). When Jung writes that the unconscious or one if its archetypes is psychoid, he means several things. Most generally, he is referring to a level of the unconscious or its content that is altogether inaccessible to consciousness (1947/1954: pars. 380, 382; 1952b: par. 840). More particularly, he is hypothesising that this inaccessible level is where the realms of the psychological and the physiological meet. The psychoid level is not equivalent or reducible to either one of these realms but, in an unknown way, combines and transcends both (1947/1954: par. 368; 1954b: 1538). Jung's aim, Marilyn Nagy suggests, is to describe 'an immaterial, autonomous psychic factor operating in organic nature according to teleological principles' (1991: 257). These formu-lations suggest that the psychoid unconscious or archetype especially has to do with the relationship between a person's psyche and body. However, Jung sometimes goes further than this and suggests that it should also refer to the relationship between a person's psyche and the physical world beyond that person's body. In the context of a discussion of miracles, he writes that synchronicity 'points to the "psychoid" and essentially transcendental nature of the archetype as an "arranger" of psychic forms *inside and outside the psyche*' (1976: 22, emphasis added; cf. ibid.: 541).

The feature that accounts for how the psychoid archetype might connect the psyche and the outer world is its ability to relativise space and time (1976: 259). As we have seen, among the kinds of incidents Jung wishes to class as synchronicities are some in which the coinciding events are widely separated either in space (as in Swedenborg's vision) or in time (as in the experience of Jung's student friend). Such incidents raise the question of how a person's mind can register images of things that are simultaneously happening a great distance away or, even more radically, have not yet happened but will do so in the future. In such cases, it seems that the way in which time and space normally operate to allow for the transmission of information between events and images has been by-passed. There seems to be an immediate connection between the events and the images regardless of their separation in space and time. Such experiences and their apparent implications led Jung to hypothesise that in the unconscious psyche the categories of space and time do not operate in the same way as they do in the world of conscious experience. He speaks of the 'relativisation' and even of the 'abolition' of time and space in the unconscious.

Summary

We can summarise some of the more salient connections between Jung's overall psychological model and the synchronicity involving the scarab beetle as follows. Jung's patient was one-sidedly rationalistic and unable from this perspective alone to gain transformative insight into her condition. Because of this impasse, we can assume that there was a withdrawal of psychic energy from consciousness and a corresponding accumulation of it in the unconscious around the archetype of rebirth. Eventually, this build-up of energy in the unconscious became so great that it burst into consciousness. The archetype of rebirth expressed itself in images gathered from the environment, which, because of the relativisation of the unconscious, could include physical as well as psychic and spatially and temporally distant as well as present events. Hence, the patient first dreamed of a scarab, a classic symbol of rebirth, then, while telling Jung this dream, encountered the real scarab that appeared at the window and was caught and shown to her by Jung. In this way, her one-sided rationalism and resulting psychological stasis were compensated by an irrational, numinous event that promoted her further psychological development or individuation.

Alternative theoretical perspectives

The basic phenomena of synchronicity can be theorised in many ways besides in terms of Jung's psychological model. What is more, the alternative models that have been proposed are in many cases more immediately consonant with current consensus world-views than is Jung's model. They are also often more straightforward and economical. If, in the face of this competition, Jung's theory is still to be taken seriously, we need to identify what is distinctive and valuable about it and how it may better account for at least some features of synchronicity than do any of the alternative theories. In order to do this, we will look briefly at a number of explanatory approaches to coincidences, including statistics, cognitive psychology, and psychoanalysis. In combination, these approaches can produce an account of meaningful coincidences that is as sophisticated as Jung's.

Mere chance

Events that appear to be meaningful coincidences can often be plausibly explained simply as products of chance. Our generally poor awareness of what can and indeed is likely to occur purely by chance may be responsible for our attributing special significance to events which in reality have no such significance. Explicitly or implicitly, this strategy for explaining coincidences appeals to considerations deriving from probability theory and cognitive psychology.

The law of truly large numbers

The most important of the considerations from probability theory is what has been called 'the law of truly large numbers'. In the words of two Harvard mathematicians, Persi Diaconis and Frederick Mosteller, this 'law' states that 'with a large enough sample, any outrageous thing is likely to happen'. They continue:

> The point is that truly rare events, say events that occur only once in a million . . . are bound to be plentiful in a population of 250 million people [the population of the USA]. If a coincidence occurs to one person in a million each day, then we expect 250 occurrences a day and close to 100,000 such occurrences a year.
>
> (Diaconis and Mosteller 1989: 859)

In view of this surprising frequency, 'we can be absolutely sure that we will see incredibly remarkable events. When such events occur, they are often noted and recorded. If they happen to us or someone we know, it is hard to escape that spooky feeling' (ibid.).

As an illustration, Diaconis and Mosteller refer to the case of a woman who won the New Jersey lottery twice within four months. A front-page story in the

New York Times hailed this as a one in seventeen trillion long shot. However, these odds were calculated on the assumption that the woman bought one ticket for exactly two lottery draws; also, that it had been predicted before her first win that precisely *she* would be the winner. In fact, she purchased multiple tickets repeatedly and no prediction was made concerning her first win. Again, in the United States there are many millions of people who buy lottery tickets, often multiple tickets on each of many lotteries. Taking these factors into consideration, it has been calculated that it is 'better than even odds to have a double winner in seven years some place in the United States' (1989: 859). For the period between the two winnings of the New Jersey woman (four months), the odds are better than one in thirty that there will be a double winner – one in thirty rather than one in seventeen trillion.

Misjudgement of probabilities

Quite apart from our general lack of awareness regarding what is likely to happen simply as a result of the law of truly large numbers, psychological experiments have suggested that people on the whole are rather poor judges of probability (see Watt 1990–1). A striking illustration of this is the so-called birthday problem. The chance that any particular person was born on a specified day of the year is roughly one in 365. Asked how many people would therefore need to be present together in a room for there to be a better than 50 per cent chance that two of them were born on the same day of the year, many people suspect the answer must be half of 365 (i.e., 182 or 183). In fact, the answer is only twenty-three. We tend to underestimate the number of different combinations of pairs of birthdays that can occur with a small number of people (ibid.: 69–70).

Diaconis and Mosteller provide formulae for calculating probabilities of the type involved in the birthday problem (1989: 857; see also Watt 1990–1: 69–70). Such formulae may be helpful in estimating the likelihood of coincidences where the number of possible categories is known or can be discovered. In most cases, however, these numbers cannot be known or discovered. In such circumstances, as Caroline Watt observes, 'people may fall back on rough "rules of thumb"; the so-called cognitive heuristics' (1990–1: 70). The suggestion is that attempts to apply these 'rules of thumb' or cognitive heuristics may again lead to serious misjudgements of probability and hence to the perception of significant coincidences where in fact there are none.

Two major cognitive heuristics are judgement by representativeness and judgement by availability. In judgement by representativeness, the claim is that when we judge the likelihood of an event we usually do so according to the frequency of its appearance within a sample group which is taken to be representative of events generally. In doing this, however, we often neglect to take into consideration the sample's size – specifically, the fact that larger samples are likely to be more representative of the parent population (i.e., 'events as a whole') than smaller samples. Applied to coincidence, this means:

if people tend not to take sample size sufficiently into account when judging likelihood, they may not appreciate that an extreme outcome is more likely to occur in a small sample, and may therefore mistakenly attribute significant rarity to a coincidence occurring under these conditions.

(Watt 1990–1: 71)

The second rule of thumb or cognitive heuristic, judgement by availability, involves estimating the frequency of an event's occurrence in terms of how easy it is to think of examples of the event. However, this can lead to biased decisions because how readily examples come to mind ('availability') is influenced not only by objective frequency but also by recency, familiarity and vividness. In particular, 'we pay less attention than we should to negative information – to non-occurrences or non-coincidences – because they are less noticeable' (Watt 1990–1: 71). Therefore, we may be led 'to overestimate the frequency of coincidences that we expect to occur (such as predicting phone calls), and to neglect actual base rate information that conflicts with our expectations or that has low salience (for example, overlooking failed predictions)' (ibid.).[3]

Further psychological considerations

Other psychological factors besides misjudgement of probabilities have also been invoked to account for why we might mistakenly perceive significance in mere chance events. Watt emphasises in particular the influence of beliefs and expectations on perception, judgement and recall (1990–1: 76–81). For example, she refers to work which suggests that beliefs can influence us to make 'illusory correlations' between events; that confidence in a theory can lead us to process information selectively so as to strengthen our beliefs; that the recency of our exposure to a theory – that is, its availability to us – can cause us to select precisely this explanatory theory rather than some alternative one; and that ambiguous information is especially easy to interpret in a way that fits our expectations (ibid.: 76–7). She also adduces considerations suggesting that information often does not influence our beliefs ('once we have made up our minds about something we are very resistant to revising our theories'), no matter whether it is a question of established beliefs, new beliefs, or even of beliefs that are discovered to have been adopted on the basis of false information (ibid.: 77–9). Similarly, she argues that recall of events can be seriously distorted by our beliefs and expectations, since 'it appears that when we recollect something we actively reconstruct our memories so as to fit with our theories and expectations' (ibid.: 79).

Normal causes

What seem to be meaningful coincidences can also be explained by demonstrating or supposing that, in spite of appearances, there is a normal causal connection between the events involved. Normal causes could create the appearance of a coincidence in various ways.

Common source

The two events in an apparent coincidence could be causally related in that they both derive from the same source. Suppose the same unlikely image appears on the same night in the dreams of two people who have not been in contact with one another. There is no way in which the dream of one person here could be considered causally responsible for that of the other in any normal sense. However, it is possible that both dreamers were exposed to the same image the previous day, perhaps on television. This televised image would then be the probable common source of the image in both dreams.

Undetected causal relationship

One's inability to discern a causal connection between two events does not mean that such a connection is not there, eluding one's present discernment. Arthur Koestler relates an intriguing incident involving crosswords appearing in the *Daily Telegraph* immediately before the allied invasion of Europe on D-Day, 6 June 1944 (Hardy *et al.* 1973: 200–1). Five of the principal codenames being used in the invasion plan appeared as solutions to the crosswords: Utah, Omaha, Mulberry, Neptune and Overlord. The composer of the crosswords was a schoolmaster living in Surrey who had been compiling crosswords for the paper for over twenty years. When MI5 questioned him, they found that he knew neither that the solutions were codewords nor how they had come into his head. Koestler therefore judged this a 'most remarkable cluster of coincidences' (ibid.: 200). However, subsequent disclosures have revealed the likelihood of a hidden causal relationship. In 1984 one of the crossword compiler's former pupils came forward and claimed that he had been responsible. He said that his former teacher had been in the habit of getting his school class to help make up the crosswords, the class suggesting words to which he (the teacher) later provided the clues. This particular pupil claimed to have suggested the codewords, having himself learnt them from the American and Canadian forces stationed nearby. In his discussion of this case, Brian Inglis (1990) finds reason to query the integrity of this claim and considers an alternative suggestion more likely. The crossword compiler was sharing his house at the time with a deputy director of naval construction who would likely have been aware of the codewords. Since the words would probably have been used openly by him – 'after all, that's what code names are for. It's the things and places they describe which are really secret' – they could easily have been overheard by the teacher (ibid.: 107–8). In either case, a causal relationship that for a long time remained undetected has subsequently turned out to be, if not proven, at least very probable.

Cryptomnesia

One specific form of undetected causal relationship is cryptomnesia, where a memory enters consciousness but is not recognised as such. For instance, William James relates the story of a young woman in Germany who, while in a fever, was heard to utter coherent but unconnected sentences in Latin, Greek and rabbinical Hebrew, even though she was a 'simple creature' and had no conscious knowledge of the languages in question. Initially, no explanation could be found other than to suggest that she was possessed by a devil. Later, however, a physician traced the girl's history and discovered that when she was nine she had been charitably taken in by an old Protestant pastor who, within the girl's hearing, used to read aloud to himself from his books which included the Greek and Latin Fathers and a collection of rabbinical writings. Within these books were found many of the very sentences spoken by the fevered girl (James 1890: 681). In addition to this kind of anecdotal evidence, the phenomenon of cryptomnesia has been demonstrated experimentally (see Zusne and Jones 1989: 138).

Subliminal or heightened perception

Causal relationships could go undetected if part of the information linking the events in question is absorbed subliminally or through a form of heightened perception. This effect is often similar to that of cryptomnesia: one's conscious actions and knowledge are influenced by information one does not know one has. However, with subliminal perception it is not a case of forgetting information that has once been in consciousness but of the information never having been in one's conscious awareness at all.

More specifically, heightened perception covers the possibility, increasingly substantiated by scientific findings, that the human organism has considerably more channels for taking in information than just the traditional five senses and, further, that even the traditional five have a vastly more extensive range and subtlety than is usually appreciated. Zusne and Jones point out, for example, that

> some people . . . can literally hear what another person may be thinking. Thinking is often accompanied by muscular movements of which the thinker is not aware. The entire speech apparatus, including the tongue and the larynx, moves. Even though the movements are slight, some people are able to pick up the air vibrations produced by these movements.
>
> (Zusne and Jones 1989: 83)

Extraordinary as this sounds, the phenomenon was clearly demonstrated in the case of a nine-year-old mentally retarded Latvian girl with apparent thought-reading abilities (ibid.: 83–4). A similar phenomenon is 'muscle-reading': certain people can learn to feel and interpret the involuntary muscular movements of others – and also various postural clues, changes in facial expression, eye movements, etc. – as indications of what those others are thinking (ibid.: 84–5).

Conscious or unconscious deception

Another way in which a normal causal relationship may be responsible for creating the appearance of a coincidence is through conscious or unconscious deception somewhere along the line of transmission of the incident. That various kinds of deception can be responsible for producing events that appear to be related other than by normal physical and psychological causes is clear enough from the existence of stage magic – where the effect can be positively uncanny even though one knows full well that deception is involved.[4] In non-theatrical contexts the motivation for and dynamics of deception are usually more complicated, but the same uncanny impression can readily enough be produced.

Psychoanalysis

The preceding considerations from probability theory and cognitive psychology provide ways of understanding apparent coincidences that challenge the case Jung would make for their improbability and acausality. However, none of these perspectives adequately accounts for the depth and subtlety of meaning that can attach to experiences of coincidence. It is, above all, this sense of meaningfulness that gives coincidences their fascination and that often leads those who experience them to consider them worthy of further attention. As we have seen, Jung's analytical psychology is able to provide a sophisticated account of the meaning experienced from coincidences and in this respect has the edge over the alternative theories so far discussed.

However, Jung's is not the only depth psychological theory capable of accounting for coincidences. Several writers working within the tradition of psychoanalysis have also addressed these events. At the same time as Jung was publishing his papers on synchronicity, George Devereux published an edited collection of papers entitled *Psychoanalysis and the Occult* (1953). This included six papers by Freud and a further twenty-five by other psychoanalysts discussing the putative occurrence, in the therapeutic context, of 'occult' events such as extrasensory perception, premonitory dreams and meaningful coincidences. Freud himself appears to have been ambivalent about such events – at once fascinated and apprehensive. His papers reveal him cautiously open to the possibility of telepathy, and he is known to have both participated in seances (Charet 1993: 210) and conducted his own informal experiments in telepathy with his daughter (Gay 1988: 443–5). However, his interest in these areas was never as extensive as Jung's, and he was reluctant to disclose even the interest he did have for fear of associating psychoanalysis too closely with the occult. As F. X. Charet has shown, conflict over the importance of these phenomena was among the reasons for the breakdown in relations between Freud and Jung (1993: 171–227).

Although coincidences and 'occult' phenomena have not been a commonly pursued theme within psychoanalysis, a number of psychoanalytic writers continue to address it. Most insist that putative synchronicities and related kinds of events are all explicable in purely naturalistic terms. This position has recently been trenchantly expressed by Mel Faber (1998), whose explanation for coincidences combines the kind of statistical argument mentioned above – that given a large enough sample, any extraordinary thing is likely to happen – with the psychoanalytic dynamic of the 'return of the repressed'. According to this view, a purely chance event becomes charged with emotional significance because it provides the occasion for a repressed wish or impulse, the trace of an event that actually occurred in the life of the experiencer, to return to consciousness. It is true that a few psychoanalytic thinkers, such as Jule Eisenbud, address such events from the position that they are indeed inexplicable and will remain so unless we postulate a paranormal human capacity or feature of reality ('psi') (see Devereux 1953; Eisenbud 1983, 1990). Eisenbud reverses the usual psychoanalytic perspective, seeing paranormal events not as mere fantasies perpetuated to defend against the admission of painful reality but as a central feature of that painful reality itself. For the possibility that our aggressive feelings and thoughts may be telepathically and psychokinetically effective has far-reaching and highly disturbing implications. From his clinical observations, Eisenbud believes in this possibility, and it is against the admission of it, he suggests, that defences, such as rationalisation and *a priori* denial of the paranormal, are employed. Thus, through invoking the concept of the unconscious and the psychodynamic processes postulated by psychoanalysis, Eisenbud, like Faber, is able to provide a highly sophisticated explanation of coincidences, including of their profound emotional significance. However, Faber's theory is probably the more articulate when it comes to accounting for the specific charge of meaning in such events.

Faber draws primarily on the work of the post-Freudian theorists Margaret Mahler, Daniel Stern and Christopher Bollas. He depicts the infant during the early period as in a condition of merger or 'dual-unity' with its mother (Faber 1998: 38–51). In this state, the relationship between the mother and infant largely takes the form of 'mirroring' or 'affect attunement' (ibid.: 51–5). Furthermore, the mother above all represents for the child a 'transformational object'. The appearance and action of the mother in the child's world usually is accompanied by some form of (mostly positive) transformation for the child: hunger is transformed into satiety, wetness into dryness, anxiety into security, and in general distress into relief (ibid.: 55–8). Faber notes the parallels between the experience of the child in this early period and the experience of synchronicity in adult life. Just as the child is inextricably connected to or merged with the mother, so the experiencer of a synchronicity seems briefly to be connected to or merged with the outer world. Just as the mother responds in a timely way to the child's needs, so in synchronistic events the outer world seems to respond in a timely way ('simultaneously') to the psychic state of the experiencer. Just as the mother's appearance and responses transform the child's state, so the occurrence of a synchronicity transforms the state of the experiencer. In view of these parallels, Faber suggests that the emotional charge or 'meaning' of a synchronicity can be accounted for as a regression to the early infantile state where dual-unity, timely attunement with the environment and transformative experience were actual conditions (ibid.: 62–4). Faber applies his model to provide a detailed alternative account of Jung's use of his sources (ibid.: 67–88), his underlying theory (ibid.: 88–105), and above all his example involving the scarab beetle (ibid.: 105–13). Stressing the analytic setting of this incident, Faber suggests that in her transference relationship with Jung the patient regressed to the early infantile period and re-experienced the condition of being merged with, attuned to, and transformed by her mother. The coincidence with the scarab was in itself nothing remarkable, since unlikely events do sometimes happen simply by chance and, besides, rose-chafer beetles are common in Switzerland. What gave this unremarkable occurrence its aura of numinosity was the patient's powerful transference to Jung – which can only have been encouraged by Jung's dramatically catching the beetle as it flew in through the window and presenting it to her.

The distinctiveness of Jung's theory of synchronicity

The explanations of coincidences based on statistics, cognitive psychology, and psychoanalysis are only a few of those that have been proposed. Other explanations have been put forward especially in terms of parapsychology (e.g., Beloff 1977; Grattan-Guinness 1978, 1983) and holistic science (e.g., Keutzer 1982, 1984; Peat 1987), and the phenomenon can also be accounted for within traditional theological frameworks both western and eastern (e.g., Polkinghorne 1998: 85; Odin 1982: 171–87). In the presence of so many alternative ways of understanding coincidence, Jung's theory of synchronicity turns out to be distinctive for its possession of three principal qualities, any one or two of which might be found in alternative theories but all of which seem to be found in developed form only in Jung's. First, Jung's theory is, or aspires to be, grounded in empirical considerations. Second, unsurprisingly for a depth psychological perspective, Jung's theory is able to provide a sophisticated account of the psychological dynamics involved in how coincidences are experienced as meaningful. Third and most decisively, Jung's theory remains open to the possibility of there being a transpersonal or spiritual dimension involved in coincidences. Many of the alternative theories mentioned are empirically grounded, and some, such as the psychological and psychoanalytic theories, can provide sophisticated accounts of the experience of meaning. However, only the theological frameworks and some holistic science models remain open to transpersonal and spiritual factors. Of these, the theological approaches generally lack empirical grounding, and the holistic science models tend to lack psychological sophistication. Only Jung's theory of synchronicity comfortably includes all three qualities of scientific grounding, psychological sophistication and spiritual openness.

However, this is not to say that possession of these three qualities is the necessary criterion of an adequate model for explaining meaningful coincidences. Faber's psychoanalytic model, for example, is explicitly presented as a challenge to the religious implications of Jung's theory in the belief that Jung is wrong to introduce such considerations (1998: 3). Faber acknowledges the impossibility of decisively proving his own model or disproving Jung's but presents the naturalistic grounding of his own approach as a reason for preferring it (ibid.: 1–3).[5] The existence of this and other kinds of naturalistic challenge heightens the urgency to understand the significance of the religious and transpersonal element within Jung's theory. More generally, the existence of a variety of alternative explanations for meaningful coincidences forces a closer consideration of the coherence and overall plausibility of Jung's theory.

Chapter 2

Intellectual difficulties

In the Foreword to his principal essay on synchronicity, Jung explains why he has waited so long before attempting to present his ideas: 'The difficulties of the problem and its presentation seemed to me too great; too great the intellectual responsibility without which such a subject cannot be tackled; too inadequate, in the long run, my scientific training' (1952b: par. 816). He recognises that he is going to make 'uncommon demands on the open-mindedness and goodwill of the reader' who is 'expected to plunge into regions of human experience which are dark, dubious, and hedged about with prejudice' (ibid.). The subject, he concedes, involves such 'intellectual difficulties' that 'there can be no question of a complete description and explanation . . . but only an attempt to broach the problem in such a way as to reveal some of its manifold aspects and connections' (ibid.). In view of this frank acknowledgement of his limitations, as well as his position as a pioneer in the exploration of a difficult and taboo subject, it is perhaps unfair to expect Jung's writings on synchronicity to exhibit the level of coherence and completeness we might ideally like to encounter. At the same time, it would be unfortunate if we were to feel so admiring of or indulgent towards Jung that we did not draw attention to the problems in his presentation where we see them. For, as I hope to show, it is often in the fault lines of Jung's thinking that there is most scope for deepening our inquiries into synchronicity; and it is there too that we might find clues as to Jung's deeper purpose in addressing the subject. With this in mind, the aim of the present chapter is to identify and examine some of the difficulties, inconsistencies and uncertainties in Jung's writings on synchronicity. Previous commentators have not neglected to point out some of these difficulties, as they appear to the perspectives of, for example, philosophy (Flew 1953; Price 1953), science (Koestler 1972; Mansfield 1995), parapsychology (Beloff 1977), religious studies (Aziz 1990), psychoanalysis (Faber 1998) and analytical psychology itself (Fordham 1993). However, the difficulties have not been addressed as comprehensively as they are here, or taken as the point of entry into deeper, sustained inquiries regarding Jung's purpose. The chapter will discuss the adequacy of Jung's definitions in relation to the actual phenomenology of synchronicity, his statements about the epistemological status of his theory, and his handling of the core concepts bound up in that theory: time, acausality, meaning and probability.

'Synchronicity: an acausal connecting principle'

First, it will be useful to provide a summary of Jung's principal essay on synchronicity (1952b). This will give a sense of the overall structure of Jung's argument regarding synchronicity and the difficulties his exposition presents to the unprepared reader. It will also confirm the embeddedness of the theory of synchronicity within the overall framework of Jung's psychology.

In his Foreword (1952b: pars. 816–17) Jung states that he is aiming 'to give a consistent account of everything I have to say on this subject'. In the first chapter, 'Exposition' (ibid.: pars. 818–71), he notes that modern physics has shown natural laws to be statistical truths and the principle of causality to be only relatively valid, so that at the microphysical (i.e., subatomic) level there can occur events which are acausal. He then addresses the question of whether acausal events can also be demonstrated at the macrophysical level of everyday experience. The most decisive evidence in support of this possibility he considers to have been provided by the parapsychological experiments of J. B. Rhine. These experiments have revealed statistically significant correlations between events in spite of the fact that the possibility of any known kind of energy transmission and hence of causal relationship between the events was completely ruled out. Jung therefore concludes that under certain psychic conditions time and space can become relative and can even appear to be transcended altogether. The fact that Rhine's positive results fell off once his subjects began to lose interest suggests to Jung that the necessary psychic condition has to do with affectivity. Affectivity in turn suggests the presence of an activated archetype, and just such an archetypal background is apparent in the kind of spontaneous acausal events Jung encountered in his therapeutic work. In these spontaneous cases, however, a certain amount of symbolic interpretation is often needed in order to detect the operation of the archetype. Jung is now in a position to define synchronicity, which he does in a variety of ways. He also suggests a possible psychological dynamic to explain how an activated archetype might result in synchronicities: the presence of the active archetype is accompanied by numinous effects, and this numinosity or affectivity results in a lowering of the mental level, a relaxing of the focus of consciousness. As the energy of consciousness is lowered, the energy of the unconscious is correspondingly heightened, so that a gradient from the unconscious to the conscious is established and unconscious contents flow into consciousness more readily than usual. Included among these unconscious contents are items of what Jung calls 'absolute knowledge', knowledge that transcends the space–time limitations of consciousness in the manner demonstrated by Rhine's experiments. If there is then the recognition of a parallel between any of this 'absolute knowledge' and co-occurring outer physical events, the result will be the experience of synchronicity. Finally in this chapter, Jung discusses a number of divinatory procedures and concludes that astrology is the one most suitable for the purposes of his investigation, which are, first, to yield measurable results demonstrating the existence of synchronicity and, second, to provide insight into the psychic background of synchronicity.

The second chapter, 'An Astrological Experiment' (1952b: pars. 872–915), describes Jung's attempt to carry out these aims. He collected and analysed 483 pairs of marriage horoscopes in three batches of 180, 220 and 83, looking for conjunctions and oppositions of sun, moon, ascendant, descendant, Mars and Venus. He found that the maximal figure for each of the three batches was one of the traditional aspects for marriage (moon conjunct sun, moon conjunct moon, or moon conjunct ascendant). Although the figures do not exceed the kind of dispersions that might be expected due to chance, Jung considers it psychologically interesting that they appear to confirm astrological expectation. Moreover, if the probabilities of the three individual sets of results are combined, the overall result does become statistically significant. In Jung's view, his results fortuitously imitate astrological expectation and therefore constitute a synchronistic phenomenon. The archetypal background to this synchronicity he finds indicated by the lively interest taken in the experiment by himself and his co-worker. Rejecting as primitive and regressive the hypothesis of magical causality, he concludes that if the connecting principle between astrological expectation and the results obtained is not causal, it must consist in meaning.

This conclusion is supported in the third chapter, 'Forerunners of the Idea of Synchronicity' (1952b: pars. 916–46). Jung surveys a range of traditional views – oriental and western; primitive, classical, medieval and Renaissance – which express the possibility of there being a realm of transcendental, objective or 'self-subsistent' meaning. In particular, he looks at the notions of Tao, microcosm and macrocosm, sympathy, correspondence, and pre-established harmony. He also notes that the idea of self-subsistent meaning is sometimes suggested in dreams.

In the fourth and final chapter, 'Conclusion' (1952b: pars. 947–68), Jung acknowledges that his views concerning synchronicity have not been proved, but he nevertheless suggests, on the basis of observations of out-of-the-body and near-death experiences, that the relationship between mind and body may yet prove to be one of synchronicity. He then elaborates on the theoretical status of synchronicity as a fourth explanatory principle, one in addition to time, space and causality (or in addition to indestructible energy, the space–time continuum and causality). According to Jung, synchronicity 'makes possible a whole judgment' (ibid.: par. 961) by introducing the 'psychoid factor' (ibid.: par. 962) of meaning into one's description of nature. It thereby also helps bring about a rapprochement between psychology and physics. More specifically, the psychoid factor at the basis of synchronicity is the archetype – a factor that Jung proceeds to characterise. Archetypes provide the shared meaning by virtue of which two events are considered to be in a relationship of synchronicity. They cannot be determined with precision and are capable of expressing themselves in physical as well as psychic processes. They manifest their meaning through whatever psychic and physical content is available, but might equally well have manifested the same meaning through other content. They represent psychic probability, making it likely that certain types of events will occur but not enabling one actually to predict the occurrence of any particular event. At this point Jung introduces the broader category of general acausal orderedness, of which experiences of meaningful coincidence are considered one particular instance. He states in conclusion that general acausal orderedness (which includes such phenomena as the properties of natural numbers and the discontinuities of modern physics) is a universal factor existing from all eternity, whereas meaningful coincidences are individual acts of creation in time. Both, however, are synchronistic phenomena occurring within the field of the contingent.

This summary gives an idea of the intellectual difficulties presented by Jung's theory of synchronicity – some of them stemming from his unorthodox range of interests and references, others from the sheer obscurity of his arguments. It is hoped that many of these difficulties will be resolved or clarified in the course of this and subsequent chapters. However, as we probe more deeply, the waters may sometimes have to get murkier before they get clearer. We can begin by looking at the relationship between the phenomena of synchronicity and Jung's definitions of the concept.

Definitions and phenomena

Even if we restrict ourselves to the examples of synchronicity provided by Jung, we find that the range of phenomena to which the notion is applied is so wide that not one of his attempts at detailed definition adequately encompasses it.

'. . . simultaneous occurrence . . . '

Consider the definition that follows Jung's paradigmatic case involving the scarab beetle. Synchronicity, states Jung, is 'the simultaneous occurrence of a certain psychic state with one or more external events which appear as meaningful parallels to the momentary subjective state – and in certain cases, vice versa' (1952b: par. 850). As we have already noted in the case of the student who dreamed of events in Spain that later occurred in reality, Jung is happy to apply the term 'synchronicity' to sets of events that conspicuously are not simultaneous (1951b: par. 973; cf. ibid.: par. 974; 1963: 169–70; 1976: 25). For this reason alone, then, the above definition is inadequate.

'. . . psychic . . . external . . . '

What about the remaining assertions in the definition? Do all synchronicities, in Jung's view, involve the paralleling of an inner psychic state with one or more outer physical events? It is true that by far the majority of the synchronistic events recounted by Jung, including the cases of the scarab beetle, Swedenborg's vision, and the student's dream of Spain, are adequately covered by this description. However, there are other events that Jung relates which fit into neither this description nor any plausible construal of what he could mean in his definition by 'vice versa'. For he also applies the term 'synchronistic' to sets of events involving a relationship either solely between two inner psychic states or solely between two outer physical events. An example of the former is where couples (or parents and children) share the same thoughts and dreams (see Jung 1976: 63). Examples of the latter would include where parallel events occur in the lives of persons born on the same day (ibid.: 353–5), or where parallel periods of style emerge at the same time in widely separated cultures (Jung 1930: par. 81; 1934–9: 228). Indeed, one of Jung's other definitions explicitly states that a synchronicity can be between two outer physical events: 'synchronicity', he writes in his 'Foreword to the "I Ching"', 'takes the coincidence of events in space and time as meaning something more than mere chance, namely, a peculiar *interdependence of objective events among themselves* as well as with the subjective (psychic) states of the observer or observers' (1950a: par. 972, emphasis added).

'. . . parallels . . .'

Further than this, it is not even certain from Jung's examples that the component events in a synchronicity, whether inner or outer, psychic or physical, always need to parallel one another. It is not just a question of some events being symbolic and requiring interpretation before the paralleling becomes evident. More than this, it seems the relationship can be one not of paralleling at all but of compensation. As Robert Aziz has observed, in some of the synchronistic events presented by Jung the psychic component consists not of an image from the unconscious that is literally or symbolically paralleled by an outer physical event but of the conscious orientation of the experiencer (Aziz 1990: 59–67, 84–90). The outer physical event does not parallel this conscious orientation but compensates it, thereby promoting individuation or providing insight into one's psychic condition in much the same way as a compensatory dream might do. Aziz suggests that the synchronistic workings of the *I Ching* should be understood in this light, since the content of the responses obtained from the oracle generally does not parallel any previously arisen unconscious image but rather compensates the conscious attitude expressed or implied in the question put to the oracle (ibid.: 62–3).

More specifically, Aziz also points to two spontaneous examples from Jung's writings where compensation rather than paralleling defines the link between the component events of the synchronicity. The first, reported by Jung in his memoirs (1963: 290–1), concerns his experience while travelling home on the train to attend his mother's funeral. Jung recounts that, in these circumstances, he was naturally filled with grief. However, he found that 'during the entire journey I continually heard dance music, laughter, and jollity, as though a wedding were being celebrated' so that 'it was impossible to yield entirely to my sorrow' (ibid.). In his discussion of the experience, Jung suggests that while from the perspective of the ego death is both physically and psychologically 'a piece of fearful brutality', from the perspective of the self it can appear as a 'joyful event', 'a wedding, a *mysterium coniunctionis*' in which 'the soul attains, as it were, its missing half, it achieves wholeness' (ibid.: 291). Aziz suggests that in this experience Jung's conscious attitude of grief is being compensated by the synchronistic appearance in his environment of the sounds of festivity that expressed the wider perspective of the self. Yet there is no inner psychic image in the event that parallels this outer physical expression of festivity (Aziz 1990: 60–1).[1]

The second example to which Aziz draws attention is the one Jung recounts in his 1952 essay alongside the incident involving the scarab beetle. Jung relates:

> The wife of one of my patients, a man in his fifties, once told me in conversation that, at the deaths of her mother and her grandmother, a number of birds gathered outside the windows of the death-chamber. I had heard similar stories from other people. When her husband's treatment was nearing its end, his neurosis having been cleared up, he developed some apparently quite innocuous symptoms which seemed to me, however, to be those of heart-disease. I sent him along to a specialist, who after examining him told me in writing that he could find no cause for anxiety. On the way back from this consultation (with the medical report in his pocket) my patient collapsed in the street. As he was brought home dying, his wife was already in a great state of anxiety because, soon after her husband had gone to the doctor, a whole flock of birds alighted on their house. She naturally remembered the similar incidents that had happened at the death of her own relatives, and feared the worst.
>
> (Jung 1952b: par. 844)

In this example, as Aziz notes, the woman's fears 'arose solely on the basis of this external synchronistic manifestation' of the alighting birds (1990: 85). There was no inner event paralleling this external manifestation. The inner event in the synchronicity was the wife's conscious attitude, which we are told was not one of any serious apprehension (Jung 1952b: 850). This attitude was compensated rather than paralleled by the external event.

It is possible that the cryptic addendum to Jung's definition – 'and, in certain cases, vice versa' – is an attempt to address the kind of experiences to which Aziz has drawn attention. If Jung means by 'vice versa' that in some cases one or more outer physical events can be paralleled by a subsequently registered inner psychic state, this arguably could apply to cases such as those just described. When the flock of birds alighted on the roof, this could have evoked the wife's already existent but unconscious apprehension concerning her husband's health. By the same line of reasoning, we could suppose that the outer manifestation of festivity that Jung encountered on the train served to evoke an already existent but unconscious appreciation of the festive, symbolically nuptial aspect of his mother's death. With his wide knowledge of myths and symbols, Jung would certainly have known these associations at the time. Again, it is conceivable that responses from the *I Ching* present outer contents that parallel already existent but unconscious images within the person asking the question. Users of the *I Ching* sometimes report that the textual image they obtain seems to correspond to their unconscious preoccupations, even if those preoccupations are not directly articulated in the question put to the oracle (e.g., Jung 1950a: par. 983; Hook 1973: 30). Jung's recognition of this dynamic is further indicated by his suggestion that cases of *déjà vu* can be understood as the recollection of unconscious knowledge in the light of an external event: 'As always when an external event touches on some unconscious knowledge', he writes, 'this knowledge can reach consciousness. The event is recognized as a *déjà vu*, and one remembers a pre-existent knowledge about it' (1952a: par. 640; see also 1951b: par. 974; 1976: 479).

If a simple reason is sought why these and similar cases have not received more emphasis in discussions of synchronicity, it may lie in the difficulty of demonstrating acausality when an outer physical event is registered before an inner psychic one, for the inner event could so plausibly be seen as a direct response to the outer event. Jung reflects on this in relation to the incident with the alighting birds. After commenting that 'The unconscious . . . often knows more than the conscious, and it seems to me possible that the woman's unconscious had already got wind of the danger' (1952b: par. 850), Jung adds a note of caution. The 'excitation of the unconscious', he says, is 'possible but still not demonstrable' because 'The psychic state . . . appears to be dependent on [i.e., caused by] the external event' (ibid.). He considers in the end that such a causal explanation is not appropriate in this particular case, since 'The woman's psyche is nevertheless involved in so far as the birds settled on her house and were observed by her. For this reason it seems to be probable that her unconscious was in fact constellated' (ibid.). However, the difficulties of maintaining the case for acausality when the first registered event is an external physical one are apparent.

' . . . state . . . events . . . '

Another point on which Jung's definition seems inadequate to the phenomenological complexity of synchronicity is in its emphasis on states and events, the former generally characterised as inner and psychic, the latter as outer and physical. Jung nowhere explains what he means by states and events, in particular whether the former are always psychic and the latter physical or whether they should be understood as synonyms. The impression given by his definitions is that the psychic states are relatively short-lived – 'momentary' (Jung 1952b: par. 850) – and the physical events even more discrete and transient. These features contribute to the sense that synchronistic experiences are brief temporal moments. However, one or both of the components of a synchronicity, if we are to follow Jung's applications of the term, can be considerably longer lived than this. In a letter to Fr. Victor White (21 September 1951), Jung refers to a particular woman as 'a synchronistic phenomenon all over' so that 'one can keep up with her as little as with the unconscious' (1976: 24). This implies that the 'inner psychic state' that contributes to the occurrence of synchronicity is in her case not something momentary but rather her ongoing subjective state. That the 'outer physical event' in a synchronicity can also be more than momentary is suggested by Jung's characterisation of the Chinese notion of Tao. 'The realization of Tao has this quality of being in a sort of synchronistic relation with everything else', he is recorded as saying in the *Visions* seminars; 'that is the general mystical experience, the coincidence of the individual condition with the universe, so that the two become indistinguishable' (1930–4: 608). Elsewhere he even equates synchronicity with Tao: 'Tao can be anything', he states in the second of his 'Tavistock Lectures'. 'I use another word to designate it, but it is poor enough. I call it *synchronicity*' (1935: par. 143). An even more decisive indication of Jung's view that the psychic and physical 'events' of a synchronicity need not be momentary is provided by his speculation that not just one or a few mental and physical events but the entire ongoing relationship between mind and body may be synchronistic (1952b: par. 948; 1935: pars. 69–70). Finally, towards the end of his 1952 essay, Jung introduced the broader category of 'general acausal orderedness' to account for phenomena such as the discontinuities of physics and the properties of natural numbers, which on the one hand are acausal but on the other hand are 'constant' and 'have existed from eternity' (1952b: par. 965).

It is clear, then, that the definition Jung provides immediately after his paradigmatic case of synchronicity – that is, at the very point where we would expect him to attempt to provide his most considered definition – is incapable of adequately accounting for the full range of phenomena that he designates as synchronistic. Indeed, as we have seen, it does not even satisfactorily account for the experiences it immediately follows. Since Jung elsewhere provides alternative definitions, we need to consider whether any of those are more successful.

' . . . three categories . . . '

As we saw in the previous chapter, in his 1951 essay Jung follows his account of the scarab coincidence with a longer definition that attempts to group synchronistic phenomena into three categories (1951b: pars. 984–5). The aim is to account for kinds of synchronicity, such as Swedenborg's vision and the student's dream of Spain, in which simultaneity between the component events is not immediately evident. In most respects, this longer definition is no more successful than the shorter one already considered. For it similarly fails to account for synchronicities in which either both component events are psychic or both are physical, in which the relationship between the events is one of compensation rather than paralleling, and in which not momentary but ongoing psychic and physical states are involved. Furthermore, the longer definition neglects to mention anything about meaning and in that respect may even be less adequate than the shorter definition.

Indeed, even in its attempt to address the lack of simultaneity in some synchronistic events, this expanded definition does not entirely account for the range of phenomena referred to by Jung. For while he provides an account of instances of apparent precognition, where an event from the future is paralleled by an image in the present, he does not similarly account for instances of apparent retrocognition, where an event from the past about which one has no conceivable knowledge is paralleled by an image in the present. Nevertheless, in his memoirs, Jung describes such an incident that occurred to him in 1923 or 1924. One night, while staying alone in his secluded tower at Bollingen, Jung had a repeated dream of a procession of hundreds of dark-clad peasant boys who had come down from the mountains and seemed to be pouring in around the tower with a great deal of loud bustling and festivity (1963: 217). He twice woke up convinced that this was taking place in reality, but when he went to the window he found only 'a deathly still moonlit night' (ibid.: 217–18). He says he was unable to account for the incident until, much later, he came across a couple of parallel experiences. In one, related in a seventeenth-century Lucerne chronicle, the procession was considered to be 'Wotan's army of departed souls' (ibid.: 218); the other involved the 'real parallel' of certain mercenaries who used to gather in the region in the spring before marching to Italy to serve as soldiers for foreign princes (ibid.: 219). After dismissing the possibility that his experience could have been a compensatory hallucination brought on by the solitude, Jung concludes that it 'would seem most likely to have been a synchronistic phenomenon' (ibid.). He omits to note, however, as he might have noted especially in relation to his knowledge about the mercenaries, that what his present dream or hallucination is paralleling is an outer physical event from the remote past. The reason for the omission may be the difficulty of establishing retrocognition convincingly, given the possibility that the past event could so easily have been known by normal means, perhaps involving cryptomnesia. In his definition, Jung prefers to direct attention to the clearer and more radical case of non-simultaneity in apparent precognition.

' . . . two different psychic states . . . '

However, Jung makes an even bolder attempt to define synchronicity, which may in part have been intended to address some of the outstanding problems we have discussed. Several paragraphs on from his paradigmatic example, and immediately following definition in the 1952 essay, he introduces an alternative definition that includes an important, at first puzzling, additional factor: a second psychic state (1952b: par. 855). Having earlier written, as in the 1951 essay, of the simultaneity of psychic and physical events (ibid.: par. 850), he suddenly shifts to speaking of 'the simultaneous occurrence of two different psychic states' (1952b: par. 855). He explains that 'One of them is the normal, probable state (i.e., the one that is causally explicable), and the other, the critical experience, is the one that cannot be causally derived from the first' (ibid.). If one wonders what has happened here to the physical event, it is understood as the 'objective existence' (ibid.) of the 'critical' psychic event. Jung is now claiming that the synchronicity consists of the coincidence not between the critical psychic event and its objective correlate but between the two psychic events: 'An unexpected content which is directly or indirectly connected with some objective external event coincides with the ordinary psychic state: this is what I call synchronicity' (ibid.). For instance, in the coincidence involving the scarab, the 'unexpected content' is the dream of the scarab jewel, while the 'objective external event' with which this unexpected content is 'directly or indirectly connected' is the appearance of the real scarab beetle. The 'ordinary psychic state' – the new presence in the definition – we must suppose to be the ongoing state of mind of the patient at the time of her dream, identified by Jung as a state of excessive rationalism. It is this ordinary state which is simultaneous with the unexpected content of the dream and which Jung, rather surprisingly, says 'coincides' with it.

This thinking receives unambiguous expression in the definition of synchronicity that occurs in the 'Résumé' added to the 1955 English translation of the principal essay. With the specific aim of clearing up misunderstandings that had arisen, Jung writes:

> By synchronicity I mean the occurrence of a *meaningful coincidence in time*. It can take three forms:
> a) The coincidence of a certain psychic content with a corresponding objective process which is perceived to take place simultaneously.
> b) The coincidence of a subjective psychic state with a phantasm (dream or vision) which later turns out to be a more or less faithful reflection of a 'synchronistic', objective event that took place more or less simultaneously, but at a distance.
> c) The same, except that the event perceived takes place in the future and is represented in the present only by a phantasm that corresponds to it.
> Whereas in the first case an objective event coincides with a subjective content, the synchronicity in the other two cases can only be verified subsequently, though the synchronistic event as such is formed by the coincidence of a neutral psychic state with a phantasm (dream or vision).
>
> (Jung 1955: 144–5)

This definition is clearly similar to the three-pronged 1951 definition quoted in the previous chapter (see pp. 13–14). Now, however, instead of the coincidence in the second and third cases being between a psychic state and an objective external event which has been 'anticipated in time', it is between one psychic state and another psychic state (a 'phantasm') which is 'a more or less faithful reflection' of an objective external event.

For Jung's purposes, the advantage of introducing the normal psychic state is that it allows him to retain the notion of simultaneity in the case of each of his three categories of synchronicity, for in each case there is both a normal psychic state and an unexpected psychic content occurring simultaneously with it. The simultaneity of these two psychic states is not compromised no matter how great a separation there is in either space or time between the unexpected psychic content and its corresponding objective external event. Referring to the occurrence of the unexpected contents which mark the actual synchronicities – of whatever kind – Jung maintains that 'we are dealing with exactly the same category of events whether their objectivity appears separated from my consciousness in space or in time' (1952b: par. 855).

However, for all its advantage in terms of preserving simultaneity, this definition is itself fraught with problems. First, it means that there are now two acausal relationships involved in the synchronicity: that between the two psychic events (1952b: par. 855), and that between the second psychic event and the physical event with which it corresponds (ibid.: par. 858). Though Jung says of the two critical events – the second psychic event and the physical event – that '[t]he one is as puzzling as the other' (ibid.), he nowhere shows explicit awareness of the fact that he is claiming they are both, in different respects, acausal. In fact, though Jung's definitions do not explicitly acknowledge this, there may be a third kind of acausal relationship possible: between the normal psychic state and the objective external event. This would be the kind of synchronicity to which Aziz draws attention, where an outer physical event does not parallel but only compensates an inner psychic state.

Second, any acausal relationship that may exist between the two psychic events will be virtually impossible to demonstrate. Since both events are intrapsychic, the possibility of there being some associative causal connection between them can scarcely be even improbable, let alone, as Jung requires, 'unthinkable' (1952b.: par. 967). At any rate, it is not acausality of this kind, but of the kind between a psychic and a physical event, that Jung's examples almost invariably try to illustrate.

A third problem is that of identifying the neutral psychic state at all in many of Jung's examples. For while we are told the neutral psychic state in the cases involving the scarab beetle and the flock of birds alighting on the roof, we are only able to guess about the normal psychic state simultaneously with which the student's dream of the Spanish city took place; and the same is true of most of Jung's other examples. If Jung thought the neutral psychic state a crucial component in his definition of synchronicity, it is surprising that he should so rarely have made this state explicit. In the light of Aziz's work, one might in general identify the normal psychic state with the conscious orientation of the experiencer (Aziz 1990: 66). The unexpected content that arises simultaneously with this conscious orientation would be, according to Aziz, an unconscious compensation serving the purposes of individuation (ibid.: 66–7). This compensatory relationship between the two psychic events is indeed acausal in that the conscious orientation does not cause the compensation but only provides the conditions in which it might occur. Again, inasmuch as the compensatory relationship is involved ultimately in the furthering of individuation, it is also meaningful. However, even if this understanding proves workable up to a point, it also involves at least one notable departure from Jung's explicit statements elsewhere: two psychic states in a compensatory relationship may be meaningfully related in terms of individuation, but they do not in any obvious sense have, as Jung specifies, 'the same or a similar meaning' (1952b: par. 849). If they did, the one would hardly be compensated by the other.

It appears, then, without our yet probing very deeply into the pivotal concepts of the notion of synchronicity – time, acausality, meaning and probability – that Jung's attempts at detailed definition of the phenomenon are inadequate even to account for his own examples. In a sense, this is not surprising, for Jung acknowledges that 'meaningful coincidences are infinitely varied in their phenomenology' (1951b: par. 995). The only definitions he offers that are not at odds with one or other of his examples are such basic ones as 'meaningful coincidence' and 'acausal connection'.

Further characteristics of synchronicity

Ambiguities surround not only Jung's definitions but also some of his general characterisations of synchronicity.

Description or theory?

In the first place, there is an ambiguity in the way Jung and others use the term 'synchronicity'. Sometimes it is used phenomenologically, simply to designate a kind of event – namely, a coincidence that is experienced as meaningful. Other times the term refers to Jung's theory of how such events come about and are to be understood psychologically. As we saw in the previous chapter, accepting Jung's theory of synchronicity entails prior acceptance of a substantial part of his psychological model. However, accepting synchronicity simply as the experiential phenomenon of meaningful coincidence does not require that one should subscribe to a Jungian psychological model.

Empiricism or metaphysics?

The ambiguity is even starker when we ask whether synchronicity is an empirical or metaphysical concept. 'Synchronicity', Jung insists, 'is not a philosophical view but an empirical concept which postulates an intellectually necessary principle' (1952b: par. 960); 'It is based not on philosophical assumptions but on empirical experience and experimentation' (1951b: par. 995). From the material before him he claims that he 'can derive no other hypothesis that would adequately explain the facts' (1952b: par. 947). Notwithstanding this last statement, he elsewhere acknowledges that it is 'only a makeshift model' and 'does not rule out the possibility of other hypotheses' (1976: 437).

Other writers, however, have found aspects of the theory of synchronicity to be less free from metaphysical presupposition than these statements imply. Explicitly or implicitly, Jung's claims to an empirical status for his work are based on an appeal to Kant's epistemological distinction between phenomena (things as they appear to human consciousness) and noumena (things as they are in themselves) – Jung's professed concern being solely with phenomena (see, e.g., de Voogd 1984). However, Wolfgang Giegerich has argued that many of the core concepts of Jung's psychology, including the concept of synchronicity, overstep the limits prescribed by Kantian epistemology: 'As long as Jung clings to his label "empiricist first and last," Kant would show him that he has no right to posit, for example, a psychoid archetypal level in which the subject–object dichotomy would be overcome' (Giegerich 1987: 111).

This issue, as Giegerich implies, goes to the heart of Jung's psychology as a whole. Jung himself does appear to have been aware that his thinking on at least synchronicity sometimes shifts into metaphysics. In a letter to Michael Fordham (3 January 1957) he congratulates Fordham on his essay 'Reflections on the Archetypes and Synchronicity' (1957) and remarks that, while he understands Fordham's emphasis on the psychologically important archetypal implications of synchronicity, he himself is 'equally interested, at times even more so, in the metaphysical aspect of the phenomena' (Jung 1976: 344).

Again, in a letter to Karl Schmid (11 June 1958) Jung admits that it can sometimes be legitimate to conceptualise beyond the bounds of what is empirically knowable so long as this conceptualisation does not come 'from my biased speculation but rather from the unfathomable law of nature herself . . . from the total man, i.e., from the co-participation of the unconscious [in the form of dreams etc.]' (1976: 448). 'This far-reaching speculation', he believes, 'is a psychic need which is part of our mental hygiene', adding, however, that 'in the realm of scientific verification it must be counted sheer mythology' (ibid.: 449). Thus, he is able to excuse some of his own more incautious statements regarding synchronicity: 'if', he concedes, 'I occasionally speak of an "organizer," this is sheer mythology since at present I have no means of going beyond the bare fact that synchronistic phenomena are "just so"' (ibid.). Again, after quoting a paragraph from his 1952 essay affirming the transcendental nature of the '"absolute knowledge" which is characteristic of synchronistic phenomena' (1952b: par. 948), he admits that 'This statement, too, is mythology, like all transcendental postulates' (1976: 449).

Irregular or regular?

Turning to the actual character of synchronistic events, Jung presents them sometimes as irregularly occurring, at other times as regularly occurring. His emphasis is on irregular occurrence. In his 1952 essay he formalises synchronicity as a principle of 'inconstant connection' (1952b: 963) and discusses at length the problems of devising experimental methods for investigating phenomena that cannot be produced to order (ibid.: pars. 821–4, 833–8, 863–71). Examples of irregularly occurring synchronicities would include the incidents with the scarab beetle and the flock of birds alighting on the roof, indeed almost all of the incidents Jung either experienced personally or observed in his clinical work.

However, at times Jung also recognises the possibility of regularly occurring synchronicities. For example, the results of Rhine's parapsychological experiments were sufficiently reproducible to be amenable to statistical evaluation

(1952b: par. 965). With divinatory methods such as astrology and the *I Ching* Jung writes that 'Synchronistic phenomena are found to occur – experimentally – with some degree of regularity and frequency' (ibid.: par. 958). Again, if the mind–body relationship were found to be synchronistic – and Jung is at least open to this possibility – then this too would imply that acausality is not just a rare and irregular phenomenon (ibid.: par. 938 n. 70). Above all, the conception of synchronicity as having to do solely with irregular one-off events was called into question for Jung by such factors as the properties of natural numbers and certain quantum phenomena such as 'the orderedness of energy quanta, of radium decay, etc.' (ibid.: par. 966).[2] These are properties of the world that appear to have no deeper cause but are 'Just-So'; that is, acausal (ibid.: par. 965).

Jung himself recognised the tension between views of synchronicity as regular or irregular and he tried to resolve it by postulating the broader category of general acausal orderedness of which synchronistic events in the more experiential sense are an important sub-category. Synchronicity in the narrow sense is distinguished from general acausal orderedness in that phenomena belonging to the latter category 'have existed from eternity and occur regularly, whereas the forms of psychic orderedness [i.e., synchronicities] are *acts of creation in time*' (ibid.).

Spontaneous or generated?

A similar tension exists in the way Jung presents synchronicity sometimes as spontaneously occurring, but at other times as amenable to conscious and repeatable generation. His emphasis is on the spontaneous character of synchronicity which, like its irregularity, is suggested primarily by personal experiences and clinical observations. However, he also finds several indications of the amenability of synchronicity to conscious and repeatable generation. One is provided by certain kinds of mediumistic personalities. Jung relates in a letter to A. D. Cornell (9 February 1960) that he has 'observed and also partially analysed people who seemed to possess a supernormal faculty and were able to make use of it at will' (1976: 542). He adds that the act of will consists 'in their being in, or voluntarily putting themselves into, a state corresponding to an archetypal constellation – a state of numinous possession in which synchronistic phenomena become possible and even, to some extent, probable' (ibid.). Another indication is the practice of divination. With the *I Ching*, for instance, answers that can stand in a clear synchronistic relationship to the underlying conscious or unconscious preoccupations of the questioner are obtained not spontaneously but by a prescribed process of consultation. This sometimes led Jung actually to recommend the use of the *I Ching* as an experimental method of generating and investigating synchronicities (ibid.: 491). Again, a measure of repeatability is suggested by the positive results of Rhine's parapsychological experiments, where some experimental subjects seemed able to generate significant numbers of 'coincidences' between their guesses and the experimental targets (1952b: pars. 833–8).

Jung was clearly aware of the apparent inconsistency between spontaneous and generated synchronicities. He attempted to resolve it through conceiving of archetypes as factors whose constellation cannot be forced but can be encouraged and which, once constellated, can make certain kinds of psychic events probable even if not certain (1952b: par. 964).

Normal or paranormal?

Jung mostly considers the component events in a synchronicity to have their own independent causal chains. There is nothing remarkable about an analysand having and telling a dream of being given a jewel in the form of a scarab beetle, nor is there anything remarkable about a scarab beetle flying against a window. Each event could be explained causally. What is remarkable, because acausal and meaningful, is the timely coincidence of these two events. However, Jung occasionally also wants to apply his concept of synchronicity to events that in themselves are radically paranormal and inexplicable in terms of ordinary causes and effects. For example, he recounts in *Memories, Dreams, Reflections* how a bread-knife once split in four in a locked drawer (1963: 108–9), how mysterious detonations occurred in Freud's bookcase when he and Freud were arguing about the paranormal (ibid.: 152), how when his house seemed to be haunted the blanket was several times invisibly snatched from his daughter's bed (ibid.: 182), and how during the same period his doorbell started ringing when there was nobody at the door (ibid.: 182–3). Each of these outer events coincided meaningfully with an intense psychic state, and so the composite event meets the criterion for being accounted synchronistic. However, these outer events are themselves inexplicable in normal causal terms, and it is not clear what Jung's attitude to such events is in relation to his theory of synchronicity. For the theory does not aim to account for the component events of a coincidence but only for the relationship between them.[3]

The solution to this dilemma probably lies in Jung's characterisation of synchronicity as a 'psychically conditioned relativity of space and time' (1952b: par. 840). If, as Jung claims, 'in relation to the psyche space and time are, so to speak, "elastic" and can apparently be reduced almost to vanishing point' (ibid.), then it is possible for physical events to occur in the absence of the spatially or temporally proximate causes that would normally account for them. This would explain the possibility of the radically anomalous physical events that happened to Jung and his household. The clue to how such an explanation could also involve coincidence (i.e., not only the physical event but also a connected psychic state) lies in Jung's statement that such 'relativity of space and time' is 'psychically conditioned'. Although such paranormal events as the shattering of a bread-knife in a locked drawer can be described and can fascinate without reference to a psychic state, they cannot, in Jung's model, be *understood* without reference to such a state. For it is this state, characterised by the 'simultaneous emergence of an archetype, or rather, of an emotion corresponding to it' (1976: 538), that psychically conditions the event.

Supporting or supported by the notion of the 'psychoid' unconscious?

There is also ambiguity about whether Jung thinks synchronicity supports the notion of the psychoid unconscious or is supported by it. Most of the evidence suggests the former. As we have seen, Jung writes that '[s]ynchronicity tells us something about the nature of what I call the *psychoid* factor, i.e., the unconscious archetype' (1950–5: par. 1208). Elsewhere he comments that '[t]his remarkable effect [i.e., synchronicity] points to the "psychoid" and essentially transcendental nature of the archetype as an "arranger" of psychic forms inside and outside the psyche' (1976: 22). Elsewhere again, he suggests that '[f]rom synchronistic phenomena we learn that a peculiar feature of the psychoid background is transgressivity in space and time' (ibid.: 259). At other times, however, Jung appeals to the notion of the psychoid unconscious as part of his explanation of synchronicity. For example, in his 1952 essay, after stating that synchronicity 'consists essentially of "chance" equivalences', he adds: 'Their *tertium comparationis* rests on the psychoid factors I call archetypes' (1952b: par. 964).

The core concepts of synchronicity

Further intellectual difficulties emerge when we examine more closely the central concepts running through Jung's theory of synchronicity: time, acausality, meaning and probability. Although there are long traditions of philosophical debate about each of these concepts, Jung does not purport to enter such debates in a rigorous manner. His understanding of each concept seems to be established through interplay between commonsense notions and some selected special meanings, either stated explicitly or emerging from the context of his discussions. Consequently, the bold and suggestive insights that he presents stand in a sometimes uneasy relationship to mainstream intellectual traditions.

Time

Jung sometimes defines synchronicity in terms of simultaneity, on the assumption that moments of time have specific qualities and therefore events happening at the same time share the quality of that moment. His early reflections stemming from investigations of astrology and the *I Ching* explicitly express this point of view. Indeed, Jung was articulating this view as late as 1949 when he wrote his 'Foreword to the "I Ching"' (1950a). Moreover, the very concept 'synchronicity', deriving as it does from Greek words for 'together' (*syn*) and 'time' (*chronos*), suggests the notion of simultaneity. However, at other times Jung categorically asserts that synchronicity does not entail simultaneity of its component events. Referring to the second and third prongs of his 1951 three-pronged definition, he writes that 'the coinciding events are not yet present in the observer's field of perception, but have been anticipated in time in so far as they can only be verified afterward. For this reason I call such events *synchronistic*, which is not to be confused with *synchronous*' (1951b: par. 985). This change of viewpoint seems to have been stimulated by his reflections on the theory of relativity in physics and the findings of parapsychology, where Rhine reported that the significant results he obtained were not affected when the senders and receivers in his experiments were separated by even great distances in space and time. Although Jung does not make this explicit, the notion of the psychic relativity of space and time accounts for coincidences in which the component events are simultaneously present in the observer's field of perception as well as for coincidences involving events that are widely separated in time or space. In a simultaneous coincidence, the very simultaneity of the events expresses a relativisation of space and time, for it is because the events are simultaneous that there is no time for a causal influence to be transmitted from one to the other.

Jung provided several hints about the outlook underlying this notion of the psychic relativisation of space and time. In his discussion of 'Forerunners of the Idea of Synchronicity' (1952b: ch. 3), he quotes Richard Wilhelm's characterisation of Tao as 'a non-spatial and non-temporal unity' (ibid.: par. 921). In equating synchronicity with such an understanding of Tao, Jung is clearly speculating about the metaphysical ground of synchronicity (what he elsewhere refers to as the '*unus mundus*' or 'one world'). This tendency is further suggested by his description of synchronistic events as 'creative acts, as the continuous creation of a pattern that exists from all eternity, repeats itself sporadically, and is not derivable from any known antecedents' (ibid.: par. 967). In a footnote on continuous creation, he cites early Christian theologians – Origen, Augustine, Prosper of Aquitaine, and an anonymous author – for whom, in Jung's words, 'Continuous creation is to be thought of not only as a series of successive acts of creation, but also as the eternal presence of the *one* creative act'; 'God is contained in his own creation'; 'What happens successively in time is simultaneous in the mind of God'; and 'Before the Creation there was no time – time only began with created things' (ibid.: par. 967 n. 17). Although all this is buried in a footnote on the penultimate page of the essay, the implication seems to be that synchronicity can be understood as expressive of the simultaneity that exists 'in eternity' in the mind of God. Generally, this simultaneity unfolds in Creation 'successively in time'. However, in moments of synchronicity, we glimpse something of the simultaneous coexistence of events in eternity; we catch a glimpse of God 'contained in his own creation' (cf. 1976: 22).

A similar resolution of the problem of simultaneity in synchronicity has been proposed by Aziz, although he appeals for support not to theology but to physics. He suggests that there is a distinction in Jung's thinking between 'the synchronicity principle' and the 'synchronistic event'. The synchronicity principle refers to the archetypal world of the unconscious in which the categories of space and time as they are experienced by ego-consciousness do not apply (as seems to be the case in the subatomic realm of physics). Within the psychoid unconscious, 'everything exists en bloc' in 'a psychophysical space–time continuum' (1990:

71). The synchronistic event, however, refers to the synchronicity as experienced by ego-consciousness in space and time. Here what is a unitary event in the unconscious has been refracted into multiple contexts in consciousness, so that the components of the synchronicity are experienced as separated in time and space as well as differentiated into psychic and physical events (ibid.: 71–2).

In spite of the explanatory potential of the notion of the psychic relativisation of space and time, Jung seeks other ways of preserving the notion of simultaneity. We have seen that this intention may have been behind his surprising and problematic reformulation of synchronicity as 'the simultaneous occurrence of two different psychic states' (1952b: par. 855). For the two psychic states, the 'normal state' and the 'unexpected state', are always simultaneous, even when there is no simultaneity between the 'unexpected state' and the 'objective event' with which it corresponds.

Acausality

We saw in the previous chapter that the notion of acausality is non-negotiable in Jung's thinking about synchronicity. As the title of his 1952 essay announces, synchronicity is 'an acausal connecting principle'. The notion is supported, in Jung's view, by data from a variety of contexts, including personal and clinical experiences, experiments in divination, the history of philosophy and religion, experimental parapsychology and developments in quantum physics. All of these influences and sources will be considered in detail in the next chapter. However, Jung's first recourse when affirming the existence of acausality is to the following argument based on quantum physics.

'The discoveries of modern physics', Jung informs us, ' . . . have shattered the absolute validity of natural law and made it relative' (1952b: par. 818). Since 'very small quantities [i.e., subatomic particles] no longer behave in accordance with natural laws', it follows that 'Natural laws are *statistical* truths' (ibid.). Further:

> The philosophical principle that underlies our conception of natural law is *causality*. But if the connection between cause and effect turns out to be only statistically valid and only relatively true, then the causal principle is only of relative use for explaining natural processes and therefore presupposes the existence of one or more other factors which would be necessary for an explanation.
>
> (Jung 1952b: par. 819)

This 'other factor' is Jung's 'acausal connecting principle'. He believes the above argument to have proved the existence of the principle in 'the realm of very small quantities' (ibid.: par. 818). Regarding its existence in the realm of normal sensory experience, he says:

We shall naturally look round in vain in the macrophysical world for acausal events, for the simple reason that we cannot imagine events that are connected non-causally and are capable of a non-causal explanation. But that does not mean that such events do not exist. Their existence – or at least their possibility – follows logically from the premise of statistical truth.

(Jung 1952b: par. 820)

Presumably, Jung emphasised this argument from physics because it promised to give his concept of acausality the greatest degree of scientific respectability and the securest epistemological grounding. However, it brings with it several problems of its own. For instance, the fact that Jung's understanding of causality and acausality is so closely tied to physics threatens to make it too restrictive. He himself clearly intended the notion of acausality to apply to psychological as well as to physical causes: synchronistic events are not caused by psychological states. Yet it is at least questionable whether physical terms alone are adequate to account for the dynamics of psychological causes. As John Beloff points out: 'the concept of cause was not invented by physicists, physics is merely one of the domains for its application, the concept as such is a very basic logical notion of wide generality' (1977: 577). In response to Jung's claim that Rhine's parapsychological data have furnished '[d]ecisive evidence for the existence of acausal combinations of events' (Jung 1952b: par. 833), Beloff writes that it is 'nonsensical to say . . . that there are events that are related experimentally that are not related causally. For the crux of the experimental method is precisely carrying out certain procedures that we may call A so as to find out whether or not they are necessary in order to obtain a result B' (Beloff 1977: 577). If Rhine's experiments are indeed statistically significant and there is no way to account for them in normal causal terms, what they demonstrate, according to Beloff, is the existence not of absolute acausality but of some form of paranormal causality.

Even if one finds reasons to differ from Beloff's understanding of causality, it remains the case that many broader conceptions than Jung's are both possible and have in fact frequently been invoked, not only in the ancient world (e.g., Aristotle's material, efficient, formal and final causes [Ross 1928]) but also in the modern period (e.g., Sheldrake's hypothesis of formative causation [1981]), and not only in the West but also in the East (e.g., in Buddhist philosophy [see Kalupahana 1975]). Whether one evaluates Jung's concept of acausality favourably or critically it is important to bear in mind the restricted understanding of causality on which it is based.

Jung's actual argument for acausality involves two stages. First, he argues that the inability of modern science to predict the behaviour of subatomic particles proves that the relationship between the particles is not only causal but must also involve some element of acausality. Second, he argues that because this acausality exists in the microphysical world of subatomic particles it ought also to exist in the macrophysical world of normal sensory experience. Both stages of the argument can be challenged.

It is certainly the case that, in Jung's day and still at present, the behaviour of individual subatomic particles cannot be predicted other than probabilistically. However, from this it does not necessarily follow that such behaviour involves an element of irreducible acausality. It is true that subatomic randomness may stem from acausality, but then again it may not. Even if it does, this is not because such randomness itself implies acausality. The acausal cannot simply be inferred from the merely probabilistic: if event A is followed by event B only 75 per cent of the time, this does not entail that B is not caused by A. For example, if it is the case that B, when it does occur, would not have done so but for A, it is reasonable to think that it has been caused by A.

It is even possible that the behaviour of subatomic particles may turn out not to be irreducibly probabilistic but the result of deterministic factors which just happen to be too complex and subtle for scientists to discern at present. Since the emergence of chaos theory in the 1980s, it has become increasingly clear that apparently random or chaotic behaviour can be just as much the product of regular causal factors as is conspicuously ordered behaviour. As the mathematician Ian Stewart has remarked, some scientists now appreciate 'the ability of even simple equations to generate motion so complex, so sensitive to measurement, that it appears random' (1990: 16). Such scientists 'are beginning to view order and chaos as two distinct manifestations of an underlying determinism' (ibid.: 22). These considerations alone should make one wary of automatically discounting the operation of causality no matter how random and unpredictable certain behaviour appears.

However, even without invoking chaos theory, a number of eminent physicists have been dissatisfied with the view which sees certain subatomic events as inescapably random and unpredictable. Einstein, for example, famously resisted the view of a universe in which 'God plays dice' – that is, allows things to happen by pure chance. He initiated a search for 'hidden variables' – as yet unknown factors that could account causally for the seemingly random behaviour of subatomic particles. More recently, this approach was also pursued by David Bohm who stressed that his was a 'causal interpretation' of quantum phenomena (1990: 276–81). Even a contemporary physicist who personally considers that there are indeed quantum phenomena for which 'both theory and experiment converge in making the prospect of a causal explanation . . . exceedingly unlikely' (Mansfield 1995: 32) nonetheless cautions that 'the key issues [in the acausality debate] are not yet fully resolved' (ibid.: 80).

Let us suppose, however, that certain events at the subatomic level are genuinely acausal. Even so, the next stage of Jung's argument – that there must also be acausal events in the macrophysical world – does not follow, as he puts it, 'logically from the premise of statistical truth'. There is no reason to expect that a property existing on the subatomic level will also exist in the realm of normal sensory experience. Perhaps what Jung had in mind was that the subatomic indeterminacy, which he thought implied acausality, could in some way be expected to be scaled up to the level of normal experience. If so, the very way in which probability operates suggests the contrary: the indeterminacy attaching to an individual event on one scale will progressively diminish as one views ever-larger aggregates of such events on a higher scale. Acausality on the subatomic level cannot prove or even make probable its existence on other levels. What it can do, however, is to make its possible existence on those higher levels less intellectually outrageous (cf. Mansfield 1995: 50).

The concept of acausality is certainly not an incoherent or absurd notion. There is strong, if not conclusive, evidence that acausality does indeed exist on the subatomic level, and there are no *a priori* reasons that it should not also exist on the level of normal sensory experience. On the normal sensory level it may not be possible actually to prove either its existence as understood by Jung or the inappropriateness of explaining it in terms of broader conceptions of causality than Jung's. Granted this limitation, a case remains for speaking of acausality in a relative and provisional sense, as applying to the relationship between events within a certain domain of consideration or level of current understanding. As the paranormal events experienced and observed by Jung indicate, 'acausality' appears to be an accurate enough term phenomenologically. As his definitions of synchronicity also emphasise, it is an extremely useful concept psychologically inasmuch as it shifts attention away from the causes of events and onto their possible meaning. Nevertheless, the tenacity with which Jung clung to the concept of acausality, in spite of the difficulties with it and the availability of alternative explanations for the phenomena he invoked in support of it, raises the question of what may have been at stake for him in maintaining the concept.

Meaning

Rather surprisingly, Jung nowhere sets out systematically his thoughts concerning what actually makes synchronicities meaningful. He does, however, provide a substantial clue to his implicit understanding when he states that 'by far the greatest number of synchronistic phenomena that I have had occasion to observe and analyse can easily be shown to have a direct connection with the archetype' (Jung 1952b: par. 912; cf. ibid.: pars. 845–6; 1976: 437, 447, 490). Though he appears to recognise not one but several kinds of meaning that can adhere to synchronicities, all of these can ultimately be related back to the single factor of the archetype. Aziz, for example, has identified four levels of meaning referred to by Jung at different times. These are: (1) simply the fact of two or more events paralleling one another (the paralleling is by virtue of a shared content or meaning); (2) the emotional charge or 'numinosity' attending the synchronicity (a source of non-rational meaning); (3) the significance of the synchronicity interpreted subjectively, from the point of view of the experiencer's personal needs and goals; and (4) the significance of the synchronicity objectively, as the expression of archetypal meaning which is transcendental to human consciousness (Aziz 1990: 64–6, 75–84).

Aziz calls this fourth level of meaning the 'archetypal level' (1990: 66). It is based on the fact that the archetype represents in itself a form of meaning which is '*a priori* in relation to human consciousness and apparently exists outside man' (Jung 1952b: par. 942). Thus in synchronicities 'one and the same (transcendental) meaning might manifest itself simultaneously in the human psyche and in the arrangement of an external and independent event' (ibid.: par. 915). In fact, each of the other three levels of meaning also depends on the presence of the archetype. The shared meaning by virtue of which two or more events are taken to be in a synchronistic relationship derives from an archetype – underlying the scarab symbol in both its psychic and its physical appearances is the archetype of rebirth. Again, the numinous charge of synchronicities derives from the presence of an activated archetype – the association with such numinosity being precisely one of the characteristics of archetypes as presented by Jung (ibid.: par. 841). Third, the subjective level of meaning, insofar as this is evaluated with reference to the process of individuation, will also be based on archetypes, since it is the archetypes – shadow, animus/anima, self, etc. – which essentially govern individuation for Jung.

At an epistemological level, Jung doubts whether objective meaning can ever be known as such. He acknowledges that 'meaning is an anthropomorphic interpretation' (1952b: par. 916), that '[w]hat that factor which appears to us as "meaning" may be in itself we have no possibility of knowing' (ibid.), and specifically that 'we have absolutely no scientific means of proving the existence of an *objective* meaning which is not just a psychic product' (ibid.: par. 915). Nevertheless, he remains committed to the notion of objective meaning and supports his stance by adducing, on the one hand, a range of eastern and western esoteric and philosophical precedents (ibid.: pars. 916–46) and, on the other hand, the evidence of synchronistic events themselves (ibid.: par. 948). This is one of the points at which Jung's 'Kantian' boundaries between the empirical and metaphysical seem to become insecure. Nor is the problem resolved by appealing to quantum phenomena as examples of acausality that does not involve human subjectivity. For, as Jung came to appreciate, the acausality of quantum phenomena is established by orderedness rather than by anything that could reasonably be called meaning. Hence his distinction towards the end of the 1952 essay between the broader category of general acausal orderedness and 'synchronicity in the narrow sense' – the latter involving 'the equivalence of psychic and physical processes where the observer is in the fortunate position of being able to recognize the *tertium comparationis*' (ibid.: par. 965; cf. ibid.: par. 942 n. 71).

Appreciation of the archetypal foundation of synchronicities helps resolve a pervasive ambiguity in Jung's use of the phrase 'meaningful coincidence'. On the one hand, the 'meaning' referred to in this phrase is clearly the significance the coincidence has for the experiencer – ultimately, its bearing on the experiencer's individuation. On the other hand, Jung also often uses the word 'meaning' to refer to the content that the coinciding events have in common: they have 'the same or similar meaning' or 'appear as meaningful parallels' (1952b: pars. 849–50). Here what the coincidence might signify for an experiencer is not germane; one could replace 'meaning' with 'content'. It is true that the two senses of 'meaning' do not exclude each other – the meaning/content can be meaningful/significant to an experiencer or observer – but it is equally true that they do not entail each other. That Jung nonetheless moves ambiguously between the two different senses probably stems from the fact that for him the content of synchronicities is generally understood to be archetypal and therefore is bound also to be meaningful in the sense of promoting individuation.

The tension between the two understandings of 'meaning' is clearest in the case of parapsychological experiments such as those of Rhine. In these experiments, what is important is primarily the paralleling of content between the image constituting the subject's guess and the target object. It is this paralleling of content which leads Jung to assert that 'Rhine's results confront us with the fact that there are events which are related to one another experimentally, and in this case *meaningfully*, without there being any possibility of proving that this relation is a causal one' (1952b: par. 840). Whether the coincidence represented by the improbable number of successful guesses is also meaningful in the sense of being significant for the individuation or other personal needs or goals of the experimental subject is a question about which Jung appears to have remained uncertain. On the one hand, he acknowledges that Rhine's experiments 'contain no direct evidence of any constellation of the archetype' (ibid.: par. 846; see also 1976: 399). On the other hand, he suggests that such a constellation may nonetheless be present inasmuch as 'the experimental set-up is influenced by the expectation of a *miracle*' and '[a] miracle is an archetypal situation' (1976: 537). Furthermore, the important emotional factor in the experiments, indicated by the decline effect (i.e., the tendency for the rate of successful guesses to decline as the subject's interest in the repetitive experiment waned), may also suggest the presence of an archetypal situation inasmuch as archetypal situations are typically 'accompanied by a corresponding emotion' (ibid.).

Probability

Jung recognises the central importance of the concept of probability for establishing synchronicity both phenomenologically and theoretically. Phenomenologically, unless an event is judged improbable, it will lack the salience to be registered as a coincidence; and theoretically, the conditions for suggesting the absence of a causal relationship between two events generally include the improbability of one of those events having caused the other. When expounding his theory, Jung therefore makes frequent reference to and use of statistics in order to persuade his readers that the component events in a putative synchronicity are so unlikely to be connected causally as to recommend their description as acausal (e.g., Jung 1952b: pars. 825, 830, 833–6).

Jung was particularly impressed by Rhine's use of statistics in his parapsychological experiments and attempted to emulate this in his own astrological experiment reported in detail in the second chapter of the 1952 essay. Rhine's work seemed to provide an example of the most rigorous methods of science being used in the service of demonstrating phenomena (extra-sensory perception, psychokinesis and precognition) whose reality was mostly denied by science. This was precisely what Jung wished to do for the related phenomena of synchronicity. However, he was also aware of a tension in using statistics for this purpose. Statistics achieve their usefulness by dealing in averages obtained from the consideration of large quantities of data. Generally, the more data that are available, the more reliable the statistics will be. Synchronicity, by contrast, is concerned with the quality of unique and unrepeatable events (1952b: par. 884). It is therefore uncertain what useful information a statistical exploration of synchronicity could yield.

It may be that Jung himself was unclear initially as to what his astrological experiment could be expected to demonstrate. Michael Fordham writes that '[a]t one time [Jung] really thought that if his [astrological] material proved statistically significant it would prove his [synchronicity] thesis' (1993: 105). This suggestion is reinforced by Jung's remark in a letter to B. V. Raman (6 September 1947): 'What I miss in astrological literature is chiefly the statistical method by which fundamental facts could be scientifically established' (1973: 476). Later, however, Jung was adamant that his experiment, as carried out, was never intended to prove anything about astrology or, through astrology, about synchronicity (1958a: 494, 497–8). He had come to appreciate, Fordham suggests, that if the astrological material did prove statistically significant, 'it would make a cause for the data more likely' (1993: 105), thereby undermining the synchronicity thesis. Rather, what Jung hoped was that his experiment would 'on the one hand demonstrate the existence of synchronicity [i.e., allow for its occurrence and make it visible in the form of measurable results] and, on the other hand, disclose psychic contents which would at least give us a clue to the nature of the psychic factor involved' (1952b: par. 863).

The key to an appreciation of the experiment is an understanding of Jung's use of statistics – a use which, as Fordham has remarked, is 'highly original and peculiarly his own' (1957: 36). As they are usually employed, Fordham explains,

> [s]tatistics distinguish between two sets of phenomena: those which are sufficiently ordered to indicate causal connections and to which the notion of prediction can be applied with considerable success, and those whose action is random and which as such obey the laws of chance where the notion of prediction is of little use.
>
> (Fordham 1957: 36)

With synchronicities, however, Jung introduces a third set of phenomena, since '[c]onsidered statistically they will appear as chance, but they will not be due to chance; i.e. he cuts right across the duality chance–cause axiom on which statistics are based' (Fordham 1957: 36). Statistically, events are considered to be 'significant' (i.e., not chance) if their improbability rises above a certain level.

When they rise above this level of improbability, events are usually expected and found to have a cause. Since none of Jung's astrological results rose to such a level, they were unlikely to have been caused but were indeed chance happenings – which is what, as acausal events, he needed them to be. Thus, Jung's use of statistics 'had an aim exactly the reverse to the usual one. He used them to define the region in which synchronistic phenomena are most likely' (ibid.: 37).

Rather than dismiss his results altogether because they did not rise to the level of statistical significance, Jung took the novel step of using the statistical distribution they presented as a monitor through which to investigate their possible psychological significance. As he remarks, 'it is just as important to consider the exceptions to the rule as the averages . . . Inasmuch as chance maxima and minima occur, they are *facts* whose nature I set out to explore' (1952b: par. 884).

Thus, analysis of the three batches of 180, 220 and 83 pairs of marriage horoscopes showed the maximum frequencies to fall on the aspects respectively of moon conjunct sun, moon conjunct moon, and moon conjunct ascendant. These are precisely the three aspects that astrological tradition would expect to turn up most frequently in marriage horoscopes, as Jung and his co-worker well knew (1952b: par. 869). Here, however, they turned up entirely randomly. The horoscopes 'were piled up in chronological order just as the post brought them in' (ibid.: par. 873), and Jung decided when to begin analysing the first batch for no better reason than that he was unable to restrain his curiosity any longer (1958a: par. 1177). As his subsequent analyses demonstrated, if the horoscopes had arrived in a different order or if he had waited until they had all come in and had analysed them together, the three traditional marriage aspects would not have shown up with the same remarkable salience (1952b: pars. 909–10). He concludes that, since the resulting figures

> actually fall within the limits of chance expectation, they do not support the astrological claim, they merely *imitate* accidentally the ideal answer to astrological expectation. It is nothing but a chance result from the statistical point of view, yet it is *meaningful* on account of the fact that it looks as if it validated this expectation. It is just what I call a synchronistic phenomenon.
> (Jung 1952b: par. 904)

The fact that the result corresponded to the expectations of his co-worker and himself suggested to Jung that their psychic state might in some way have been involved in 'arranging' it; that there may have existed, in their case as with practitioners in the past, 'a secret, mutual connivance . . . between the material and the psychic state of the astrologer' (1952b: par. 905). This conclusion was further suggested by his realisation that in working on the statistics 'use had been made of unconscious deception', that he had been 'put off the trail by a number of errors' (ibid.: par. 906). The curious thing about these errors was that they '*all tend[ed] to exaggerate the results in a way favourable to astrology,* and add[ed] most suspiciously to the impression of an artificial or fraudulent arrangement of the facts' (ibid.). Jung remarks:

> I know, however, from long experience of these things that spontaneous synchronistic phenomena draw the observer, by hook or by crook, into what is happening and occasionally make him an accessory to the deed. That is the danger inherent in all parapsychological experiments.
>
> (Jung 1952b: par. 907)

Fortunately, the errors in the astrological experiment were discovered in time and corrected (1952b: par. 906). However, in the light both of these errors and of the remarkable correspondence between his expectation and the results he obtained, Jung conducted a further experiment to test for indications of possible psychic participation. He invited three people 'whose psychological status was accurately known' (ibid.: par. 897) to draw by lot twenty pairs of marriage horoscopes from a random assortment of 200. In each case, he found that the person's random selection of twenty horoscopes produced maximal figures which, while not statistically significant, corresponded surprisingly well with the known psychic state of the subject (ibid.: pars. 897–900). For example, one woman 'who, at the time of the experiment, found herself in a state of intense emotional excitement' drew horoscopes in which there was 'a predominance of the Mars aspects' (ibid.: par. 897). Inasmuch as '[t]he classical significance of Mars lies in his emotionality', this result 'fully agrees with the psychic state of the subject' (ibid.). This informal experiment appeared to confirm what had happened under more rigorously controlled circumstances in the main experiment. Without exceeding the levels of dispersion that would be expected due to chance, the data nonetheless patterned themselves in ways that corresponded to a known psychic disposition.

In sum, Jung seems to have considered synchronistic events to lie between mere chance events and caused events. He believed statistics to be useful both for establishing the existence of synchronistic events (after the manner of Rhine) and for monitoring their activity (through paying attention to deviations from chance expectation that do not rise to the level of statistical significance). However, for learning in detail about the complex phenomena associated with synchronicity, he considered that statistics were of little use compared with the study of richly described individual cases.

Inexplicability

Jung's presentation of synchronicity involves numerous intellectual difficulties. There are questions concerning the adequacy of his definitions to account for the range of phenomena that he wishes to call synchronistic. There is uncertainty about the extent to which the concept of synchronicity should be considered empirical or metaphysical. It is unclear whether and to what extent synchronistic events can occur regularly as well as irregularly, can be consciously generated as well as spontaneous, can consist of paranormal as well as normal component events, and support or are supported by the notion of the psychoid unconscious. There are problematic issues surrounding the role in synchronicity of each of the central concepts of time, acausality, meaning and probability.

Some of these difficulties can be at least partly resolved with reference to the theory of analytical psychology. For instance, the various kinds of meaning that Jung implicitly attributes to synchronicity are all explicable if synchronistic events are assumed to have an archetypal basis. Other difficulties may be the result of incomplete, inadequately grasped, or out-of-date knowledge and can be resolved if the relevant knowledge is supplemented, corrected, or updated. Parts of Jung's argument for acausality based on an appeal to quantum physics could be redeemed in this way. Further difficulties can be eased if we bear in mind that Jung's thinking on synchronicity developed. For example, it appears that he first conceived of synchronicity in terms of simultaneity and the quality of moments of time, then later re-conceived it in terms of the psychic relativisation of space and time. While Jung did not systematically absorb the earlier conception into the later one, it is possible for us, following the direction of his development, to attempt this. Other difficulties again can be most effectively addressed by simply abandoning parts of Jung's formulation. For example, his attempt to define synchronicity in terms of 'two different psychic states' generates problems from which there seems to be no effective escape other than to jettison that definition. However, none of these resolutions is entirely satisfactory, and there remain many other difficulties that such approaches do not even partly resolve.

Overall, the impression gained from our so far primarily theoretical consideration of synchronicity is of a theory that is richly suggestive and constitutes a significant addition to the overall framework of analytical psychology but is full of remaining difficulties. This situation may be partly due to Jung's acknowledged intellectual and methodological limitations. However, it may also partly be due to the rationally ungraspable nature of synchronicity itself, its inherent 'inexplicability' (Jung 1952b: par. 967). We noted this irrationality of synchronicity in the incident involving the scarab, where indeed it proved to be the decisive therapeutic factor. Unfortunately, the ability to work effectively with an irrational factor in therapeutic situations does not entail that the factor can equally effectively be articulated in theory. However, rather than be discouraged by these outstanding difficulties and the possibly ungraspable nature of the phenomenon, we can attempt to gain further understanding by shifting perspective and turning from a theoretical consideration of Jung's work on synchronicity to a fuller examination of its contexts.

Part 2

Synchronicity in context

Chapter 3

Sources and influences

The previous chapter demonstrated the range and number of intellectual difficulties that Jung encountered in attempting to provide a coherent theoretical account of synchronicity. Since Jung did not satisfactorily address many of these difficulties, readers of his texts on synchronicity are themselves forced to engage with them. In doing so, it can be helpful, even indispensable, to bear in mind the sources of and influences on Jung's ideas: their personal, professional and intellectual contexts. For these will enable us to understand more clearly why Jung articulated his theory in the terms he did.

Contextual work on Jung began in earnest with Henri Ellenberger's *The Discovery of the Unconscious* (1970), was raised to a higher level of theoretical and sociological sophistication by Peter Homans's *Jung in Context* (1979/1995), and has subsequently burgeoned (see, for example, Papadopoulos and Saayaman 1984; Papadopoulos 1992; Clarke 1992, 1994; Shamdasani 1990, 1993, 1994, 1995, 1996, 1998, 2003; Charet 1993; Noll 1992, 1994, 1997; Douglas 1997; Bishop 1995, 1999, 2000, 2002; Bair 2004). However, contextual studies specifically of synchronicity have been few: the only book-length study is Paul Bishop's *Synchronicity and Intellectual Intuition in Kant, Swedenborg, and Jung* (2000). F. X. Charet's *Spiritualism and the Foundations of C. G. Jung's Psychology* (1993) provides a great deal of pertinent background information but stops short of engaging in detail with synchronicity. Moreover, each of these works primarily focuses on only one major context of Jung's thinking (in Bishop, philosophy; in Charet, spiritualism), whereas, as we shall shortly see, there are at least eight major contexts that clearly influenced Jung. Some of the general studies of synchronicity, such as those by Progoff (1973), Aziz (1990) and Mansfield (1995), do include discussion of contexts. However, such discussion is subordinate to other emphases and hence tends to be more selective than what is attempted here.

In the present chapter I shall look in detail at a wide range of contexts, focusing on those that had a demonstrable impact on Jung's actual writing about synchronicity. I shall examine the influence on him of the following areas: paranormal experiences and spiritualism; philosophy; astrology; the *I Ching*; analytical psychological theory and practice; psychical research and parapsychology; physics; and the history of religion and western esotericism. Where relevant I will also consider the general social and cultural milieu within which Jung grew up, lived, and worked. However, discussion of the wider significance of that milieu will be reserved for subsequent chapters. Here, the emphasis will be on Jung's specific intellectual sources and influences and the perspectives, insights and encouragement he derived from each.

Paranormal experiences and spiritualism

One of the most important influences on Jung's theory of synchronicity was his frequent experiencing and witnessing of seemingly paranormal events and the lifelong interest in spiritualistic speculations and practices that went with this.[1] His early life was spent in a milieu conducive to his developing these interests. Living in the Swiss countryside, he continually heard stories of uncanny happenings (Jung 1963: 102) such as 'dreams which foresaw the death of a certain person, clocks which stopped at the moment of death, glasses which shattered at the critical moment' (ibid.: 104). The reality of these events, he says, was 'taken for granted in the world of my childhood' (ibid.). More specifically, paranormal experiences were virtually commonplace in Jung's family. His maternal grandfather, Samuel Preiswerk, had believed himself to be continually surrounded by ghosts and would devote one day every week to conversing with the spirit of his deceased first wife, for whom he kept a special chair in his study (Jaffé 1984: 40). Jung's grandmother Augusta, Prieswerk's second wife, was believed to be clairvoyant (ibid.). The couple's daughter, Jung's mother, experienced 'strange occurrences' with suffi-cient regularity to write a diary exclusively dedicated to them (Jaffé 1971: 2).

Jung's own experiences of the paranormal began at the age of seven or eight. During a period when his parents were sleeping apart and there was considerable tension in the house, he would sometimes see nocturnal apparitions: 'One night I saw coming from [my mother's] door a faintly luminous, indefinite figure whose head detached itself from the neck and floated along in front of it, in the air, like a little moon' (Jung 1963: 31).

When Jung was twenty-three, and by that time a medical student, a couple of incidents happened which he says were 'destined to influence me profoundly' (1961: 108). On one occasion a round walnut table in his family home suddenly and inexplicably split with a loud bang. Two weeks later another loud explosion was heard, and it was discovered that a steel knife which was in perfect condition and had been used to cut bread just an hour before had miraculously shattered into four in a closed drawer (ibid.: 107–9). These experiences contributed to his decision to enter the then widely despised field of psychiatry (ibid.: 107, 110–11; also Baumann-Jung 1975: 46).

Jung's own account presents these incidents as mysteriously anticipating a series of seances which he claims he heard about and started attending a few weeks later (1963: 109; 1973: 181). In fact, he had already been attending the seances for several years and had even initiated them (Hillman 1976: 125; Charet 1993: 155–6). His observations at the seances formed the basis for his doctoral dissertation, later published as 'On the Psychology and Pathology of So-Called Occult Phenomena' (1902). The desire to present his findings in an optimally objective light is undoubtedly why this and his various subsequent accounts (1925: 3–6, 9–10; 1973: 181–2; 1963: 109–10) all conceal to various degrees the full extent of his personal involvement. Charet summarises what is now known:

> the séances were conducted in Jung's own home, the medium was his cousin, and the participants, members of his own family. In addition, several of the spirits with which the medium was allegedly in communication were none other than Jung's ancestors.
>
> (Charet 1993: 288)

This degree of engagement is supported by other information about Jung's interests at the time. In particular, the second of the lectures he delivered to his student fraternity, the Zofingia Society, consists largely of an impassioned and informed appeal for the serious scientific study of spiritualistic phenomena (1896–9: pars. 67–142; see also Oeri 1970: 187–8). Indeed, several of the principles that Jung asserts here in relation to spiritualism later appear in more sophisticated form as central assumptions of his theory of synchronicity: for example, that matter is animated by a life force that is unconscious, intelligent, and beyond space and time (1896–9: pars. 95–9).

Jung describes his experiments with his medium cousin as 'the one great experience which wiped out all my earlier philosophy and made it possible for me to achieve a psychological point of view. I had discovered some objective facts about the human psyche' (1963: 110). The primarily descriptive account given in his dissertation prefigures several of the themes of his mature psychology. The medium's ability when in the trance state to manifest a variety of seemingly autonomous personalities provided evidence for the dissociability and unconscious functioning of the psyche – observations that would eventually lead to the formulation first of complexes and later of archetypes. While analysing his cousin's trances psychiatrically, Jung did not dismiss the psychic dissociation as simply pathological. The secondary personalities she was manifesting could also be therapeutic, representing 'attempts of the future character to break through' (1902: par. 136).[2] The emphasis here on the positive, prospective tendency of apparently pathological symptoms foreshadows Jung's later ideas of compensation and individuation, while the practice of consciously interacting with fantasy images prefigures his method of active imagination. As we have seen, all of these concepts are integral to his understanding of synchronicity, especially of the meaning of synchronistic events.

Jung continued to attend seances for another thirty years (Charet 1993: 172–4, 197, 269). Already by 1905 he could report that he had investigated eight mediums (1905: par. 724). His publicly expressed view at this time was that the results were 'of purely psychological interest . . . Everything that may be considered a scientifically established fact belongs to the domain of the mental and cerebral processes and is fully explicable in terms of the laws already known to science' (ibid.).

Jung's continuing interest in spiritualistic phenomena, even after he had established himself as a respectable psychologist, is, far from being eccentric, simply an instance of the intimate relationship that had long existed between depth psychology and anomalous phenomena. As Ellenberger (1970) and Charet (1993) have argued, the origins of depth psychology can largely be traced to such movements as mesmerism, hypnotism and spiritualism that flourished throughout the nineteenth century. Among the originative depth psychologists, Jung was not alone in exploring such areas. Frederick Myers, William James, Granville Stanley Hall, Pierre Janet, Théodore Flournoy, Sigmund Freud and Sandor Ferenczi are just some of the other pioneers of depth psychology who are known to have visited mediums (Shamdasani 1994: xi). Indeed, as we have already noted, discussions of anomalous phenomena continued within Freudian psychoanalytic circles concurrently with, yet independently of, Jung's work throughout the first half of the twentieth century (see Devereux 1953).

Jung's interest in the paranormal played a critical role in his relationship with Freud between 1907 and 1913. Initially, Freud was highly sceptical and dismissive about the entire field – an attitude expressed most vividly in his exhortation to Jung to make the sexual theory 'a dogma, an unshakeable bulwark' against 'the black tide of mud . . . of occultism' (Jung 1963: 147–8). This resistance eventually mellowed to the point where Freud was actually encouraging Jung's experiments and even attending seances himself (Charet 1993: 196–7).[3] 'In matters of occultism', he wrote to Jung on 15 June 1911, 'I have grown humble . . . my hubris has been shattered' (in Jung 1963: 335). However, he was still not willing to expose publicly the full extent of his interest, nor would he accede to Jung's demand that the theoretical basis of psychoanalysis be broadened to take account of spiritualistic phenomena that were inadequately explained in terms of sexuality.[4]

On one occasion, this tension between Freud and Jung resulted in an argument that had an interesting psychological and political context and an even more interesting parapsychological outcome. Earlier in the evening Freud had, as he afterwards wrote in a letter to Jung, 'formally adopted you as an eldest son, anointing you as my successor and crown prince' (in Jung 1961: 333). Later in the evening, however, in the course of an argument about paranormal phenomena, a seemingly unaccountable detonation went off in Freud's bookcase. When Freud dismissed Jung's parapsychological interpretation of this event, Jung predicted that the same thing would happen again, and so, to Freud's consternation, it did (ibid.: 152). Freud's letter to Jung continues by remarking of this phenomenon, by which he admitted to having been impressed, that it 'then and there [i.e., immediately after his 'anointing' of Jung] . . . divested me of my paternal dignity' (in ibid.: 333). Whether or not consciously realised at the time, this incident symbolised the inevitable divergence between the two psychologists. One of the main causes of this divergence was the significance each attached to paranormal phenomena.

Nevertheless, Jung's understanding of paranormal phenomena undoubtedly benefited from his association with Freud. For he was helped by Freud to appreciate the important role that sexuality can indeed play in spiritualistic phenomena. As he recognised only after he had written his dissertation, the medium had fallen in love with him (Jung 1925: 5) and her inadmissible passion for her cousin – which may have been reciprocal[5] – had contributed significantly to her experiences, many of which involved supposed romances of past members of their shared ancestry.

In effecting his break with Freud, Jung was greatly assisted by the psychologists Théodore Flournoy and William James (Shamdasani 1995: 126–7). Like Jung, both of them were deeply interested in psychical research and had made close observations of mediums. Moreover, they were willing, as Freud was not, to consider the phenomena that emerged in these contexts in a non-pathological light. While James's influence on Jung was mainly through his writings (Jung 1976: 452), Flournoy's was more personal. In an appendix contained in the Swiss edition of *Memories, Dreams, Reflections*, but omitted in the English one, Jung recounts that during the period of his disaffection with Freud he regularly visited Flournoy, who both helped him formulate his understanding of Freud's limitations and encouraged him in his own researches on somnambulism, parapsychology, and the psychology of religion (summarised in Charet 1993: 235). It was also through Flournoy that Jung became interested in the creative imagination and specifically in the 'Miller Fantasies', which were to form the basis for his *Psychology of the Unconscious* (1911–12/1952) – the work in which Jung first openly expressed his divergence from Freud (Jung 1963: 158; Charet 1993: 235).

Validating the creative or, as he came to call it, the 'active' imagination was also important to Jung personally. He had a facility for imaginative thinking, and what he learned about this faculty from the Miller material enhanced his ability to cope with the deluge of dreams, visions, and paranormal experiences that were released in him in the years following his rupture with Freud (Jung 1963: 165–91).

Prominent among these experiences were Jung's inner encounters with a variety of seemingly autonomous fantasy figures with whom he conversed as though they were spirits (1961: 174–8). The most important such figure was 'Philemon', whom Jung described as his 'ghostly guru', his 'psychagogue', a representation of 'superior insight' who 'conveyed to me many an illuminating idea', above all 'the insight that there are things in the psyche which I do not produce, but which produce themselves and have their own life' (ibid.: 176–7). This notion of the autonomy of the psyche is central to Jung's understanding of both archetypes and synchronicity. One of the earliest experiences Jung mentions specifically of a meaningful coincidence concerns Philemon: the 'ghostly guru' had appeared in Jung's dreams with kingfisher's wings, and Jung, in order to understand the image better, did a painting of it. While engaged on this, he happened to find in his garden, for the first and only time, a dead kingfisher (ibid.: 175–6).

Later, in 1916, Jung relates that he felt 'compelled from within, as it were, to formulate and express what might have been said by Philemon' (1961: 182). The composition of the resulting *Septem Sermones ad Mortuos*, a series of texts addressed to the spirits of the dead, was immediately preceded by a remarkable haunting of Jung's house, involving an 'ominous atmosphere' and various apparitional and poltergeist phenomena experienced not just by himself but by his children and other members of the household (ibid.: 182–3). As several writers have noted, the *Septem Sermones* – whose relation to spiritualistic communications is obvious, if also rather eccentric (see Segal 1992: 37–8) – express in germinal form many of Jung's developed ideas: the nature of the unconscious, individuation, the problem of opposites, the archetypes, and the self (see, e.g., Heisig 1972; Charet 1993: 265–7).

In 1919, while in England, Jung delivered to the Society for Psychical Research a lecture on 'The Psychological Foundations of Belief in Spirits' (1920/1948). In this lecture he explained experiences of one's own soul in terms of complexes of the personal unconscious, while seemingly autonomous spirits were explained in terms of complexes of the collective unconscious; that is, archetypes (ibid.: pars. 585–91). Towards the end of the lecture he admitted to having 'repeatedly observed the telepathic effects of unconscious complexes, and also a number of parapsychic phenomena' (ibid.: par. 600). But on the question of the objective existence of spirits he took a cautious position, in spite of his own experience of three years earlier. While acknowledging that, from the point of view of feeling, it might well be legitimate to believe in spirits, he considered that, from the point of view of thinking, there are no grounds for holding that spirits can be known to exist other than as 'the exteriorized effects of unconscious complexes': 'I see no proof whatever', he remarked, 'of the existence of real spirits, and until such proof is forthcoming I must regard this whole territory as an appendix of psychology' (ibid.).

However, Jung later became less sceptical than he says here. For, in a footnote added at this point to the 1948 revision of the lecture, he admits:

> After collecting psychological experiences from many people and many countries for over fifty years, I no longer feel as certain as I did in 1919, when I wrote this sentence. To put it bluntly, I doubt whether an exclusively psychological approach can do justice to the phenomena in question.
>
> (Jung 1920/1948: par. 600 n. 15)

In the year following his lecture to the Society for Psychical Research, Jung was again in England and had some disturbing experiences while staying over a series of weekends in a house that he afterwards learned was reputed to be haunted. He heard loud thumping and dripping noises, smelled foul odours, and on one occasion saw a figure with part of its face missing lying in the bed beside him – all of which phenomena simply disappeared at the first light of dawn (Jung 1950b: pars. 764–74). For at least one of these phenomena, the loud dripping noise, he could find no adequate physical or psychological explanation (ibid.: par. 778).

Jung was also influenced by his continued witnessing of spiritualistic trance phenomena. We are told, for instance, of his attendance at seances with Rudi Schneider in 1925 at which 'telekinetic phenomena and the materialization of human limbs were observed' (Charet 1993: 282–3 n. 230).[6] At a seance with Oscar Schlag in 1931 'a sample of ectoplasm was secured', and on another occasion Jung 'embraced Schlag when suddenly Schlag's Jacket dematerialized' (ibid.: nn. 230–1).[7] On the 'question of materialization' Jung wrote in 1945: 'I have seen enough of this phenomenon to convince me entirely of its existence' (1973: 390). Regarding the objective existence of spirits, he recalled in 1946 his discussions many years earlier with the American psychologist and psychical researcher James Hyslop:

> He [Hyslop] admitted that, all things considered, all these metapsychic phenomena could be explained better by the hypothesis of spirits than by the qualities and peculiarities of the unconscious. And here, on the basis of my own experience, I am bound to concede he is right. In each individual case I must of necessity be sceptical, but in the long run I have to admit that the spirit hypothesis yields better results in practice than any other.
>
> (Jung 1973: 431)

Of Jung's experiences in this period after 1919 one more deserves mention for the significant bearing it had on the development of his concept of the self as the centre of psychic totality (1963: 188). He relates that after he had worked this concept out in isolation, he experienced a powerful confirmatory coincidence in which a painting he had done, based on a dream, was paralleled by the core idea of a Taoist-alchemical treatise, *The Secret of the Golden Flower*, sent to him by Richard Wilhelm (ibid.: 188–9). The timely receipt of this treatise was, he says, 'the first event which broke through my isolation. I became aware of an affinity; I could establish ties with something and someone' (ibid.: 189).

Finally, Jung's thinking was also furthered by his experiences while recovering in hospital from a heart attack in 1944. A series of altered states of consciousness, including a near-death experience, attendant coincidence, and some profound states of mystical union, gave him the insight, and ultimately the courage, to express himself much more forthrightly on a number of controversial topics, including synchronicity (1963: 270–7).[8]

Jung's paranormal experiences, and the resulting need to understand them adequately, arguably were the greatest influence on the development of his theory of synchronicity. Such intimate personal engagement both gave him an inside view of the kind of psychological dynamics that can be involved in paranormal experiences and, even more importantly, impressed on him the extent to which the experiences can be meaningful. Thus, Jung's own experiences seemed to occur at critical junctures in his life: paranormal events accompanied his decision to make a career of psychiatry, his conflict and eventual breach with Freud, his relationship with his 'ghostly guru' Philemon, the writing of the *Septem Sermones ad Mortuos* in which he adumbrated much of his later psychology, his formulation of the concept of the self as the centre of psychic totality, and his heart attack and transformative near-death experience of 1944.

Philosophy

Jung insists that his theory of synchronicity 'is not a philosophical view' (1952b: par. 960) and is not based on 'philosophical assumptions' (1951b: par. 995). Nevertheless, he acknowledges that the 'obscure field' it opens up is 'philosophically of the greatest importance' (1952b: par. 816), and his thinking on the subject was undoubtedly influenced by his own philosophical reading.

While generally careful to distinguish his therapeutic and empirical work in psychology from the more argumentative and speculative tendencies of the philosophers, Jung nonetheless was explicit throughout his career about the important relationship between psychology and philosophy (see Nagy 1991). Especially important influences on his intellectual development were the German philosophers Immanuel Kant (see Jung 1963: 77; Bishop 2000), Arthur Schopenhauer (see Jung 1963: 76–7; Jarrett 1981; Charet 1993: 93–123), and Friedrich Nietzsche (see Jung 1963: 105–7; Bishop 1995). In his writings on synchronicity, the two philosophers that Jung most fully discusses are Schopenhauer and Gottfried Wilhelm von Leibniz, since both directly addressed the problem of meaningful coincidence. There are also occasional references to Heraclitus (1952b: par. 916), Plato (ibid.: par. 942), Plotinus (ibid.: par. 927), Arnold Geulincx (ibid.: pars. 860, 937 n. 58, 948), and Kant (1950a: par. 967; 1952b: pars. 829 n. 19, 840, 912 n. 15). Nietzsche is not mentioned.

Although Jung's principal essay on synchronicity contains a discussion of Schopenhauer (1952b: pars. 828–9) and several shorter references (ibid.: pars. 928, 937, 948, 966), these seem to have been included only at the specific prompting of Wolfgang Pauli, to whom Jung had shown an early draft of his 1952 essay (Meier 2001: 36–8). They do not reflect the deeper influence of Schopenhauer on Jung, reaching back into Jung's student years. The references concern Schopenhauer's essay 'On the Apparent Design in the Fate of the Individual', whose 'almost friendly and optimistic tone' Jung finds uncharacteristic of Schopenhauer and somewhat alienating (1952b: par. 829). Jung acknowledges Schopenhauer's perspicacity in having identified the phenomenon of meaningful coincidence as 'a problem of principle of the first order' (ibid.), one that 'is concerned with the foundations of our epistemology' (ibid.: 828). However, while he takes the trouble briefly to expound Schopenhauer's proposal, he never seriously entertains it as an adequate theory. Schopenhauer suggests that 'the simultaneity of the causally unconnected, what we call "chance"' (quoted in ibid.) can be accounted for if we postulate that there is a first cause – for Schopenhauer, the transcendental Will – from which, as Jung summarises it, 'all causal chains radiate like meridian lines from the poles and, because of the circular parallels, stand to one another in a meaningful relationship of simultaneity' (ibid.).

However, Jung rejects on empirical as well as philosophical grounds both of the main assumptions in this view: that natural processes are determined absolutely and that there is a unitary first cause. He especially notes Schopenhauer's inability to escape thinking in terms of causes. 'Schopenhauer thought and wrote', Jung comments, 'at a time when causality held sovereign sway as a category *a priori* and had therefore to be dragged in to explain meaningful coincidences' (ibid.). Jung, by contrast, considers meaningful coincidences to be a manifestation of acausality. Moreover, Schopenhauer's view 'credits meaningful coincidences with occurring so regularly and systematically that their verification would be either unnecessary or the simplest thing in the world' – which Jung considers to be contradicted by the available empirical evidence (ibid.).

Jung discusses Leibniz's work as the last full flowering of the ancient and medieval view that the human soul is a microcosm, mirroring in itself the macrocosm of the universe (1952b: pars. 937–9). Leibniz postulates the existence of an infinity of simple, unitary substances or 'monads', each of which is entirely independent of all others. Nevertheless, they have been created and are maintained by God in a state of perfect pre-established harmony such that each one expresses and accords with all the others. For Leibniz, souls, as the monads of living organisms, 'are the living mirrors or images of the universe of created things' (cited in ibid.). The idea of pre-established harmony implies that there is 'an absolute synchronism of psychic and physical events' (ibid.). Because this view preceded the dominance of science, it escapes the causal thinking which Jung thought a limitation in Schopenhauer's theory. Nevertheless, Jung still rejects it on empirical grounds. For whereas Leibniz's view implies that synchronicity would become 'the absolute rule in all cases where an inner event occurs simultaneously with an outside one', synchronistic events empirically 'are so exceptional that most people doubt their existence' (ibid.).

Although Jung takes very little from his explicit, if brief, discussions of these two philosophers, other important philosophical influences on him have been proposed. Marilyn Nagy, discussing the implications of synchronicity on Jung's theory of archetypes, suggests a Platonic influence. She writes:

> In spite of Jung's caveat against philosophical interpretation, [his late formulation of the archetype based on synchronicity] resembles nothing so much as Plato's vision of a universe ordered by eternal forms, directed by the World Soul, and limited in the perpetration of divine order only by the parallel existing facts of Necessary Cause.
>
> (Nagy 1991: 185–6)

Charet, in greater detail, argues that Jung's response to spiritualism was largely based on his reading of Kant's pre-critical *Dreams of a Spirit Seer*, especially as interpreted by Schopenhauer in his *Essay on Spirit Seeing* (Charet 1993: 93–123). Kant distinguished between unknowable noumena (things-in-themselves) and knowable phenomena (things-as-they-appear), and argued that spirits belong to the former category. He therefore rejected claims, such as those of Swedenborg, to have knowledge of spiritual reality. He suggested that such claims were instances of pathological fantasy and recommended that more attention be paid to knowable phenomena rather than unknowable noumena (ibid.: 99–108, 114). Schopenhauer interpreted Kant not to be denying the existence of noumenal or spiritual reality but to be clearly separating it from phenomenal reality. However, for Schopenhauer communication between the noumenal and phenomenal worlds is possible by an inner course involving the operation of a 'dream-organ' that can provide intuitive perception independently of external sense impressions. Noumenal reality enters human consciousness by this means and, as it does so, becomes subject to the conditions of phenomenal reality: time, space and causality. This view provides both a non-pathological account of fantasy as a process taking place between noumenal and phenomenal reality and a way of understanding spiritualistic and paranormal phenomena as occasions when noumenal reality (where the categories of time, space and causality do not apply) enters into phenomenal reality (where the categories do apply) (ibid.: 108–15). Although Charet discusses Schopenhauer's interpretation of Kant in the context of Jung's engagement with spiritualism, his findings clearly also suggest an important influence on the later theory of synchronicity.

The most thorough discussion of philosophical influences on Jung's theory of synchronicity has been provided by Bishop (2000). He argues that Jung's concept of synchronicity can be seen as 'an analytical psychological equivalent of intellectual intuition' (ibid.: 20). Intellectual intuition, a notion found in Kant (where it is criticised), and much of the German idealist philosophy of the nineteenth century and the early twentieth (where it is often championed), is 'a non-rational, extra-spatial and extra-temporal form of knowledge' (ibid.: 17). Bishop notes many connections between intellectual intuition and synchronicity: both are concerned with the possibility of directly obtaining knowledge by non-sensory means – what Jung calls 'absolute knowledge'; both provide knowledge deriving from the unconscious rather than from ego-consciousness; both involve a kind of immediate representation of the knowing subject; both involve an exit from time; both are conceived as productive or creative processes; both provide knowledge that is irrational in the sense that it is obtained intuitively; and both presuppose the idea that the microcosm of the human mind mirrors the macrocosm of the universe (ibid.: 45–8). With these parallels in mind, Bishop considers that Jung's theory of synchronicity is part of his attempt to harmonise teleology with mechanism (ibid.: 54), to support the notion of a philosophical Absolute in the guise of the *unus mundus* (ibid.: 54–7), to resolve the mind–body problem (ibid.: 57–9), and in general to pursue 'the old, Romantic yearning for totality' (ibid.: 21). Like Charet, Bishop notes the importance for the development of the concept of synchronicity of how Jung misreads Kant through focusing on but missing the irony in Kant's pre-critical *Dreams of a Spirit Seer*. However, Bishop provides a more detailed account of how this misreading resulted from the influence on Jung of the spiritualistic interpretation of Kant offered by Carl du Prel (2000: 371–3).

The notion of intellectual intuition can be understood as part of the wider movement of thought known as *Naturphilosophie*. This approach to knowledge combined empirical science with philosophical and literary speculations and, although it had many variants (Noll 1994: 40), was most definitively articulated by the philosopher Friedrich Wilhelm von Schelling (1775–1854). Among the basic assumptions of *Naturphilosophie* was 'that nature and spirit both sprang from the Absolute and constituted an indissoluble unity' (Ellenberger 1970: 202). Matter, living nature and human consciousness were considered to arise successively from a common spiritual principle, the World Soul, and to obey the same laws. Accordingly, 'human life was regarded as a participation in a kind of cosmic movement within nature. The universe was an organized whole in which each part was connected to all others through a relation of sympathy' (ibid.: 203). Of central importance in this way of thinking was the notion of the unconscious, considered to be 'the very fundament of the human being as rooted in the invisible life of the universe and therefore the true bond linking man with nature' (ibid.: 204). Intellectual intuition figures as the '"inner" or "universal sense" (*All-Sinn*) by which man, before the fall, was able to cognize nature' and which, though deteriorated, 'still enabled us . . . to gain some direct understanding of the universe, be it in mystical ecstasy, poetic and artistic inspiration, magnetic somnambulism, or dreams' (ibid.). Ellenberger comments that 'there is hardly a single concept of Freud or Jung that had not been anticipated by the philosophy of nature' (ibid.: 205). Although Jung does not specifically refer to this tradition in his writings on synchronicity, it is clearly significant as an intellectual context for his theory.

Jung's lack of discussion of the substantial influence on his theory of Kant, Schopenhauer and other German idealistic philosophers can perhaps be explained by his general reluctance to subject his epistemological Kantianism to critical scrutiny. The references he does make to Schopenhauer and Leibniz, as well as to other philosophers, mainly serve rhetorically to provide his writings on synchronicity with a respectable intellectual pedigree. On examination, there is very little serious engagement with philosophical arguments in Jung's essay. For example, as we noted in the previous chapter, he for the most part simply sidesteps the profound philosophical issues involved in such central concepts of his theory as time, causation, meaning and probability – all of which are long-standing and deeply pondered problems in European philosophy.

Astrology

Around 1911, Jung developed an interest in astrology. In a letter to Freud (12 June 1911), he reports:

> My evenings are taken up very largely with astrology. I make horoscopic calculations in order to find a clue to the core of psychological truth. Some remarkable things have turned up . . . I dare say that one day we shall find in

astrology a good deal of knowledge that has been intuitively projected into the heavens. For instance, it appears that the signs of the zodiac are character pictures, in other words libido symbols which depict the typical qualities of the libido at a given moment.

(Jung 1973: 24)

This interest continued to the end of Jung's life. For example, in a letter to B. V. Raman dated 6 September 1947 he reaffirmed the practical importance of astrology for the psychologist:

In cases of difficult psychological diagnosis I usually get a horoscope in order to have a further point of view from an entirely different angle. I must say that I very often found that the astrological data elucidated certain points which I otherwise would have been unable to understand.

(Jung 1973: 475)

That Jung should have become interested in astrology when he did is not especially remarkable. It was at a time when mythology and ancient knowledge were increasingly becoming the focus of psychoanalytic inquiries, and when both popular and scholarly texts on astrology were becoming widely available, largely due to the recently formed theosophical presses (see Noll 1994: 68). As Jung notes in his essay 'The Structure of the Unconscious': 'The truth is that astrology flourishes as never before. There is a regular library of astrological books and magazines that sell for far better than the best scientific works' (1916: par. 494). Jung's distinction was to be the first to relate astrology to depth psychology, not just as a cultural phenomenon to be analysed by depth psychological methods but as an adjunct to those methods.

Jung's practical involvement with astrology provided data that seemed to support the idea of moments of time having particular qualities. Thus, in a letter to B. Baur (29 January 1934), after discussing the precession of the equinoxes, he remarks:

The fact that astrology nevertheless yields valid results proves that it is not the apparent positions of the stars which work, but rather the times which are measured or determined by arbitrarily named stellar positions. Time thus proves to be a stream of energy filled with qualities and not, as our philosophy would have it, an abstract concept or precondition of knowledge.

(Jung 1973: 138–9)

Initially, Jung seems to have hoped that astrology might be able to demonstrate objectively a relationship of synchronicity between temporal determinants (i.e., planetary and stellar positions) and individual character (1976: 476; 1952b: pars. 867–9). Later, however, his attitude became more complex and ambivalent. This change stemmed partly from his own astrological experiment, which, as we saw in the previous chapter, revealed the extent of the astrologer's psychic participation in the handling of astrological material (1952b: pars. 872–915; see also Hyde 1992: 121–39). However, it seems also to have been influenced by recent discoveries concerning the possible effect of planetary positions on solar proton radiation. Those discoveries suggested to Jung that there might after all be a causal basis for the apparent efficacy of astrology (1951b: par. 987; 1976: 23–4) – or that astrology might be partly causal and partly synchronistic (1976: 177, 421, 428–30). Finally, for all his early enthusiasm for the idea of qualitative time, which he articulated even more fulsomely in relation to the *I Ching*, Jung eventually expressed dissatisfaction with this notion. In a letter written in 1954 in response to questions about astrology he rejected the notion as tautological and claimed that, rather than using it as the basis for an explanation of synchronicity, he had replaced it with the idea of synchronicity (1976: 176). He came to consider that synchronistic events were not expressions of the already existing quality of a moment of time but created and were constitutive of that quality.

I Ching

Around 1920, Jung began experimenting with the ancient Chinese oracle the *I Ching*, or *Book of Changes*. He may have been made aware of this text by his former patient and later colleague and lover Toni Wolff, who had learned about eastern philosophy and religion from her Sinologist father (Douglas 1997: 28). However, Jung would also have had ample opportunity to encounter the *I Ching* on his own, as the English translation by James Legge that he first obtained (Legge 1882) was readily available as one of the volumes in Friedrich Max Müller's scholarly series *Sacred Books of the East*.[9]

Jung was deeply impressed by the effectiveness of the *I Ching* in yielding pertinent answers to his questions. He relates how, one summer, he

> resolved to make an all out attack on the riddle of this book . . . I would sit for hours on the ground beneath the hundred-year old pear tree, the *I Ching* beside me, practising the technique by referring the resultant oracles to one another in an interplay of questions and answers. All sorts of undeniably remarkable results emerged – meaningful connections with my own thought processes which I could not explain to myself . . . Time and again I encountered amazing coincidences which seemed to suggest the idea of an acausal parallelism (a synchronicity as I later called it).
>
> (Jung 1963: 342)

Jung's appreciation of the *I Ching* deepened considerably a couple of years later when he met the German missionary and Sinologist Richard Wilhelm, who had just produced a new German translation of the book. Jung refers to his friendship with Wilhelm as 'one of the most significant events of my life' (1930: par. 74). He appears to have been particularly impressed by Wilhelm's own mastery of the *I Ching*:

At his first lecture at the Psychological Club in Zurich [in 1923], Wilhelm, at my request, demonstrated the use of the *I Ching* and at the same time made a prognosis which, in less than two years, was fulfilled to the letter and with the utmost clarity.

(Jung 1930: par. 84)

It was with reference to the *I Ching*, at a memorial address for Wilhelm in 1930, that Jung made his first public use of his new concept: 'The science of the *I Ching*', he asserted, 'is based not on the causality principle but on one which – hitherto unnamed because not familiar to us – I have tentatively called the *synchronistic principle*' (1930: par. 81). He referred to 'psychic parallelisms which simply cannot be related to each other causally, but must be connected by another kind of principle altogether' (ibid.). The essence of this other principle he considered to consist 'in the relative simultaneity of the events'. For time, as he still understood it,

far from being an abstraction, is a concrete continuum which possesses qualities or basic conditions capable of manifesting themselves simultaneously in different places by means of an acausal parallelism, such as we find, for instance, in the simultaneous occurrence of identical thoughts, symbols, or psychic states.

(Jung 1930: par. 81).

Referring also to the data and claims of astrology, he asserted that 'whatever is born or done at this particular moment of time has the quality of this moment of time', adding confidently that '[h]ere we have the basic formula for the use of the *I Ching*' (1930: pars. 82–3).

A fuller exposition of the principle, again preceding the publication of his main essays on synchronicity, was also made with reference to the *I Ching* in Jung's Foreword to the English rendering of Wilhelm's German translation (Jung 1950a: pars. 967–74; see also Wilhelm 1950). Here, as late as 1949, Jung was still emphasising the factor of the quality of moments of time. He writes that 'synchronicity takes the coincidence of events in space and time as meaning something more than mere chance, namely, a peculiar interdependence of objective events among themselves as well as with the subjective (psychic) states of the observer or observers' (1950a: par. 972). The specific style of thinking implied in this is then explicated as follows:

How does it happen that A', B', C', D', etc., appear all at the same moment and in the same place? It happens in the first place because the physical events A' and B' are of the same quality as the psychic events C' and D', and further because all are the exponents of one and the same momentary situation. The situation is assumed to represent a legible or understandable picture.

(Jung 1950a: par. 973)

Apart from consolidating his understanding of qualitative time, the divinatory method of the *I Ching* provided Jung with a means of generating experiences of meaningful coincidence with some measure of regularity. For he realised that, like other mantic procedures, the *I Ching* can 'create favourable conditions for the occurrence of meaningful coincidences' (1952b: par. 911). At times, he practically recommended the *I Ching* to others for such experimental purposes (1976: 491). Again, largely because of this amenability to experimental investigation, the system offered a context for looking at some of the dynamics of synchronicity. The *I Ching* hexagrams, for example, seemed to Jung to be a kind of readable representation of archetypes (1963: 294; 1976: 584). This connection between hexagrams and archetypes, combined with the fact that the method of consulting the oracle is essentially based on number, led Jung to speculate on the archetypes of natural numbers and on the possibility of their having a special relationship to synchronicity (1952b: pars. 870–1). Finally, that the *I Ching* was such a significant cultural presence throughout Chinese history encouraged Jung's efforts to present his ideas on synchronicity by providing him with a major precedent for the recognition of an acausal principle of connection between events.

Analytical psychological theory and practice

We noted in Chapter 1 the principal ways in which the concept of synchronicity integrates with the rest of Jung's psychological model. This is hardly surprising and largely stems from Jung's thinking about synchronicity having been influenced by his already worked-out framework of psychological ideas. For example, his formulation of synchronicity as the complementary opposite of the principle of causality reflects his understanding of the psyche as a system composed of a balancing of opposites. The meaningfulness of synchronicities largely presupposes a teleological understanding of psychic processes such as is implied in the notion of individuation. The independent origin of the psychic and physical events that compose a synchronicity accords with the way Jung characterised archetypal events as being able to arise spontaneously and independently. In general, the notion of synchronicity could not have meant what it did to Jung if it were not supported by the various structural and dynamic features of his model of the psyche. As we saw towards the end of Chapter 1, the bare phenomena of coincidence, encountering a different set of theoretical assumptions, could be interpreted in a radically different way.

Jung's observation of synchronicities in the clinical setting, far from being eccentric, is an instance of the intimate relationship that, as we have already noted, had long existed between depth psychology and anomalous phenomena. However, Jung's specific interest in meaningful coincidence dates, by his own account, from the mid-1920s; that is, just at the time when he had clarified and was beginning to expound his distinctive psychological model. At this time, he writes:

I was investigating the phenomena of the collective unconscious and kept coming across connections which I could not explain as chance groupings or 'runs.' What I found were 'coincidences' which were connected so meaningfully that their 'chance' concurrence would represent a degree of improbability that would have to be expressed by an astronomical figure.

(Jung 1952b: par. 843)

In his analytic practice, Jung was impressed both by the frequency with which coincidence phenomena occurred and by their meaningfulness to those who experienced them:

As a psychiatrist and psychotherapist I have often come up against the phenomena in question and could convince myself how much these inner experiences meant to my patients. In most cases they were things which people do not talk about for fear of exposing themselves to thoughtless ridicule. I was amazed to see how many people have had experiences of this kind and how carefully the secret was guarded.

(Jung 1952b: par. 816)

The example involving the scarab beetle, discussed at length in Chapters 1 and 2, is an instance of the kind of clinical experiences Jung has in mind. The special value of such events for the development of the theory of synchronicity lay in the fact that they occurred in a psychotherapeutic context, so that their accompanying psychological dynamics could be observed particularly closely. Jung noted, for instance, that the meaning which coincidences have for their subject, including their attendant emotional charge or numinosity, seems to stem from the underlying presence of an archetype, activated usually in response to the person having reached some kind of psychological impasse. Thus, in the scarab case, Jung believed the archetype of rebirth had been activated by the patient's inability to see beyond her rationalism, by her need for 'psychic renewal' (1952b: par. 845). As we have seen, implicit in Jung's analysis of this and other cases is his understanding of synchronicity as an expression of the process of individuation furthered through compensation. Thus only after the excessive rationalism of the patient's conscious attitude had been compensated from the unconscious by the powerful irrational event of the synchronicity, could her 'process of transformation [i.e., her individuation] . . . at last begin to move' (ibid.). Cases such as this also enabled Jung to observe that coincidences can be symbolic in their meaning. His reason for supposing the archetype of rebirth to have been active in the woman's experience was his knowledge that '[t]he scarab is a classic example of a rebirth symbol' (ibid.).

Considering the importance Jung attaches to his observations of synchronicities in the clinical setting, it is surprising how few clinical synchronicities are to be found in his work, and of these few the scarab incident alone is analysed in any detail. Rather than treating the clinical synchronicities he mentions as cases to be analysed, Jung generally uses them as passing illustrations of particular points. Nevertheless, we do gain a few insights into how synchronicities can manifest, how Jung understands the psychic background of synchronicities, and how he used synchronicities in his clinical work.

Regarding the way synchronicities manifest, Jung provides other explicit examples where symbolic interpretation is needed in order to establish the parallel between the events. One such example is the incident (also discussed in Chapter 2) where the wife of a patient of Jung's became anxious at home just when her husband elsewhere suffered a fatal collapse in the street. The immediate reason for her anxiety was that a flock of birds had alighted on the roof of her house, something that had previously happened on the deaths of her mother and grand-mother. Accordingly, she associated flocks of birds with imminent death. Jung later provided comparative mythological material to substantiate the association of birds with death (1952b: pars. 844–5). Here, without the wife's personal association, no synchronicity would have been recognised, and without Jung's mythological amplification, the personal association might have seemed arbitrary.

A frequent theme in the synchronicities Jung relates that have a clinical reference is the apparent connection such incidents demonstrate between the human psyche and the natural world. This is again evident in the scarab incident, where the behaviour of an insect reflects what is being discussed between analyst and analysand. Elsewhere, Jung describes a woman patient who was attacked by birds whenever she was in the country, while her companions (on one occasion, Jung) were unmolested (Aziz 1990: 139). Another woman, suffering from unconscious guilt at having murdered her best friend out of jealousy, experienced the human and natural worlds turn against her (Jung 1963: 143–5). Once, Jung was walking in a wood with a patient who was telling him about an important early dream of a spectral fox. At that moment, a real fox came out of the wood and walked on the path ahead of them for several minutes (Jung 1973: 395). In another case, a patient kept trying to explain her dreams symbolically in spite of their obvious sexual content and Jung's sexual interpretation of them. At the next appointment, 'two sparrows fluttered to the ground at her feet and "performed the act"' (in McGuire and Hull 1978: 182–3).

Accounts of Jung's synchronicities also sometimes provide glimpses into how he made use of them in the clinical setting. Once more, the scarab incident provides the richest detail.[10] Additionally, we are told that when analysing in his garden room by the lake, Jung would take the behaviour of insects and the lake water as a synchronistic commentary on what was going on in the analytic session (Aziz 1990: 85–6, citing Hannah 1977: 202).

As we saw in Chapter 1, Jung notes a connection between transference and countertransference phenomena and synchronicity. 'The relationship between doctor and patient,' he writes, 'especially when a transference on the part of the patient occurs, or a more or less unconscious identification of doctor and patient, can lead to parapsychological [i.e., synchronistic] phenomena' (1963: 159). By way of illustration, he recounts how, one evening while staying in a hotel, he had felt uncharacteristically restless and nervous (ibid.: 136–7). During the night, he was awakened by a feeling of dull pain, as though something had struck his forehead and then the back of his skull. He also had the impression that someone had hastily opened the door and entered his room. The following day he received news that one of his patients had shot himself, learning later that the bullet had come to rest in the back of his patient's skull. Jung follows this account with further theoretical reflections on the nature of synchronicity – its connection with archetypal situations (such as death) and the relativisation of time and space in the unconscious. However, he does not pursue further the connection with the dynamics of the transference.

The consulting room was not the only analytical psychological context to provide Jung with data that influenced his formulations of synchronicity. From 1925 to 1939 Jung held a series of English language seminars on his psychological ideas at the Psychological Club in Zurich,[11] during which meaningful coincidences sometimes occurred. Indeed, during the 1928–30 seminars on dream analysis, we can observe Jung moving towards a first definition and characterisation of synchronicity.

On 14 November 1928 the seminar group was discussing the meaning of certain forms of ritual sport, since one of the dreams being examined (the important 'initial dream' of the analysis) contained an image of a square amphitheatre which made the dreamer think of the game of *jeu de paume*, an early form of tennis. Amplifying on the idea that this game could be viewed as a form of symbolic ceremonial, Jung associated it with the sport of bullfighting, which in turn he connected with the ancient cult of the bull god Mithras (1928–30: 24–5). It happened that, unknown to Jung, one of the participants at the seminar had dreamed the night before that she had been present at a bullfight in Spain (ibid.: 35).

When this dream was mentioned at the next meeting a week later, on 21 November, it was followed by a discussion of its meaning and the meaning of the bull symbol generally, during which Jung reported that 'not long ago I had a letter from a patient [in Mexico], a lady who had just been to a bull-fight' (ibid.: 36). Then, at the meeting following this, on 28 November, Jung began by announcing that the discussion of the bull dream and the meaning of the bullfight had 'brought interesting coincidences to light' (ibid.: 43). For he had just received another letter from the woman in Mexico in which she commented on the bullfight she had been to in terms very similar to those used by Jung in the seminar. Allowing time for postage, Jung calculated that the letter must have been written 'just about the day when we first spoke of the bull in the seminar' (ibid.: 44). He remarks: 'My friend is a quite independent observer, but she got the gist of [the symbolic significance of the bullfight] and in that moment found it necessary to convey it to me' (ibid.).

Further, Jung reported that the person whose dreams were being analysed in the seminar (a patient not a participant) had spent from the 20th to the 24th of November 'making a picture which he could not understand' (1928–30: 43). It was of a bull's head holding the disc of the sun between its horns, as in representations of sacred bull gods. Thus he drew just what was being discussed by the seminar group and over the very period when they were discussing it. 'I told him', Jung reported, 'that we were talking of the bull in connection with his dream, and that his drawing *synchronizes* with that' (ibid.; emphasis added).

Coincidences such as these, Jung told the seminar group, have a sort of 'irrational regularity' (ibid.), which is why we notice them. 'The East bases much of its science on this irregularity', he continued, 'and considers coincidences as the reliable basis of the world rather than causality. *Synchronism* is the prejudice of the East; causality is the modern prejudice of the West' (ibid.: 44–5; emphasis added).

In November 1928 Jung is recorded as having used the words 'synchronize' and 'synchronism'. A year later, on 4 December 1929, another incident occurred. The five-year-old child of one of the participants at the seminar made two drawings incorporating symbols (principally the cross and the crescent) that were being talked about, yet the child had not actually been exposed to any information about the seminars. Jung remarks:

> Since I have seen many other examples of the same kind in which people not concerned were affected, I have invented the word *synchronicity* as a term to cover these phenomena, that is, things happening at the same time moment as an expression of the same time content.
>
> (Jung 1928–30: 417)

From this series of incidents two important points can be noted about the way Jung was initially conceiving of synchronicity. First, he understood it to be a phenomenon that could have its impact on the widest collective level. Thus, the whole nexus of bull coincidences manifested via four different people: Jung himself, who first mentioned the cult of the bull god Mithras; the seminar participant who dreamed of a bullfight the night before Jung mentioned the bull god; the person whose dreams were being analysed and who felt moved to draw a bull's head; and the correspondent who wrote to Jung with her symbolic interpretation of the bullfight she had recently attended. The last two of these people were not even present at the seminars, and one of them was many thousands of miles away in Mexico. Again, concerning the dream of the bullfight Jung remarked that 'any one of us might have dreamt it' (1928–30: 36).

The second point is that Jung was stressing the idea of the quality of particular moments of time. 'In 1929', he remarked at the end of one seminar (27 November 1929), 'everything has the cast and brand of this year. And the children born in this year will be recognisable as part of a great process and marked by a particular condition' (1928–30: 412). As we have seen, this idea also played a central role in the way Jung generally articulated his understanding of astrology and the *I Ching*.

Psychical research and parapsychology

At around the same time as the early depth psychological theories began to appear in the late nineteenth century, there also emerged the new discipline of scientific psychical research. Its formal beginning can be dated to 1882 with the founding of the Society for Psychical Research (SPR). The scientists and scholars involved in this society especially wished to investigate claims of the by now rampant spiritualist and theosophical movements concerning various alleged paranormal phenomena that were being taken as proof of post-mortem survival and the existence of higher planes of reality. In his student days and throughout his professional life, Jung maintained a keen interest in psychical research. He was an honorary member of the SPR and, as we have seen, lectured to the society in 1919. His familiarity with the field is evident from the numerous references to psychical researchers in his 1952 essay on synchronicity. Those named include Edmund Gurney, Frederick Myers, Frank Podmore, Xavier Darieux, Charles Richet, Camille Flammarion, G. N. M. Tyrell, Robert McConnell, J. W. Dunne, S. G. Soal, K. M. Goldney and J. B. Rhine. For Jung, the work of the early psychical researchers represented not only the application of science to a range of obscure phenomena but also an indirect revival of the correspondence theory and hence of the 'magical world of earlier ages' (1952b: par. 939).

Although he would not have thought of himself as a psychical researcher, the Austrian biologist Paul Kammerer can also be mentioned here. For, like the early psychical researchers, he applied scientific methods – in his case the methods of descriptive biology – to the investigation of anomalous phenomena. Thus, he meticulously observed selected everyday situations, noting the tendency of the same or similar events to occur in clusters within those situations. As Arthur Koestler summarises:

> Kammerer spent hours sitting on benches in various public parks, noting down the number of people that strolled by in both directions, classifying them by sex, age, dress, whether they carried umbrellas or parcels. He did the same on his long tram journeys from suburb to office. Then he analysed his tables and found that on every parameter they showed the typical clustering phenomena familiar to statisticians, gamblers, and insurance companies. He made, of course, the necessary allowances for such causal factors as rush-hour, weather, etc.
>
> (Koestler 1975: 135)

Considering chance alone insufficient to explain this kind of clustering, Kammerer proposed what he called the 'law of seriality'. Koestler explains the central idea as being that

> side by side with the causality of classical physics, there exists a second basic principle in the universe which tends towards unity; a force of attraction comparable to universal gravity. But while gravity acts on all mass without

discrimination, this other universal force acts selectively to bring like and like together both in space and in time; it correlates by affinity, regardless whether the likeness is one of substance, form or function, or refers to symbols.

(Koestler 1975: 138)

Koestler considers Jung's theory of synchronicity to be in many respects simply a renaming of the law of seriality (1975: 141), and it may be significant that Kammerer published his theory and some of his data in a book, *Das Gesetz der Serie*, which was published in 1919 – around the time Jung says he became particularly interested in coincidences.[12] However, in his 1952 essay on synchronicity Jung is mostly critical of Kammerer. He considers that Kammerer's data are fully explicable in terms of 'statistical and mathematical probability' and that 'there is no apparent reason why he should look behind them for anything else' (1952b: par. 825). That Kammerer does nevertheless look behind his data and postulate his law of seriality Jung explains by supposing that he had 'a dim but fascinated intuition of an acausal arrangement and combination of events' (ibid.). Jung laments that Kammerer did not attempt a quantitative evaluation of seriality. However, one suspects that what he really misses in Kammerer's data and theory is an account of the meaningfulness that can attach to coincidences.

While Jung was actively interested in psychical research throughout his life, few bodies of work within this field made such a deep impression on him as the parapsychological experiments carried out by Rhine in the first parapsychology laboratory, established at Duke University in 1932.[13] These experiments, which involved guessing the signs on a series of cards, appeared to give statistical, that is to say, scientifically respectable, confirmation of the reality of both extrasensory perception (ESP) and psychokinesis (PK). More importantly, the positive results of Rhine's experiments did not diminish if the subjects attempting the ESP or PK tasks were separated from the target objects by even great distances in space or time. Jung concluded that 'in relation to the psyche space and time are, so to speak, "elastic" and can apparently be reduced almost to vanishing point' (1952b: par. 840). Another of the ways in which Jung came to characterise synchronicity was therefore as 'a psychically conditioned relativity of time and space' (ibid.). In fact, Jung suggests that spatio-temporal relativity of this kind is the basic condition within the unconscious psyche, as though space and time 'did not exist in themselves but were only "postulated" by the conscious mind' (ibid.). Knowledge of events at a distance or in the future is possible because, within the unconscious psyche, all events coexist beyond time and space:

For the unconscious psyche space and time seem to be relative; that is to say, knowledge finds itself in a space–time continuum in which space is no longer space, nor time time. If, therefore, the unconscious should develop or maintain a potential in the direction of consciousness, it is then possible for parallel events to be perceived or 'known'.

(Jung 1952b: par. 912)

This space–time relativity is different from the notion of qualitative time. In qualitative time the idea of a 'moment', and hence of relative simultaneity, is of paramount importance. In space–time relativity any natural understanding of 'moments', and certainly of simultaneity, becomes irrelevant, as precognitive coincidences clearly indicate.

Apart from experimental confirmation of this crucial insight concerning space–time relativity, Rhine's work also appeared to support Jung's observation that paranormal experiences are usually attended by heightened emotionality. For Rhine's work identified the so-called 'decline effect', the fact that the most significant results were generally obtained towards the beginning of the experimental session when the subject's interest (emotional engagement) can be supposed to have been at its greatest (1952b: pars. 838, 841).

On Rhine's initiative, a correspondence between him and Jung developed which continued intermittently from 1934 to 1954. Rhine repeatedly pressed Jung to write down accounts of his paranormal experiences and observations as well as his theoretical reflections concerning them (see Jung 1973: 180–2, 378–9). Though reluctant, because fearing incomprehension on the part of the public (ibid.: 190), Jung did comply to a certain extent and in a letter of November 1945 gave in response to a series of direct questions submitted by Rhine a tentative preliminary formulation of the theory of synchronicity as he would eventually present it in terms of the psychic relativisation of space and time (ibid.: 493–5). However, probably the strongest testimony to Rhine's influence on him is that Jung modelled his own astrological experiment on Rhine's work, attempting, like Rhine, to use the statistical method to demonstrate and elucidate phenomena not recognised by the dominant science of the day.

Physics

Jung's language in discussing the implications of Rhine's experiments – his references to 'relativity' and a 'space–time continuum' – is clearly reminiscent of Einstein's theories of relativity in physics, and Jung did indeed acknowledge the influence on him of Einstein's theories. When the physicist was working in Zurich in 1909 and 1912, he was Jung's dinner guest on several occasions, and, as Jung recalls, 'tried to instil into us the elements of [his first theory of relativity], more or less successfully' (1976: 109; see also Jung 1935: par. 140). Jung continues:

> It was Einstein who first started me off thinking about a possible relativity of time as well as space, and their psychic conditionality. More than thirty years later this stimulus led to my relation with the physicist Professor W. Pauli and to my thesis of psychic synchronicity.
>
> (Jung 1976: 109; see also Progoff 1973: 151–2)

However, even more influential on Jung were certain developments within the other great physics theory that arose in the early part of the twentieth century:

quantum mechanics. Jung was impressed above all by both the principle of complementarity and the ability to predict subatomic events only probabilistically. As we saw in the previous chapter, it was to the legitimacy of mere probabilistic prediction that Jung most often appealed in support of his concept of acausality. With reference to one such subatomic event, radioactive decay, he quotes James Jeans: 'Radioactive break-up appeared to be an effect without a cause, and suggested that the ultimate laws of nature were not even causal' (in 1952b: par. 959).

There was nothing unusual about Jung seeking support from physics for his psychological views. Theories in physics underpinned assumptions in much of the psychological thinking of the late nineteenth century and the early twentieth. An instance is Hermann von Helmholtz's principle of the conservation of energy, the materialistic implications of which influenced Ernst Brücke and through him the early Freud. Jung, already in the Zofingia lectures of his student years, boldly addressed fundamental questions in physics, such as the law of universal gravitation, in order to lay the ground for his approach to psychology (1896–9: pars. 49–50).

The principle of complementarity was utilised by Jung in his presentation of the status of synchronicity. Niels Bohr considered that one of the central paradoxes of quantum physics – that subatomic entities behave in contradictory ways, either as particle or as wave, depending on the method by which they are observed – cannot be resolved by considering one of the forms of manifestation more fundamental than the other. Both, in his view, are fundamental: the two forms of manifestation *complement* each other and together give as complete a picture of the subatomic entity as is possible given the intrinsic limitations of human cognition (see Honner 1987). Jung saw causality and acausality as standing in a similar relationship. As the title of his principal essay indicates, synchronicity is for him 'an acausal connecting principle'. As such, it is 'a hypothetical factor equal in rank to causality as a principle of explanation' (1952b: par. 840). It is 'equal in rank' in the sense of being complementary to the principle of causality: causality accounts for one kind of connection between events – 'constant connection through effect', as Jung epitomises it – while synchronicity accounts for the complementary kind of connection – 'inconstant connection through contingency, equivalence, or "meaning"' (ibid.: par. 963). Together, the two principles give, in Jung's view, a complete account of the kinds of connections that can exist between events.[14]

The implications of these points from physics were explored by Jung largely through his friendship with the physicist Wolfgang Pauli, which lasted from 1932 until Pauli's death in 1958. The full extent of Pauli's and Jung's influence on each other has only recently begun to be evaluated (see, e.g., van Erkelens 1991, 1999; Zabriskie 1995; Lindorff 1995a, 1995b; Meier 2001). One can note in particular that Jung's principal essay on synchronicity was originally published in the same volume as a companion essay by Pauli on 'The Influence of Archetypal Ideas on the Scientific Theories of Kepler' (Jung and Pauli 1955). In letters to Pauli and another physicist Markus Fierz (both dated 22 June 1949) Jung refers to a draft of his essay on synchronicity as having been written at Pauli's prompting and with his encouragement (Meier 2001: 36; Jung 1973: 530). In the essay, Jung credits Pauli with having helped him formulate the *quaternio* diagram in which the complementary relationships between causality and synchronicity and between indestructible energy and the space–time continuum were set out (1952b: par. 963). He also refers to Pauli's proposal to develop a 'neutral language' in which to express the unity of being suggested by recent findings in physics and psychology (ibid.: par. 960). There is, in addition, a sprinkling of footnotes in which Jung acknowledges Pauli for drawing his attention to a parapsychological paper by McConnell (ibid.: par. 839 n. 33), Niels Bohr's use of the term 'correspondence' (ibid.: par. 924 n. 13), and Arnold Geulincx's priority over Leibniz in the use of the idea of synchronised clocks to express the relationship between body and soul (ibid.: par. 937 n. 58).

However, the recently translated Jung–Pauli letters (Meier 2001) reveal that this is only a fraction of Jung's debt to Pauli. In letters exchanged between 7 November 1948 and 2 February 1951, Pauli recommends that Jung sharpen up his use of each one of the notions of acausality (ibid.: 38), time (ibid.: 38–9), meaning (ibid.: 44) and statistics (ibid.: 53, 64), as well as of terminology from physics (ibid.: 57–8, 65–6); that he note the limitations of the astrological experiment (ibid.: 37); that he refer to qualitative mathematics (ibid.: 44); that he distinguish and explain differently synchronicities involving two physical events, two psychic events, or one psychic and one physical event (ibid.: 60, 64); that he also distinguish between spontaneous and induced synchronicities (ibid.: 44); that he include more on the archetypal basis of parapsychological experiments, since it is not evident that the results of these experiments qualify as synchronicities (ibid.: 36); that he consider broadening the concepts of both synchronicity and the archetype (ibid.: 65) and viewing archetypes in terms of psychic probability (ibid.: 64); and that he refer to Schopenhauer's essay 'On the Apparent Design in the Fate of the Individual' (ibid.: 37). Jung followed most of these recommendations and thereby gained Pauli's strong endorsement, especially for the final chapter of the essay which Pauli gives his 'wholehearted approval' since it 'reflects faithfully the state of affairs with the problems at the moment and, from the standpoint of modern physics, is now unassailable' (ibid.: 71).[15]

History of religions and western esotericism

Also significant for the development of the concept of synchronicity was Jung's extensive research into the history of religion and western esoteric thought, as evinced by several volumes in his *Collected Works* (especially *Symbols of Transformation*, *Aion*, *Psychology and Religion: West and East*, *Psychology and Alchemy*, *Alchemical Studies* and *Mysterium Coniunctionis*). Again, Jung's involvement in these areas was not idiosyncratic but part of a widespread cultural movement. *Religionswissenschaft*, the non-theological study of religions, had established itself as an academic discipline in German universities by the end of the nineteenth century and the beginning of the twentieth. Max Müller (1823–1900), who coined the term '*Religionswissenschaft*', made a particularly notable contribution to this development with his editorship of the translations published in the *Sacred Books of the East* series. At a more popular level, the Theosophical movement was a major influence. For its publishing ventures had made widely available many accessible, if not always reliable, accounts of past and present world religions – Egyptian, Hindu, Judaic, Buddhist, Graeco-Roman, Christian, Islamic – as well as of esoteric traditions such as astrology, magic, Gnosticism, alchemy, Kabbalah, Yoga, together with their various rituals, meditations and occult techniques (see Noll 1994: 64–9).

From his study of religions, Jung found especially relevant the philosophical Taoism of the Chinese sages Lao-tzu and Chuang-tzu (1952b: pars. 916–24). He notes that the Chinese concept of 'Tao' has been variously translated as 'Providence', 'God' and, most interestingly for Jung, 'Meaning' (ibid.: par. 917; the last translation was proposed by Richard Wilhelm). The Chinese conception implied that there is a latent rationality or meaning in the cosmos, which is also the viewpoint that Jung believed was suggested by synchronistic experiences. In other contexts, Jung had already equated Tao with synchronicity (see 1930–4: 608; 1935: par. 143). In the 1952 essay he quotes Chuang-tzu's description of a state in which 'the soul can become empty and absorb the whole world. It is Tao that fills this emptiness.' With the insight based on this, says Chuang-tzu, 'you use your inner eye, your inner ear, to pierce to the heart of things, and have no need of intellectual knowledge' (in 1952b: par. 923). Jung comments: 'This is obviously an allusion to the absolute knowledge of the unconscious, and to the presence in the microcosm of macrocosmic events' (ibid.). Finally, Jung's conception of synchronicity as an ability to see meaningful connections regardless of causal relationships resonates with his view of Chinese thinking as 'a thinking in terms of the whole' (ibid.: par. 924).

There are a few hints in his writings on synchronicity that Jung was also keeping in mind works within the tradition of Christian theology. Thus, in a footnote on the penultimate page of his principal essay, he refers to Origen, Augustine, Prosper of Aquitaine and an anonymous theologian (1952b: par. 967 n. 17) in relation to the notion of continuous creation. Mostly, however, Christianity does not appear to have influenced him directly but only in terms of the history of its symbols. Thus, he writes: 'my researches into the history of symbols, and of the fish symbol in particular, brought the problem [of synchronicity] ever closer to me' (ibid.: par. 816). The reference here is to the coincidence, mapped out in detail in *Aion* (Jung 1951a), 'between the life of Christ and the objective astronomical event, the entrance of the spring equinox into the sign of Pisces'. His discovery of this was another of the factors which, he says, 'led to the problem of synchronicity' (1961: 210).

These researches into the history of Christian symbols also confirmed for Jung that alchemy and esotericism in general constituted an underground counter-current to mainstream Christianity (see 1944: pars. 1–43). Among the forerunners of his theory of synchronicity, Jung names many of the major figures who either influenced or were representatives of the western esoteric tradition: Hippocrates on the 'sympathy of all things' (1952b: par. 924), Philo Judaeus on the microcosm and macrocosm (ibid.: par. 925), Theophrastus on the bond joining the sensuous and supersensuous worlds (ibid.: par. 927), Plotinus on the possibility of sympathy regardless of distance (ibid.), Pico della Mirandola on organic unity (ibid.), Agrippa von Nettesheim also on the microcosm and macrocosm (ibid.: par. 930), Paracelsus on correspondence theory (ibid.: par. 932) and Johannes Kepler on astrological synchronicity and the animation of the earth (ibid.: par. 933–5). At times Jung presents his theory of synchronicity as simply an updating of these esoteric views: 'Synchronicity', he writes at the end of his 1951 Eranos lecture, 'is a modern differentiation of the obsolete concept of correspondence, sympathy, and harmony' (1951b: par. 995). Nevertheless, he is careful to distinguish his own position from the tendency sometimes found in these earlier views to assume the existence of 'magical causality', so that coincidences, rather than being acausal, would be 'somehow due to magical influence' (1952b: par. 941). What the early theories suggest to Jung is the same as was suggested by his consideration of philosophical Taoism: that there may be a dimension of meaning that does not depend on human subjectivity or projection but is 'transcendental' or 'self-subsistent' – 'a meaning which is *a priori* in relation to human consciousness and apparently exists outside man' (ibid.: par. 942).

A motley of insights

We have noted a wide range of sources and influences that shaped Jung's thinking about synchronicity. The list could certainly be extended if we were also to focus on unacknowledged influences[16] and Jung's broader cultural and social milieu. Moreover, in the case of some influences, such as philosophy, we have seen reason to suspect that the specific nature of the influence may have been somewhat different and more far-reaching than Jung presents it. Nevertheless, we are left with an overall impression of openness and thoroughness in Jung's admission and discussion of his sources. What he seems less explicit about, perhaps because he was not sufficiently aware of it, is that these diverse sources, while all providing him with much-needed encouragement to develop and publish his ideas, also stimulated him to heterogeneous and sometimes incompatible insights. Appreciation of this motley of sources and insights may help us to understand why Jung's writings about synchronicity should be so replete with intellectual difficulties. Not all of these difficulties necessarily stem from the inherent irrationality of the phenomenon, which we noted at the end of Chapter 2. However, while we have thus been helped to understand another possible origin of the difficulties, we have not yet considered how they might be more fully resolved.

Chapter 4

Religion, science and synchronicity

In view of the wide diversity of influences on Jung's theory of synchronicity, it is perhaps not surprising that there should be a number of apparent inconsistencies among his insights. Later in this chapter we will directly address the question of whether these apparent inconsistencies can be resolved. Before that, however, it is worth asking *why* Jung appealed to so many sources. If it turns out that he was governed by an overarching purpose, this might provide the key to understanding why he pursued the lines of thought and invoked the kinds of support he did.

One reason for Jung having ranged so widely could be that he recognised the controversial and, to the mainstream, thoroughly objectionable nature of the ideas he was presenting and so wished to draw support for them from as many quarters as possible. That Jung did have an eye to making his ideas acceptable is suggested by his conspicuous foregrounding of the scientific evidence for his theory while downplaying its religious influences (a point to which I shall return). However, it is unlikely that Jung's concern was solely with optimising the mainstream credibility of his ideas. Were that the case he would hardly have devoted so much time to sources that, in mainstream terms, are highly dubious, however much of a scientific spin he gives to them: for example, paranormal experiences, parapsychological experiments, astrology, Chinese divination, and ancient and medieval cosmology. More probably, Jung's exceptionally wide range of sources should be understood as part of an earnest attempt to illuminate a fundamentally enigmatic phenomenon from as many perspectives as possible. Certainly, this is suggested by his admission that he could not hope to describe and explain synchronicity completely but only 'to broach the problem in such a way as to reveal some of its manifold aspects and connections' (1952b: par. 816). However, a further, arguably even more important, reason for Jung having appealed to the sources he did can be found, I think, in his attempt to engage with a particular problem that affected both him personally and the intellectual and cultural milieu into which he was born: the impact of the rise of science on religion and, more broadly, of modernity on tradition. Because he was engaging with interactions between such vast cultural forces, interactions taking place on many different fronts, Jung's explorations needed to be wide-ranging and multi-faceted if they were to be even representatively encompassing.

Several previous studies have examined synchronicity in relation to both science and religion (e.g., Peat 1987; Combs and Holland 1994; Mansfield 1995). However, they have tended to do so in terms of the possible contribution of synchronicity to resolving a present tension between these fields rather than, as here, exploring how the relationship between religion and science might provide a key to understanding the motivation of Jung's work on synchronicity and resolving some of its theoretical difficulties. In this chapter I shall first provide a brief sketch of some of the historical phases in the interaction between religion and science. This will extend up to, through, and beyond Jung's lifetime, in order to provide background not only for Jung's work on synchronicity but also for the continuing appeal of the phenomenon (a topic which we will examine in Chapter 6). Keeping in mind the limitations of the sketch, especially the risk it runs of oversimplifying, I shall then discuss Jung's complex relationship to the interaction between religion and science and the significance of this for his theory of synchronicity. Finally, in the light of these discussions, I shall revisit some of the outstanding intellectual difficulties in Jung's presentation of synchronicity and assess to what extent they may have been clarified.

Religion and science

Of all the influences on religion during Jung's lifetime (and continuing into the present), few have been as pervasive as modern science. However, precisely because this influence has been so profound and far-reaching, it is difficult to specify its nature. We can note the immense role that science, especially in the form of technology, has played in promoting some of the broad processes identified by sociologists as shaping the world within which contemporary religion exists – for example, modernisation, secularisation and globalisation. Indeed, for some commentators, 'Modernity is co-extensive with science' (Segal 1999a: 548). We can also note that science has provided explanations for the way the world is and for the way the human being is that are different from and, for many people, more satisfactory than the explanations traditionally provided by religion. Conspicuous examples concern the nature of the physical universe, the development of organic life on earth, the history of cultures and communities, and the functioning of the human mind. In numerous practical and ethical areas, too, developments in science have prompted a rethinking of traditional religious attitudes. For example, where the technology and resources exist with which to mitigate major sufferings such as poverty and sickness, it is understandable that for some the appeal of religious consolations should diminish. However, while at a general level we can readily acknowledge the rise of science, the challenges it has presented and the impact it has had, when we turn to the level of particular interactions between religion and science the picture quickly becomes complicated. Religion, after all, is a global phenomenon with thousands of variants, and science, itself not a unified phenomenon, has had different kinds of impact on different cultures and individuals at different times. Cautious historical discussions generally reveal that the interactions between religion and science vary enormously, are often not what one expects, and can be minutely sensitive to context (e.g., Brooke 1991; Brooke and Cantor 1998).

A thumbnail historical sketch

A widespread popular account of the interaction between religion and science pictures religion as having been more or less undisputedly the dominant worldview up until the seventeenth century. After that time, developments in natural science presented a series of increasingly compelling challenges to the claims of religion, and eventually, in the late nineteenth and early twentieth centuries, science supplanted religion altogether as the intellectually most satisfying and credible explanation of the world and our being in it. According to this account, the contemporary persistence of religion indicates an inability or refusal on the part of many people to take on board the implications of science and rationality. The prevalence of this account of the interactions between religion and science make it particularly important to appreciate the actual complexity of the situation, both historically and now.

The fields of both religion and science are extraordinarily vast and by no means static, so any attempt to discuss them in general terms is bound to be selective and questionable. I will highlight some of these difficulties shortly. Before that, however, I offer a very brief historical sketch of some of the major episodes in the interaction between religion and science in the West from the beginning of the seventeenth century to the end of the twentieth – the period during which the supplanting of religion by science supposedly occurred.

Before the seventeenth century, the dominant world-view in Europe was the one endorsed by the Roman Catholic Church: a synthesis, largely worked out by Thomas Aquinas (c. 1225–74), of Christian doctrine with the philosophical and scientific views of Aristotle (384–322 BCE) and the cosmology of Ptolemy (85–160). This world-view pictured a created hierarchy with the earth and human beings at the centre of a cosmic drama of redemption. Events in the physical world were explained in terms of their purposes. God was known through revelation and reason as the creator of the cosmos, the guarantor of purpose, and the redeemer of fallen humanity (Barbour 1998: 3–9).

During the seventeenth century, this traditional cosmology underwent a series of profound shocks, epitomised by the works of Galileo Galilei (1564–1642) and Isaac Newton (1642–1727). Rather than simply accept the authority of Aristotelian science and Ptolemaic cosmology, Galileo made his own observations of how phenomena actually behave. Combining these observations with mathematical calculations, he made significant discoveries – especially in the field of mechanics. Most controversially, however, his refined telescopes enabled him to make observations of celestial phenomena – mountains on the moon, spots on the sun, moons around Jupiter – that called into question the Ptolemaic cosmology in which the Church had embedded many of its doctrines. Instead, they seemed to lend support to the rival Copernican cosmology according to which the earth revolved around the sun. This raised serious questions for the Church both about the authority of those scriptures that implied that the sun revolved around the earth (e.g., Joshua 10:13) and about the status of a humanity no longer at the centre of the cosmos (Barbour 1998: 9–17). When in 1687 Newton published his *Mathematical Principles of Natural Philosophy* formulating the laws of motion, many of Galileo's mechanical and astronomical theories, and especially his method of testing his theories against observation, received cogent endorsement. So, in addition, did the principle of explaining events not in terms of their purposes but in terms of their causes. Indeed, such was the explanatory efficiency of Newton's laws that they inspired the image of the physical universe as a perfectly law-abiding machine, a cosmic clock. This image was used to support the design argument for God's existence, for such an efficiently functioning clock seems to imply an intelligent clockmaker. This, and variants, forms one of the staple arguments of natural theology, the understanding of God held to be obtainable through rational reflection on the world rather than through revelation (Barbour 1998: 17–24).

In the eighteenth century, Pierre Laplace and others extended Newton's mechanical model. Where Newton had believed that certain unexplained features of planetary motion left room for occasional, necessary divine intervention, Laplace later provided the data and theories that rendered this 'God of the gaps' redundant. A world-view was becoming prominent whose main features were determinism (the view that all things are determined by causes) and reductionism (the view that complex data can be explained in terms of something simpler). Newton's own determinism had been applied to the natural world but not to the human mind. Other eighteenth century thinkers saw no reason to draw this distinction and conceived of human mental life as equally determined. Again, Newton and many others had considered the extraordinary mechanical orderliness of the world as evidence for an intelligent creator. However, when Napoleon observed that Laplace's book on astronomy contained no mention of the Creator, Laplace famously replied: 'I had no need of that hypothesis' (quoted in Barbour 1998: 35). Thus, the eighteenth century saw the rise of materialistic atheism in the West (ibid.: 34–9).

The tendencies of determinism, reductionism and materialism provoked reactions from various quarters. One reaction was Romanticism, which considered that not only reason but also the irrational faculties of imagination and intuition were essential modes of understanding the world. The Romantics rejected determinism and celebrated human freedom and creativity; they rejected the view of nature as a machine and embraced the view of nature as a living companion; they rejected materialism and acknowledged a spiritual reality (Barbour 1998: 39–41). Another reaction was the revitalisation of personal religion in such forms as Pietism in Germany and Methodism in Britain. The achievements of Newton had led to the view of a mechanical nature. Newton himself, and many others, continued to believe in God, but it was a God very different from the medieval one.

Rather than being the source of revelation, miracles and providence, and the guarantor of human redemption and immortality, God was increasingly conceived as a being who had created the world in the beginning but did not afterwards intervene in the course of natural and human affairs. This Deist understanding, of which there were many variants, failed to satisfy the need, to which Christianity had traditionally catered, for a more personal relationship with a redeeming God. It was to this neglected need that Pietism, Methodism and related movements responded (ibid.: 41–2).

The eighteenth century also saw the emergence of two contrasting philosophical viewpoints on the relationship between religion and science that were to have a profound impact on subsequent debates. The Scottish philosopher David Hume (1711–76), holding that all knowledge is derived from sensory experience, argued that there were no cogent grounds for believing anything about either the existence or nature of God or any of the other metaphysical claims of religion. His arguments have had a profound and continuing influence on secular humanism. More particularly, Hume formulated some telling objections to natural theology. For example, he pointed out that even if one could, on the analogy of clocks and clockmakers, infer a maker of the world mechanism, there is nothing to guarantee that there would be only one such maker rather than a plurality of makers – a view that would not sit comfortably with monotheistic Christianity (Barbour 1998: 42–5). Kant (1724–1804), responding to Hume, agreed that the claims of knowledge must be restricted to what can be empirically observed. However, he argued that sense experience alone is not sufficient for knowledge but that the human mind supplies conceptual categories in the interpretation of sense data. In the realm of morality, he suggested that God is a necessary postulate; that is, for our assertions of moral law to make any sense they have to presuppose a lawgiver who is the source and guarantor of that law. Kant agreed with Hume that *theoretical reason* cannot prove the existence of God, but he maintained that *practical reason* requires us to presuppose this existence (ibid.: 45–7). Kant's manoeuvre here of assigning separate realms and functions to science (empirical knowledge) and religion (morality) is a common feature of many contemporary discussions of the relationship between religion and science.

The major event for our theme in the nineteenth century was the publication by Charles Darwin (1809–82) of his *On the Origin of Species by Means of Natural Selection* in 1859 and the subsequent debates about evolution. Darwin's theory proposed that biological species did not spring into being in their present forms through an act of divine creation but were the products of a long process of evolution governed by the principles of random variation and natural selection. Evolutionary ideas had existed before Darwin but only Darwin's work provided a cogent theory and adequate supporting data (Barbour 1998: 49–57).

The theory of evolution had a profound impact on perceptions of the natural world and the role of humans within it. The theory gave new importance to the concepts of change and development; it highlighted the interdependence of organic forms; it greatly extended the scope of scientific law; and, above all, it placed human beings within the animal kingdom rather than as a species altogether apart. The theory presented some particularly strong challenges to religion. First, it challenged scripture. If Darwin's theory was correct then many passages in the Bible, especially concerning creation, could not be taken literally. This was far from being a new problem and there was already a long tradition, fully sanctioned by the Catholic Church, of interpreting biblical passages non-literally. However, non-literal interpretation of the Bible was never endorsed lightly, and Darwin's theories made particularly heavy demands on this exegetical strategem. Actual responses to this problem ranged from outright rejection of evolution to various forms of accommodation between evolution and scripture to outright rejection of scripture (Barbour 1998: 57–8).

Second, evolutionary theory challenged the design argument for God's existence, which, in spite of the philosophical criticisms of Hume and others, still held considerable sway. William Paley, for example, in his book *Natural Theology* (1802) argued that the complex structure of the eye is co-ordinated to the one aim of vision and that such co-ordinated structure naturally leads us to infer the existence of an intelligent designer. However, evolutionary theory could now provide an account of how the complex structure of the eye came about that appealed only to natural causes: random variation, the struggle for survival and the survival of the fittest. Proponents of natural theology, if they accepted evolutionary theory, now had to detect God's intelligent design in the laws by which evolution proceeds or in a supposed providential guiding of the variations (Barbour 1998: 58–9).

Third, evolutionary theory challenged the status of humanity. Many people felt that seeing human beings as continuous with animals compromises human dignity. Particularly objectionable was seeing the human moral sense and other higher human faculties as having evolved by natural selection, for these were traditionally the marks of our affinity with the divine. Alfred Russel Wallace (1823–1913), who independently discovered the principle of natural selection, was among those who claimed that it could not account for the higher human faculties (Barbour 1998: 59–61).

The twentieth century saw scientific developments that were at least as significant as anything that had gone before. In physics the theories of relativity and quantum mechanics revolutionised ways of thinking about matter and energy as well as about such fundamental categories as space, time and causality. No longer, as in classical Newtonian physics, can we describe the world 'realistically', as though it is unaffected by our observations. For experiments have shown that if we observe certain subatomic phenomena such as photons in one way, they behave as particles, while if we observe them in another way, they behave as waves. Our method of observation crucially influences what we observe. Nor, as in classical physics, can we describe the world deterministically. For there are events, such as the disintegration of a particular atom in a radioactive substance, that we can only predict with probability, never with certainty. Nature, it seems, is in some respects inherently indeterministic. Nor again, as in classical physics, can we explain all physical processes reductively; that is, we cannot explain all higher-level processes and entities in terms of increasingly more fundamental principles and particles. For at the subatomic level there are particles, such as quarks, which seemingly cannot exist except as parts of a larger whole. At least some phenomena appear irreducibly holistic. These challenges to realism, determinism and reductionism have opened new possibilities for engagement between religion and science, for the contrary principles of participation, indeterminacy and holism have seemed to some to be more compatible with traditional theological notions (Barbour 1998: 165–94; Brooke 1991: 326–36).

In astronomy, there have been equally significant discoveries. Most conspicuous is Big Bang cosmology – a plausible reconstruction of cosmic history based on a series of theoretical and observational developments in physics and astronomy over the course of the twentieth century. According to this widely accepted theory, the origin of the universe can be calculated back to a hypothetical 'Big Bang' approximately 15 billion years ago. The inability of scientists even in principle to offer any picture of the situation before the initial moment of the Big Bang has encouraged some to appeal to an act of divine creation at this point. Further, calculations about the rate of expansion of the universe following the Big Bang have shown that if this rate had been smaller by one part in a hundred thousand million million or greater by one part in a million, it would either have re-collapsed before reaching its present size or expanded too rapidly for stars and planets to form. This has led some to suggest that the universe has been designed as though specially to enable the development of beings such as we are – the so-called 'Anthropic Principle' (Barbour 1998: 195–220). Writes Stephen Hawkins: 'The odds against a universe like ours emerging out of something like the Big Bang are enormous. I think there are clearly religious implications' (quoted in ibid.: 205).

In biology, the outstanding events of the twentieth century must include the discovery of DNA and the subsequent gradual deciphering of the genetic code. This has resulted in a sharpening of the evolutionary debates of the nineteenth century. All that exists in nature, no matter how marvellous, is even more fully explicable in materialistic terms than the early proponents of evolutionary theory conceived. Theologians have again responded by suggesting that God either controls events that seem to be random or designed the system of law and chance by which evolution proceeds. The pattern of these debates is broadly the same as in the nineteenth century, though conducted at a greater level of sophistication. Additionally, some theologians have suggested that God takes a continuous active role in evolution – not through controlling events with coercive power but through influencing them with persuasive love (Barbour 1998: 221–49).

Issues arising

The preceding sketch, fragmentary as it is, demonstrates that developments in modern science, in terms of both methodology and particular theories, brought into prominence ideas that traditional religions had to engage with in one way or another. All of this provides the deeper context for appreciating the influence of interactions between religion and science on Jung's psychology and theory of synchronicity. Immediately, however, we need to qualify our account in some important ways.

First, we need to note that the above account is, given the magnitude of the topic, necessarily very selective. Other writers than the ones upon whom I have drawn might have highlighted different events in the history of science or have handled the same ones differently. Moreover, simply by focusing more closely on any one of the areas covered, we will find that the issues become increasingly ambiguous. For example, we have noted that Galileo championed the Copernican cosmological view according to which the earth revolves around the sun. In 1616, the Catholic Church issued an injunction forbidding him to hold or promote this view and when, in 1632, Galileo published a work that seemed to disregard the injunction, he was tried, found guilty, forced to recant, and condemned to house arrest for the remainder of his life. This episode continues to be used as a paradigmatic example of the inveterate hostility between religion and science, with religious authority impeding the development of scientific truth (for example, Wilber 1998: vii–viii). However, closer historical examinations of the case have revealed that the conflict was at least as much between different scientific models and methods or between different interest groups within religion as it was between religion and science. Many of the clerics involved in Galileo's trial were sympathetic to scientific investigations and even to much of Galileo's own work. Meanwhile, Galileo was, and was acknowledged to be, a devout Catholic and argued that his cosmological views actually provided stronger support for Catholic doctrine than the traditional Ptolemaic views. Moreover, though Galileo may have been correct about the earth revolving around the sun, his telescopic observations did not decisively prove this and the main supporting argument he adduced, that the earth's motion can be inferred from the tides, is now known to be incorrect. Again, historians have shown that in important respects the trial of Galileo was not about religion and science at all. The instigator of the trial was Pope Urban VIII, formerly a friend and sympathetic patron of Galileo. At a moment of acute political vulnerability Urban was led to believe that he had been personally insulted by Galileo's writing and wished to make an example of him (Brooke 1991: 77–80, 97–108; Brooke and Cantor 1998: 106–38).

Second, the above account, for all its ambitious scope and skipping over particulars, focuses narrowly on the Christian religion and on understandings of science that originated and developed in modern Europe. This neglects all the other religious traditions of the world, as well as such alternative and arguably no less sophisticated approaches to scientific understanding as existed in ancient China (Needham 1962), ancient Greece (Tambiah 1990: 8–11), or medieval Islam (Brooke 1991: 43).

Third, even within the temporal, geographical and cultural limits I have set myself, the way people have understood the terms 'religion' and 'science' has shifted continuously. Regarding religion, in medieval Europe this concept tended to be used exclusively to signify Christianity, with emphasis on the notions of faith and an organised community or church (Tambiah 1990: 4). During the Reformation there emerged a greater emphasis on personal, inner, transcendental experience rather than on community organisation (ibid.). Later, from the Enlightenment through to the modern period, it was neither the organisational nor the experiential dimensions that were emphasised but the philosophical and doctrinal aspects. Religion came to be conceived primarily as a system of ideas and beliefs (ibid.: 4–5). This coincided with an increased awareness of other systems of ideas and beliefs, in India and China for instance, which could therefore also be designated religions. Hence arose the comparative study of religions. The objectivist emphasis further developed through an increasing application of historical methods in the study of religious texts and institutions (ibid.: 5–6).

Regarding science, it is important to remember that as a discipline this was not clearly differentiated until the nineteenth century. Galileo, for instance, referred to himself as a mathematician or philosopher, and John Brooke notes the following about Isaac Newton:

> His most famous book, in which planetary orbits were explained by his gravitational theory, was entitled *Mathematical principles of natural philosophy* (1687). It was not entitled *Mathematical principles of natural science*. When seventeenth-century students of nature called themselves philosophers, they were identifying themselves with intellectual traditions in which broader issues than immediate scientific technicalities were discussed. Newton himself remarked that it was part of the business of natural philosophy to discuss such questions as the attributes of God and His relationship to the physical world.
>
> (Brooke 1991: 7)

Further, even after William Whewell coined the term 'scientist' in the 1830s, there were continual open and covert struggles over who should be entitled to apply the term to themselves – struggles bound up with the whole issue of the professionalisation of science (ibid.: 49–50). Throughout the twentieth century, psychologists, sociologists, anthropologists and others frequently had to defend the scientific status of their disciplines. Ambiguities of language further complicated the situation. When Max Müller introduced the term *Religionswissenschaft* for the academic study of religions, he himself translated it into English as 'science of religion'. However, *Wissenschaft* means not just science but also learning and knowledge more broadly and so can refer to the humanities as well as the sciences. Therefore, other scholars have preferred to translate *Religionswissenschaft* as 'comparative religion' or 'history of religion' (Hinnells 1997: 416–17). Even at the end of the twentieth century the boundaries of science were being vigorously contested, with debates as to whether the term can legitimately be applied to, for instance, psychoanalysis, parapsychology, or the knowledge systems of the indigenous peoples of Africa, New Zealand or the Americas.

A fourth difficulty is that, even allowing for problems of definition and demarcation, the interactions between religion and science have been immensely complex. In the late nineteenth and the early twentieth century, when the depth psychological theories were being developed, much of the most vocal discussion of the relationship between religion and science presented them as irreconcilable and engaged in an epic battle for intellectual and spiritual hegemony. For example, in 1875, the year of Jung's birth, J. W. Draper published a book entitled *History of the Conflict between Religion and Science*. Twenty years later, in 1895, A. D. White's volume *A History of the Warfare of Science with Theology in Christendom* appeared.[1] Recent contextual history has ensured that such simplified accounts, though still frequently promulgated, are no longer sustainable. Accordingly, responsible present-day discussions have had to find ways to acknowledge a wider range of actual and possible positions. In what follows, I shall make use of the four main categories of interaction between religion and science articulated by Ian Barbour, a professor of both physics and religion (Barbour 1998: 77–105). First is *conflict*, in which religion and science provide competing and mutually exclusive explanations for the same phenomena (for example, fundamentalist creationist accounts versus Neo-Darwinian evolutionary accounts of the origin of human life). Second is *independence*, in which religion and science either account for different phenomena (for example, material and spiritual) or provide different kinds of account for the same phenomena (for example, science explains the mechanisms, religion explains the purpose). Because there is no direct competition between them, these accounts are, at least in principle, compatible. Third is *dialogue*, in which religion and science, for all their differences, have sufficient areas of overlapping interest to allow for a fruitful exchange of insights and ideas (for example, Fritjof Capra [1976] highlights a shared concern with interconnectedness in some Eastern religions and some theories of modern physics). Fourth and last is *integration*, in which religion and science are capable, at least at certain points, of unification into a single discourse (for example, Teilhard de Chardin [1959] weaves together biological and spiritual evolution).

Bearing in mind this historical background and its complexities, we can now return to consider Jung's views on the relationship between religion and science and the significance of these for his theory of synchronicity.

Jung on the relationship between religion and science

Jung was preoccupied with the relationship between religion and science throughout his life. As we shall need to discuss in more detail in the next chapter, he used the terms 'religion' and 'science' in different ways on different occasions. Briefly, when he speaks of religion, he generally means either a distinctive kind of attitude or experience consisting of 'a careful consideration and observation of certain dynamic factors that are conceived as "powers"' (1938/1940: par. 8), or the organisation into a creed of the beliefs and practices relating to this attitude or experience. When he speaks of science, he generally means either a particular experimental approach to the acquisition of knowledge, based on reductive and materialistic premises, or a more phenomenological approach to the acquisition of knowledge, based on observation but not presupposing materialism. In the case of both religion and science, it is usually clear from the context in which sense Jung is using the term.

In one of the chapters he himself wrote for *Memories, Dreams, Reflections* Jung recalls his youthful interest in both science and religion:

> The older I grew, the more frequently I was asked by my parents and others what I wanted to be. I had no clear notions on that score. My interests drew me in different directions. On the one hand I was powerfully attracted by science, with its truths based on facts; on the other hand I was fascinated by everything to do with comparative religion . . . What appealed to me in science were the concrete facts and their historical background, and in comparative religion the spiritual problems, into which philosophy also entered. In science I missed the factor of meaning; and in religion, that of empiricism.
>
> (Jung 1963: 79)

Jung's reference here to his 'inner dichotomy' – between one part of him oriented towards mystery and inner experience and another part oriented towards rationalism and social adaptation – testifies to the personal dimension of his struggle with religion and science. The problem of their relationship was made even more acute for Jung when he witnessed his father, a Protestant pastor, undergoing a crisis of faith largely precipitated by the ascendancy of materialistic science. Writes Jung:

> My father was obviously under the impression that psychiatrists had discovered something in the brain which proved that in the place where mind should have been there was only matter, and nothing 'spiritual'. This was borne out by his admonitions that if I studied medicine I should in Heaven's name not become a materialist.
>
> (Jung 1963: 98)

Even more forcefully, though, Jung's father advised him that he 'should keep away from theology. "Be anything you like except a theologian", he said emphatically' (ibid.: 81).

This is not to suggest that personal factors alone were responsible for Jung's interest in the relationship between religion and science. A fuller contextualisation would have to consider a whole range of other contributory influences

– intellectual, professional, social, geographical, economic and political. However, the personal factors most vividly convey the urgency of the problem presented to Jung by the dominant narrative of conflict between religion and science. As someone who could count numerous clergymen among his relatives and ancestors, and who himself had a strong disposition towards personal religious experience, Jung would likely have experienced materialistic science not just as a threat to religion but as a threat to his own identity.

A survey of Jung's work at any stage in his long career shows that this early problem never left him. It is a dominant theme in the five lectures he delivered as a medical student to his fraternity the Zofingia Society (1896–9). In these lectures he acknowledges the usefulness of science but vigorously protests against the materialism and inertia of current science. He favours a more vitalistic understanding, asserts the inseparability of morality from science, and even argues that religion is the natural endpoint of science. The same problem is implicit in his decision to base his doctoral dissertation on a case study of a spirit medium (1902). Much of the nineteenth-century interest in spiritualism had been motivated by the aim of providing 'empirical' evidence to support the traditional claims of religion about the existence and survival of the soul, and Jung was in part heir to these concerns (see Charet 1993). Again, the relationship between religion and science was one of the main issues that led to his parting of the ways with Freud and psychoanalysis. Freud was a staunch atheist and relentlessly reduced all religious phenomena to natural causes (see Freud 1927). Jung, by contrast, wished to find an honourable place for religious phenomena within psychoanalytic thinking (see Jung 1911–12/1952; McGuire 1974). In developing and articulating his mature psychological theory, Jung always insisted that he was working as a scientist and empiricist, but he increasingly applied his 'empiricism' to the investigation of religious phenomena (1928–54). His dual interest is conspicuous in the three 'Terry Lectures' on 'Psychology and Religion' that he delivered at Yale University in 1937. These were part of a series of 'Lectures on Religion in the light of Science and Philosophy' (1938/1940: 3). They focused on a set of dreams of a scientist, showing, Jung argued, the spontaneous operation of a religious function in the psyche of someone sceptical about religion. The scientist we now know to have been Wolfgang Pauli, with whom Jung was later to collaborate in developing his ideas on synchronicity (Jung and Pauli 1955; Meier 2001). Pauli's dreams and visions also provided material for one of Jung's major works on alchemy (Jung 1944). This subject, which occupied Jung in the last thirty years of his life (see 1929–54, 1944, 1946, 1955–6), again joins religion and science: for alchemy, Jung shows, was not just a precursor of modern chemistry concerned with material transformations but also, in many cases, an esoteric religious discipline concerned with the spiritual transformation of the personality. Many of Jung's other late works – *Aion* (1951a), 'Answer to Job' (1952a), 'On the Nature of the Psyche' (1947/1954), and not least 'Synchronicity: An Acausal Connecting Principle' (1952b) – also evince this preoccupation with religion, science, and the relationship between them.

Jung's guiding motive throughout all of this appears to have been to promote religion in the face of science. In a letter to Pastor Josef Shattauer (20 February 1933), Jung confided that

> it is exceedingly difficult nowadays to inculcate into people any conception of genuine religiosity. I have found that religious terminology only scares them off still more, for which reason I always have to tread the path of science and experience, quite irrespective of any tradition, in order to get my patients to acknowledge spiritual truths.
>
> (Jung 1973: 118)

Apparently, this was his motive not just with patients but also with professional colleagues. Writing to Father Victor White (5 October 1945), Jung claimed that his 1911–12 book translated as *The Psychology of the Unconscious* 'was written by a psychiatrist for the purpose of submitting the necessary material to his psychiatric colleagues, material which would demonstrate to them the importance of religious symbolism'. In the same letter he explained: 'My personal view . . . is that man's vital energy or libido is the divine pneuma all right and it was this conviction which it was my secret purpose to bring into the vicinity of my colleagues' understanding' (1973: 383–4; see also ibid.: 349–50).

At early stages in his career, Jung toyed with the conflict model of the relationship between religion and science. In doing so, his hope was that religion might win out. For example, in the last of his Zofingia lectures he longs for the return of a mystical approach to religion, even if this entails 'the possibility of social and scientific indifference and call[ing] into question the further progress of civilization' (1896–9: par. 290). However, Jung quickly recognised that on most points of direct confrontation and conflict between religion and science, science was likely to prove the victor. 'The imposing arguments of science', he later acknowledges, 'represent the highest degree of intellectual certainty yet achieved by the mind of man. So at least it seems to the man of today' (1957: par. 543). Consequently, 'the guardians and custodians of symbolical truth, namely the religions, have been robbed of their efficacy by science' (1911–12/ 1952: par. 336).

Jung therefore increasingly appealed to the independence position. 'My subjective attitude', he wrote to Paul Maag (12 June 1933), 'is that I hold every religious position in high esteem but draw an inexorable dividing line between the content of belief and the requirements of science' (1973: 125). At a talk he gave in London in 1939, a questioner put it to him that 'There is obviously, and always has been, a conflict between religion and science . . . How do you bring about a reconciliation, which obviously is the sort of thing that is needed?' Jung replied: 'There is no conflict between religion and science. That is a very old-fashioned idea. Science has to consider what there is. There is religion . . . Science cannot establish [or, Jung implies, refute] a religious truth . . . Our science is phenomenology' (1939: pars. 691–2). Again, no less explicitly, he wrote to Pastor Max

Frischknecht (8 February 1946): 'Science is human knowledge, theology divine knowledge. Therefore the two are incommensurable' (1973: 411; see also ibid.: 119, 124, 346, 350, 384).

From the safety of this basic position of independence, Jung explored bolder possibilities for dialogue and integration between religion and science. 'A rapprochement between empirical science and religious experience', he writes in *Mysterium Coniunctionis*, 'would in my opinion be fruitful for both. Harm can result only if one side or the other remains unconscious of the limitations of its claim to validity' (1955–6: par. 457). He notes that 'inside the religious movement there [have been] any number of attempts to combine science with religious belief and practice, as for instance Christian Science, theosophy, and anthroposophy' (1936b: par. 863). However, he held these particular attempts in low esteem, and this may account for his occasional repudiation of any integrative intent on his own part. For example, to one of the same correspondents to whom he had declared his belief in the independence of religion and science, he wrote: 'I am wholly incorrigible and utterly incapable of coming up with a mixture of theology and science' (1973: 125). Nevertheless, as he admitted in a letter to H. Irminger (22 September 1944), he did aim to promote dialogue:

> I start from a positive Christianity which is as much Catholic as Protestant, and I endeavour in a scientifically responsible manner to point out those empirically graspable facts which make the justification of Christian and, in particular, Catholic dogma at least plausible, and besides that are best suited to give the scientific mind an access to understanding.
>
> (Jung 1973: 349–50)

Certain statements even point directly towards integration – at least if we bear in mind Jung's insistence that his psychology was scientific: 'I would surely be among the first to welcome an explicit attempt to integrate the findings of psychology into the ecclesiastical doctrine', he wrote to Father White (5 October 1945) (ibid.: 385).

Jung was enabled to explore these integrative possibilities by the phenom-enological emphasis within his psychological theory.[3] Basing himself on his understanding of Kant's epistemology, Jung argued that things in themselves, whether material things or spiritual things, cannot be known other than as mediated to consciousness in the form of psychic images. Our primary reality, he repeatedly stated, the only reality of which we can be immediately aware, is psychic reality (e.g., 1939/1954: par. 760; 1963: 323–4). This notion provides a middle ground in which images stemming from the realm of matter (the traditional province of science) and images stemming from the realm of spirit (the traditional province of religion) can be treated even-handedly within the same field. The primary reality of these images, whatever their putative origin, is psychic.[4] The mere fact that they occur as psychic images guarantees them reality and importance and some basic affinity with one another. Particularly important for Jung is the implication that religious images no less than any other kind deserve to be taken seriously (1938/ 1940: pars. 4–5).

Combined with the specific structures and processes postulated in his psychological theory, this perspective of the primacy of psychic reality provided Jung with a vantage point from which he could, reflexively, comment back on religion and science. For instance, he argues that 'it is out of himself and out of his peculiar constitution that man has produced his sciences. They are *symptoms* of his psyche' (1930–1: par. 752). He remarks on the presence within both religion and science of guiding images and myths (1919: par. 278; 1927/1931: par. 327; 1963: 313). Above all, he enjoyed pointing to the hidden presence of religious attitudes within science: he quotes with approval William James's statement that 'our scientific temper is devout' (1921: par. 528) and makes similar references of his own to the deification of matter (1938/1954: par. 195), the asceticism of the scientist (1939/1954: par. 786), and the way faith in science can act as a defence or compensation for superstitious impulses (1916: par. 495; 1938/1940: par. 81). We will discuss Jung's critique of religion and science more fully in Chapter 5. Here we can just note how the implication that both religious phenomena (including experiences, doctrines and rituals) and scientific phenomena (including observations, theories and practices) present themselves as psychic images enabled Jung to discuss any of these phenomena as relative, conditioned, susceptible to pragmatic and psychological evaluation, and both open to and often requiring change – all of this without making any judgement about the spiritual or material reality or truth that may underlie the phenomenal images.

The influence of religion and science on the theory of synchronicity

However, Jung also made a bolder attempt at rapprochement between religion and science in the form of his theory of synchronicity. This theory does not pivot so much on the notion of psychic reality. Indeed, as we shall see later, it arguably represents an attempt by Jung to extricate his psychology from the charge of reductionism prompted by his emphasis on psychic reality.

As we saw in detail in the previous chapter, the theory of synchronicity drew on both religious and scientific influences. The scientific influences are the more obvious, as Jung pushed these to the fore when presenting his theory. In the first place, there was Jung's usual 'empiricism'; that is to say, his accumulation of observational data. He refers to 'the innumerable cases of meaningful coincidence that have been observed not only by me but by many others, and recorded in large collections' (1951b: par. 983). In the second place, there was Jung's familiarity with recent discoveries in physics, including the inspiration he received from Einstein and his collaboration with Pauli. Through discussions with Pauli, Jung deepened his understanding of such features of quantum physics as complementarity and acausality, both of which were to figure in his presentation of synchronicity. In the third place, there was Jung's interest in the newly developed field of experimental parapsychology, particularly in the work of Rhine. For Rhine's experiments at Duke University seemed to provide robust statistical evidence for the existence of extra-sensory perception and psychokinesis: connections between events that do not depend on any known form of psychophysical causation and even seem to transgress the barriers of time and space.

The religious influences on Jung's theory of synchronicity are less explicit – interestingly so. In his efforts to highlight the scientific evidence for his theory, Jung introduces the religious influences on it covertly in scientific, philosophical, or historical disguise. For example, one major influence is the Chinese divinatory system of the *I Ching*. This is deeply embedded in Chinese religious thought, but Jung emphasises its 'experimental foundation', its 'experiment-with-the-whole' (1952b: par. 865); in an earlier discussion he had referred to the *I Ching* as the 'standard text book' of Chinese science (1930: par. 80). Again, instead of referring to the traditional religious concern with the post-mortem existence of the soul, Jung refers to out-of-body and near-death experiences as studied empirically by psychical researchers (1952b: pars. 949–55). Where he might have discussed religious experiences of mystical unity, he refers to the philosophical Taoism of Lao-tzu and Chuang-tzu (ibid.: pars. 916–24). Where he might have discussed religious notions of Providence, he refers to philosophical notions of pre-established harmony in Leibniz (ibid.: pars. 937–9). In his major essay on synchronicity, discussion of the religious concept of continuous creation, very suggestive for Jung's theme, is relegated to a footnote on the penultimate page (ibid.: par. 967 n. 17). Jung mentions Christian religious thought as having influenced him: not in terms of its doctrines and theology but primarily through providing historical instances of synchronicity encountered in the course of his research into symbols (1951a; 1963: 210). Other demonstrable religious influences go unmentioned in the writings on synchronicity: for example, Jung's personal religious experiences, which included spiritualistic encounters with otherworldly beings and mystical visions of unity (1963: 174–8, 270–7).

This foregrounding of the scientific evidence for his theory and downplaying its nevertheless easily detectable religious influences illustrate Jung's awareness that the route to intellectual respectability lay through science. Nevertheless, it is interesting that, in covertly introducing the religious influences, Jung sometimes implicitly demonstrated the extent to which he felt the religious and scientific categories could interact – and no longer simply on the basis of their shared grounding in psyche. For example, he implies that the concept of science should be broad enough to accommodate the kinds of 'experimental' observation involved in divination, and that the concerns of religion, such as the survival of the soul, should not be kept insulated from the investigative procedures and insights of the sciences. Further, if we recall Jung's complaint that 'In science I missed the factor of meaning; and in religion, that of empiricism' (1963: 79), we can sense the measure of integration he has achieved for himself with his theory of synchronicity. For in this theory Jung has championed precisely the factor of meaning; and he has done so on as solid a base of empiricism as he could manage.

If we look not only at sources and influences but also at the contexts in which Jung presented and discussed his work on synchronicity, we find the same double engagement with religion and science. Jung's three most significant writings on synchronicity are his 'Foreword to the "I Ching"' (1950a), his lecture 'On Synchronicity' (1951b), and his monograph 'Synchronicity: An Acausal Connecting Principle' (1952b). The first of these accompanies the translation of a Chinese religious-philosophical text. The second was presented at one of the Eranos conferences, initiated in 1933 by Olga Froebe-Kapteyn, the original purpose of which was 'the encounter between Eastern and Western religions, philosophy, and psychology' and which later 'developed far beyond [their] original boundaries and became a meeting place where ideas were exchanged on science, the humanities, mythology, and psychology' (Kirsch 2000: 6). The third was published in a volume entitled *The Interpretation of Nature and the Psyche* alongside an essay on Johannes Kepler by the Nobel Prize-winning physicist Pauli.

Again, if we look at those of Jung's published letters in which the notion of synchronicity is discussed, we find that the recipients include a Dominican priest (1973: 479–81, 516–17), a professor of philosophy and comparative religion (ibid.: 522–3), an anonymous theologian (1976: 21–3), and a Protestant pastor (ibid.: 257–64), as well as three physicists (1973: 176–8, 529–30; Meier 2001), a mineralogist (1976: 351–2), and an electrical engineer (ibid.: 425–6). Other recipients include parapsychologists, analytical psychologists, various non-Jungian psychologists and psychotherapists, writers, philosophers and astrologers. The topics synchronicity is mentioned in relation to are variously parapsychological, religious, scientific, therapeutic, philosophical and esoteric.

The same wide-ranging application – sometimes religious, sometimes scientific, sometimes in areas between the religious and scientific or otherwise connected to both – is evident from the occasional discussions of, or references to, synchronicity that occur in other published works of Jung. These include works on alchemy (1944: par. 415; 1946: par. 468 n. 8; 1955–6: par. 662), the history of Christian symbols (1951a: 140, 233, 257, 287; 1942/1948: par. 174), resurrection (1954d: par. 1573), eastern thought (1949: par. 1485), the myth of flying saucers (1958b: pars. 593, 660, 682, 780), the theory and dynamics of analytical psychology (1935: par. 143; 1947/1954: pars. 394, 418, 440–1; 1934/1950: par. 608), parapsychology (1950b: par. 761; 1958a: par. 1175) and conscience (1958c: pars. 849–50).

Intellectual difficulties revisited

In Chapter 2 we noted a large number of apparent confusions and inconsistencies in Jung's presentation of his theory of synchronicity. It was suggested that these might partly be explained as the inevitable consequence of trying to grasp rationally a phenomenon that is intrinsically irrational. However, our examination in Chapter 3 of the sources of and influences on Jung's theory suggests that a further reason for his difficulties might be that he was drawing on such a wide range of contexts, with different and not always obviously compatible perspectives and insights emerging from each. So far in the present chapter, we have outlined the background to the tension between traditional religion and modern science into which Jung was born and have traced his lifelong attempt to find a satisfactory resolution of this tension. In this light, we have noted that some of the contexts informing his work on synchronicity can be most readily characterised as scientific, while others are more religious in character. Moreover, many of the religious contexts are presented in such a way as to enhance their scientific credibility, while many of the scientific contexts are pushing at the boundaries of mainstream science and touching on more mystical territory (empirical observations of anomalous phenomena, parapsychological experiments, mysterious quantum physical properties). Indeed, many of Jung's sources and influences already consist of bodies of knowledge that stem either from a time before there was a notable split between religion and science (for example, alchemy and pre-modern philosophy) or from cultures considered to be distant from the tension between religion and science (for example, Chinese philosophical Taoism and divinatory practices). Other fields that influenced Jung specifically arose as attempts either to provide empirical evidence for some of the central claims of religion (notably, spiritualism) or to investigate that purported evidence (notably, psychical research). In sum, it seems reasonable to view Jung's theory of synchronicity as an attempt, his most ambitious, to resolve the tension between traditional religion and modern science. We can now revisit the intellectual difficulties noted in Chapter 2 to consider to what extent this conclusion helps us to clarify them.

Jung's characterisation of synchronicity

We have seen that Jung writes about synchronicity sometimes as a descriptive and sometimes as an explanatory concept; again, sometimes as an empirical concept and sometimes as a metaphysical one. Writing about it as a descriptive and empirical concept keeps it within the bounds of scientific consideration, while writing about it as an explanatory and metaphysical concept allows some of the religious implications of the theory to be articulated. Jung's desire to achieve scientific respectability for his religious concerns and, conversely, religious depth of meaning for his scientific work would account for why he characterises synchronicity in these seemingly incompatible ways.

More generally, Jung writes of synchronicity, albeit in passing, sometimes as a quantity (1952b: par. 947) and sometimes as a relationship based on quality (1950a: par. 973). The former suggests something amenable to experimental investigation, belonging to the domain of science. The latter, by contrast, suggests something more concerned with subjective evaluation and the domain of religion and the humanities. The double characterisation reflects Jung's statement in the Foreword to his 1952 essay on synchronicity that his interest in the problem 'has a human as well as a scientific foundation' (1952b: par. 816).

We noted that, at different times, Jung writes of synchronicity as an irregular and unrepeatable phenomenon or as a regular and repeatable one. Irregular occurrence would have been suggested by his personal experiences and clinical observations, regular occurrence by some of the instances of acausality in physics, as well as by reflections that synchronicity might be able to help solve the traditional philosophical problem of the relationship between mind and body (1952b: par. 948). Again, Jung's emphasis depends on which facet of synchronicity he is trying to promote. His religious influences and concerns tend to pull the theory towards a conception of synchronicity as irregular and unrepeatable, while his scientific influences and concerns tend to pull it towards a conception as regular and repeatable. That both tendencies are present suggests that Jung is trying to hold together the religious and the scientific implications of the theory.

Jung's attempt to fuse the religious and scientific influences on and implications of his theory is evident in his appeal to divination and mediumistic trance phenomena as suggesting the partly repeatable nature of synchronicity. Divination and mediumistic trances would normally be thought of as religious practices, yet repeatability is usually presented as one of the defining features of scientific methodology. Perhaps with this in mind, Jung feels he can characterise the *I Ching* as the standard text book of Chinese science. He would also doubtless be aware that many spiritualists consider their repeatable contacts with departed souls and allegedly verifiable communications from them as constituting a scientific approach to religion. That divinatory and mediumistic synchronicities are only partly repeatable places them midway between the spontaneously occurring events that are mostly associated for Jung with the domain of religion and the regular events associated with the domain of science. The implication is that synchronicity can straddle both domains.

Jung's dual commitment to the scientific and religious outlooks can also help account for his vacillation between, on the one hand, presenting synchronicities as involving component events that in themselves are naturalistic and causally explicable and, on the other hand, including synchronicities whose component events are radically anomalous and causally inexplicable. Focusing on naturalistic events, and emphasising the bare fact that coincidences happen, optimises the scientific image of his theory. Referring also to radically anomalous or paranormal events assists his further aim of lending credibility to religious phenomena such as miracles, revelations, acts of providence and experiences of mystical union.

Jung usually specifies that synchronicities occur between a psychic event and a physical event. However, we have seen that he also includes examples of synchronicities either between two psychic events or between two physical events, and some of his definitions explicitly allow for these possibilities (1950a: par. 972; 1952b: par. 855). Most of Jung's sources and influences provide examples of synchronicities between a psychic and physical event. However, his personal experiences, clinical observations, and reading in psychical research additionally provided examples of synchronicities between two psychic events, such as shared thoughts or dreams. Meanwhile, Jung's awareness of developments in physics provided examples of synchronicities between two physical events, and indeed Pauli urgently drew Jung's attention to this as a correction, or expansion, of his earlier formulations (Meier 2001: 60, 64). That Jung nevertheless gives salience to synchronicities involving a combination of psychic and physical events may reflect his aim of connecting and integrating the domain of the psychic (including subjectivity, value and the spiritual/religious) with the domain of the physical (including objectivity, facts and the scientific). Other kinds of synchronicities may occur and equally express a principle of acausal connection through meaning, but they serve Jung's integrative purpose less well and so receive less prominent treatment.

Time

Jung's apparent vacillations on the role of time in synchronicity can also be understood in the light of his attempt to resolve the tension between his commitments to religion and science. His most conspicuous inconsistency is between defining synchronicity as involving simultaneous events then later admitting that the events need not be simultaneous. The simultaneity in synchronicities is suggested by many of Jung's personal experiences and clinical observations, as well as by his philosophical reading and engagement in the divinatory practices of astrology and the *I Ching*. Related to this and stemming particularly from his work on astrology and the *I Ching* are his reflections on 'qualitative time': the idea that 'whatever happens in a given moment of time inevitably has the quality peculiar to that moment' (1950a: par. 970). Jung's contrary realisation that, after all, simultaneity is not a necessary criterion for synchronicity probably stems from personal experiences of 'precognitive' events, together with the evidence for such occurrences provided by Rhine's parapsychological experiments and the suggestion of them provided by Einstein's theory of relativity and the space–time continuum in physics. From these sources Jung derived his definition of synchronicity as 'a psychically conditioned relativity of space and time' (1952b: par. 840).

We saw that Jung was not just aware of the existence of synchronistic events that do not involve obvious simultaneity but went to great lengths to try to preserve the notion of simultaneity even where in the obvious sense it clearly was not present, as in experiences of precognition (1952b: pars. 855, 858; 1955: 144–5). As we have noted, this attempt landed his theory in even greater difficulties. Not surprisingly, several commentators have therefore wondered why Jung did not simply abandon the idea of simultaneity as a criterion of synchronicity (e.g., Pauli in Meier 2001: 38–9; Koestler 1972: 95; Aziz 1990: 71, 149). The answer may be that Jung was attracted to the notion of simultaneity because it could be used to support both the scientific and the religious dimensions of his theory. The scientific dimension of the theory is supported because simultaneity enables acausal events to be immediately observed (see Pauli in Meier 2001: 39) and thus more convincingly presented as scientific or 'empirical' data. Meanwhile, the religious dimension of the theory is supported because the transcendental unity of the unconscious, which, according to Jung, is implied by synchronistic events (1958b: par. 780), can be characterised in terms of simultaneity (see Pauli in Meier 2001: 39). Jung writes of 'the "timeless" quality of the unconscious, where conscious succession becomes simultaneity, a phenomenon I have called "synchronicity"' (1946: par. 468 n. 8). In his 1952 essay on synchronicity, he draws attention to the theological proposition that '[w]hat happens successively in time is simultaneous in the mind of God' (1952b: par. 967 n. 17).

A further uncertainty we noted relating to the role of time in synchronicity is whether the states or events involved are momentary or longer lasting. Probably with his mind on personal experiences and clinical observations, Jung generally suggests that they are momentary. However, we saw that, based on his awareness of Taoism, quantum physics, and some exceptional mediumistic personalities, he also acknowledges that they can be longer lasting and even, in the case of acausal phenomena in physics permanent – a possibility also suggested by philosophical considerations relating to the mind–body problem. This uncertainty about the duration of synchronicity and its component events may again reflect the difficulty of specifying the relationship between the time-bound phenomenal world in which synchronicities manifest (the domain of science) and the timeless noumenal world of which Jung considers them to be an indication (the domain of religion).

Acausality

The main difficulties that emerged from the discussion of acausality in Chapter 2 concerned Jung's narrow understanding of causality, his selective appeal to those theories in physics that postulated acausality while ignoring others (including Einstein's) that questioned it, and his dubious inferences from the supposed existence of acausality in subatomic physics to its existence at the level of everyday experience. Here it appears to be less a case of Jung's holding diverse views than of his being insufficiently cautious and critical about the views he does hold, in both philosophy and physics. On the one hand, these weaknesses in his presentation are understandable, as he was neither a professional philosopher nor a professional physicist. Furthermore, he closely discussed his use of physics with Pauli and eventually obtained Pauli's 'wholehearted approval' (Meier 2001: 71) for the chapter in which most of his arguments from physics were presented; so he had good reason to think that he was being cautious enough. On the other hand, a study of the correspondence between Jung and Pauli reveals that on many points Pauli had to temper Jung's enthusiastic co-opting of physics by making clear that its relationship to psychology and synchronicity was more complex and ambivalent than Jung supposed. For example, Pauli twice points out the lack of precision in Jung's use of concepts from physics: 'When you use physical terms in order to explain psychological terms or findings', he writes, 'I often have the impression that with you they are dreamlike images of the imagination; this impression is usually accompanied by the feeling that the sentences you write here stop at the very point where they should begin' (Meier 2001: 57). This 'dreamlike nature', he comments in another letter, 'brings out analogies and ignores differences' (ibid.: 66). Jung's aim of resolving tension between religion and science can again be suggested here as the motivation for both his highly selective engagement with physics and his tendency to 'soften' physics concepts by treating them as though they were psychological images.

More generally, the concept of acausality, for all Jung's attempts to support it scientifically, relates most obviously to the sphere of religion, where meaningful events that lack a mundane cause are a common part of theological discourses. In proposing acausality, with these religious associations, as the necessary complement of causality, which is the fundamental principle of science, Jung again seems to be attempting to integrate religion and science into a single overall world-view.

Meaning

In Chapter 2 we saw that Jung speaks ambiguously about the meaning in synchronicities, using the word 'meaning' to refer sometimes to the significance of a coincidence for its experiencer, at other times to the content that coinciding events have in common. The first use stems most obviously from Jung's personal experiences, clinical observations, and experiments in divination, the second use from his reflections on recent findings in parapsychology and physics. We saw that this ambiguity can be largely resolved through considering the archetypal foundation of synchronicities, even though Jung was not totally certain that they always have such a foundation. Here we can further suggest a reason for the emergence of this ambiguity. When drawing on data from parapsychology and physics, Jung's focus was on proving the existence of acausal combinations of events according to the standards of rigorous experimental science. For this purpose, it was expedient to restrict the understanding of 'meaning' to something observable and quantifiable, such as parallel content, and to avoid introducing the qualitatively complex notion of archetypes. However, when drawing on the data of personal experience, clinical observation, and divinatory practice, Jung's concern was with demonstrating the profound emotional and religious dimension of synchronistic events. For this purpose, it was more relevant to emphasise the personal and transpersonal significance synchronicities can have for their experiencer; that is, their archetypal character. For this purpose, too, the relationship between the coinciding events need not be so obvious but can involve more complex psychological dynamics such as symbolisation and compensation. Ultimately, Jung wants to present a phenomenon and principle that is located between, and is equally relevant to, both scientific and religious perspectives. However, he approaches that mid-point now from one side, now from the other, and the terrain through which he passes is sometimes more conspicuous than his destination.

Jung's treatment of the relationship between the notions of synchronicity and the psychoid unconscious is another instance of this dual movement. Sometimes Jung infers the psychoid unconscious from the experience of synchronicity, at other times he invokes the psychoid unconscious as part of his explanation of synchronicity. In the first case, Jung is moving from the empirical towards the metaphysical; in the second case, from the metaphysical towards the empirical. Both moves arguably stem from Jung's tacit conception of synchronicity as an experience and principle that participates in the empirical and the metaphysical domains alike.

Probability

Finally, we noted in Chapter 2 Jung's apparent indecisiveness regarding the value of statistics for establishing and investigating synchronicity. Jung's general position is that statistics are antithetical to the appreciation of synchronicity, since synchronistic events are individual and unique, whereas statistics only deal in averages (1950–5: par. 1198). Synchronicity, says Jung, 'plays havoc with statistical material' (1958a: par. 1175). However, impressed by the success of Rhine's experiments, he believed that statistics are capable of proving at least the bare fact that synchronistic events exist (ibid.: 1952b: par. 833). Again, most originally, he proposed that statistics provide a means of investigating the psychological significance of events even when those events do not rise to the level of statistical significance (1952b: par. 884).

The statistical method is the instrument *par excellence* of quantitative science. When Jung negates its value for investigating synchronicity he implies that synchronicity is concerned with properties of nature that cannot be demonstrated by science – its 'background of acausality, freedom, and meaningfulness' (1958a: par. 1186), properties that point towards the religious domain. When he nevertheless accepts that the statistical method can prove the existence of synchronistic events he asserts that synchronicity is an empirical phenomenon whose nature and implications deserve serious scientific and intellectual attention. When he further proposes that the statistical method can be used to investigate the psychological significance of chance combinations of events he employs a scientific tool in a way that undercuts its usual purpose and turns it into an instrument for the disclosure of psychological meaning. Since this psychological meaning is specifically archetypal (1952b: pars. 897–900) it reaches beyond the merely personal into the transpersonal dimensions of the psyche. In other words, Jung employs a paradigmatically scientific method for the elucidation of transpersonal meaning. The procedure may be highly questionable, but it again evinces his concern to connect the domains of science and religion.

A mediating position

In this chapter we have suggested that Jung's lifelong struggle with the relationship between religion and science might provide a perspective from which the confusions, uncertainties and other difficulties in the presentation of his theory of synchronicity might be better understood. We considered analytical psychology as an attempt to integrate the domains of religion and science – or at least to articulate a third domain that inalienably participates in and connects the other two – and saw the especially important role that the theory of synchronicity plays in this. The period during which Jung developed his psychological model and theory of synchronicity saw science very much in the ascendancy over religion, and psychology – including psychoanalysis – increasingly aligning itself with science. If Jung wished to keep his psychological model poised between religion and science his task predominantly would have been to support its religious component in order to prevent the model from being absorbed into a purely scientific and secular framework. We have seen some of the subtle ways in which he attempted this, introducing religious concerns and implications while trying not to compromise his commitment to science. Looking back from the perspective of these integrative aspirations of Jung's, we found that many of the intellectual difficulties noted in Chapter 2 can be understood as the result of incomplete approaches from opposite sides towards the same mediating position between religion and science.

Part 3

Synchronicity applied

Chapter 5

Synchronicity and Jung's critique of science, religion and society

In the previous chapter, we saw that the theory of synchronicity can be better understood by viewing it in terms of Jung's aim of resolving the tension he experienced between the conflicting claims of traditional religion and modern science. In a sense, the theory of synchronicity, like analytical psychology as a whole, emerged out of this tension. Having emerged, both analytical psychology and synchronicity then provided Jung with perspectives from which he could comment back on science and religion. In the present chapter, we will examine this reflexive commentary or critique. In view of the central role that science and its complicated relationship with religion have had in fashioning modern culture in the West, an examination of Jung's critique of science and religion will also in large measure be an examination of his critique of modern western culture as a whole. In his writings, Jung addressed many specific areas of modern culture – among them art, education, ethics, gender, literature, myth, personal and social relationships, politics, and psychotherapy, as well as science and religion themselves. However, it is in his writings about science and religion that he addresses the problem of modern culture most directly. Moreover, his comments on science and religion underpin much of what he has to say about the other areas. Our focus in this chapter, therefore, will primarily be on science and religion. However, we will also look in some detail at Jung's general understanding and critique of society. The importance of the theme of society in relation to synchronicity, unlike those of science and religion, may not be immediately obvious. However, as we shall see in the course of this chapter, in Jung's view, the theme of society was intimately bound up with the other two and no less important, not least because society is the arena in which the implications of issues in and between religion and science play themselves out most visibly and pressingly.

Jung and modern western culture

A pertinent overall characterisation of modernity and the particular manner in which Jung's psychology can be seen as a response to it has been presented by Peter Homans in his book *Jung in Context: Modernity and the Making of a Psychology* (1979/1995). Homans surveys several theorists of modernity

– including David Riesman, Philip Rieff, Edward Shils, Peter Berger, Fred Weinstein and Gerald Platt, E. C. Tolman, Erik Erikson, Allen Wheelis, Robert Lifton and Marthe Robert (ibid.: 3–8, 135–40, 148–60) – and finds them in broad agreement about many (though by no means all) of the salient features of modernity. One central feature, clearly relevant to a study of Jung, is the emergence of 'psychological man', a new kind of person who is 'self-sufficient in relation to the past and to the existing social order and . . . capable of relating to both without commitment or loyalty because he is equipped with psychological ideas' (ibid.: 4, summarising Rieff; cf. Jung 1928/1931: pars. 167–9). This phenomenon has been recognised by various sociologists and discussed by them in different ways. However, all the analyses agree on the following major points summarised by Homans: that the modern, psychological person is 'characterized by inner diffuseness: he can organize or structure the inner, personal, and private dimension of his experience of the contemporary world only through psychology'; that 'meaning . . . tends to be realized in the personal sector of life'; that the person's 'relation to social institutions is precarious'; that there is 'no firm, synergic connection between personal identity and the social order'; and that this condition is 'rooted in the decline of the power of religious thought and institutional practices to organize the forces of personality and society' (ibid.: 5). The analyses propose a fundamental distinction between traditional western culture, associated with religion, and modernity, associated with lack of religion and the rise of both psychological man and the discipline of psychology (ibid.).

Focusing on the specific theory of Weinstein and Platt's *The Wish to Be Free* (1973), Homans reviews their thesis that the novel social conditions created by the industrial revolution 'moved the father out of the family circle and into the economic order and segregated the mother from wider social involvement, confining her to the family' (Homans 1979/1995: 135). This produced 'a capacity for separating the emotional functions and abstract mental functions' (ibid.: 136). Traditional societies, for Weinstein and Platt, are characterised by dependency and exclusion: 'subjects are dependent upon authorities for nurture and protection, and they are excluded or removed from the sources of power' (ibid.). Modern societies, by contrast, are characterised by autonomy and inclusion: the individual is 'free from dependency upon authority figures – he is self-nurturant and self-protective', is able to exercise 'self-control, active mastery of both inner and outer worlds, self-denial, and competitiveness', and 'demands and receives inclusion: he identifies with and internalizes the values of authority figures, and this permits him to be included in the economic processes that surround him' (ibid.). As a result, 'Modern societies . . . do not display an unconscious adherence to the common culture but instead – by virtue of the collective presence of autonomous, included members – are pluralized and undergo a fundamental separation between public and private morality' (ibid.).

Weinstein and Platt argue that Freudian psychoanalysis emerged out of and indeed is a codification of this social process of modernisation (Homans 1979/1995: 137–8). Homans sees Jung's psychology also as such a codification, but with a difference. For Jung's psychology, unlike Freud's, does not fully commit to the demands of modernity but rather is 'an attempt to integrate traditional and modern orientations to life' (ibid.: 140). Homans finds the modern commitment to autonomy and inclusion encapsulated in the Jungian concept of the persona, 'especially the rigid persona of the modern man, associated as it was with rationality and the extraverted attitude' (ibid.). However, 'Jung's psychology . . . contains, alongside its perception of modernity, an even stronger appreciation of tradition' (ibid.: 142). For, inasmuch as Jung's archetypes of the collective unconscious 'consist of the oldest and most fundamental psychic contents of mankind', they 'constitute the essence of tradition' (ibid.: 141). Further, Homans argues that while Freud's psychology provides a means by which the private individual as well as being separated from the public order can also maintain contact with it, Jung's psychology 'locates psychological reality and the nature of the self more within the private sector' (ibid.: 142–3). In Jung's process of individuation, according to Homans, 'The collective consciousness gives way to the collective unconscious, which is entirely psychical, not social. The end point of individuation is a pure and intensely privatized self, liberated from all obligation imposed from without by the social order' (ibid.: 143). (We will later have occasion to take issue with this characterisation.)

Homans sees Jung's psychology as having emerged out of the tension he experienced between traditional religion (represented by Christianity) and modern secularity (epitomised by Freudian psychoanalysis). This tension 'forced a heightened self-consciousness, a new inwardness, an intense, introspective preoccupation with the self' and also 'a crisis in thought' as a means was sought to 'bridge the gap between the religious orientation and the attractiveness of secularity or modernity' (1979/1995: 156–7). Concludes Homans:

> The crisis was resolved by the emergence of a new form of thinking that was neither wholly scientific, in the sense of experimental science, nor wholly religious, in the sense of traditional religion, but that was instead 'psychological'. This form of thinking supported the new introspective orientation; and it allowed Jung, the innovative thinker, to separate himself from, and also relate himself to, both the old world, organized by religion, and the new world, organized by modernity or secularity.
>
> (Homans 1979/1995: 157)

Homans's account here is precisely supported by the account in the previous chapter of how Jung's theory of synchronicity arose as part of his attempt to resolve the tension between his dual commitments to religion and science.

Jung's own characterisation of modernity is fully consistent with the socio-logical accounts summarised by Homans, though it has its own distinctive emphases. Jung was already aware of modernity as a problem during his student years and commented in his lectures to the Zofingia Society on the dangers of materialistic science, the crisis of faith brought about by an overly rational approach to religion, and the 'terrifying lassitude' in contemporary politics (1896–9: pars. 11–66, 151–8, 243–91). Broadly speaking, these remained his main points of criticism throughout his professional life. They were, however, continually deepened and enriched with detail, as he better understood the phenomena of modernity and the interconnections among them.

Jung's specific observations and insights on modernity, though often made in passing, together provide a vivid and consistent picture. For example, his awareness of some of the social conditions of modernity is evident in his essay on 'New Paths in Psychology' (1912), where he suggests that the 'sexual problem' of his day may stem partly from 'the rapid development of the towns, with the specialization of work brought about by the extraordinary division of labour, the increasing industrialization of the countryside, and the growing sense of insecurity [which] deprive men of many opportunities for giving vent to their affective energies' (ibid.: par. 428). Later, with an eye to 'The political and social conditions, the fragmentation of religion and philosophy, the contending schools of modern art and modern psychology', he characterises modernity as 'a time of dissociation and sickness' in which 'no-one feels quite comfortable' (1933/1934: par. 290; cf. 1957: par. 552). There has been a dangerous break with tradition, which has led to a condition of 'uprootedness, disorientation, meaninglessness' (1934a: par. 815), and 'profound uncertainty' (1928/1931: par. 155). Because of this sudden rupture with the past, 'a lot of vitally necessary things have become obsolete', including traditional Christianity (McGuire and Hull 1978: 245–6). In the absence of a vital religious tradition we find 'spiritual confusion' (1933/1934: par. 313), 'loss of myth' (1963: 142, 165–6, 306), and alienation from nature (1945: pars. 1360–8). There is a general trivialisation of life in which the modern person seeks distraction in 'numerous activities and boundless extraversion' (1933/1934: par. 296) and is prevented from concentrating by 'cinema, radio, television, the continual swish of motor cars and the drone of planes overhead' (McGuire and Hull 1978: 248–9).

No longer sustained and restrained by the moral force of religion, the modern person succumbs to 'unbridled materialism . . . coupled with either maniacal arrogance or else the extinction of the autonomous personality' (1945/1948b: par. 393). This last is among the most serious symptoms of modernity for Jung, when the modern person 'loses all capacity for introspection', 'feels totally dependent on his environment', and 'looks to the State for salvation' (1954c: par. 479). For, in Jung's view, this condition makes individuals vulnerable to the 'spiritual and moral darkness of State absolutism' (1957: par. 488) such as had existed in Nazi Germany, still existed in Communist Russia and China, and, Jung believed, was in danger of coming about in America (ibid.: par. 523).

The immediate cause of the predicament of modernity lies for Jung in the rise of scientific rationalism, which he considers has led to 'a new one-sidedness, the overvaluation of "scientifically" attested views' (1947/1954: par. 426). Because 'scientific knowledge not only enjoys universal esteem but, in the eyes of modern man, counts as the only intellectual and spiritual authority' (1957: par. 496), the authority of traditional religion has correspondingly waned, leaving no adequate symbolic container for the irrational forces of the unconscious (ibid.: par. 512). These irrational forces then play havoc with culture and society: 'The tempo of the development of consciousness through science and technology', Jung considers, 'was too rapid and left the unconscious, which could no longer keep up with it, far behind, thereby forcing it into a defensive position which expresses itself in a universal will to destruction' (1934/1950: par. 617) – epitomised in the development of the hydrogen bomb (1957: par. 488). Jung elaborates on many of these themes in 'The Undiscovered Self (Present and Future)' (1957), published after two world wars and in the shadow of the Cold War.

Jung's critique of science

As well as being partly the product of scientific sources and influences, synchronicity both supports Jung's overall critique of science and is his boldest instance of that critique. In order to demonstrate this, we need to look first at Jung's understanding of science, then at his general analytical psychological critique of science, and finally at the specific contribution of synchronicity to this critique.[1]

Jung's understanding of science

Throughout his life, and even when working on religion and esoteric thought, Jung claimed primarily to be a scientist or empiricist. However, his understanding of science is not straightforward. Different understandings come to the fore during different periods of his career: when a student, when working at the Burghölzli, when involved with Freud and psychoanalysis, when developing analytical psychology, and when theorising about synchronicity. Furthermore, even within the same period of his career, what he means by 'science' often depends on the context in which he is writing – his particular purpose and audience.

This absence of a uniform understanding of science is not unique to Jung. As we have already had occasion to note, the terms 'science' and 'scientist' are historical constructions whose meaning has been a matter for continual debate and negotiation (see Brooke 1991; Brooke and Cantor 1998). In Jung's day, the professionalisation of science was a recent phenomenon, and such history of science as there was tended to be dominated by accounts that viewed the past as so many right and wrong turns – the former celebrated, the latter marginalised – leading to the truth that was enshrined in present knowledge and practice. There was little attempt to understand the activities of even recent past scientists in terms of either their own perception of their practices and problems or, more broadly, their intellectual, social and cultural contexts. Consequently, there was a multiplicity of understandings of science, with only limited reflection on the origins and significance of that multiplicity. Different versions of science tended to exist in ignorance of or competition with one another rather than in conscious pluralism.

With this background in mind, we can better appreciate Jung's uses of the term 'science' and more easily discern their underlying consistency.

Jung used the term 'science' in two main ways. Narrowly, he used the term to refer to the dominant science of his day: a science based on assumptions of materialism and reductionism. More broadly, he used the term to refer to any empirical approach to the acquisition of knowledge, any systematic study based on careful observation of facts.[2] When Jung criticises science, he generally has in mind the narrower understanding of the term. When he presents himself as a scientist, he has in mind the broader understanding. Clearly, the broader understanding encompasses the narrower, and much of what Jung finds to praise about science applies to both understandings. However, because of his alignment with the broader understanding, he is able to modify his specific use of the term several times throughout his career. Each modification represents a move away from materialism and reductionism towards a more holistic position that acknowledges psychological and spiritual as well as material reality and other principles of explanation than efficient causality. In the background of all these developments, we can sense the continuing influence on Jung of German Romantic *Naturphilosophie* (see Ellenberger 1970: 202–5; Noll 1994: 40–2).

Briefly, the main developments in Jung's understanding of science are as follows. As a student, while acknowledging the usefulness of science, he protested against the materialism and inertia of current science, favouring a more vitalistic understanding that asserted the inseparability of morality from science (1896–9). In his work during the early period of his appointment at the Burghölzli (1900–1907), the scientifically most respectable methods of contemporary experimental psychology were to the fore, especially in his word association tests (Jung 1904–37). However, there was also an openness of approach – for example, in his continuing investigation of mediums (Jung 1905) – that clashed with the more reductive materialistic orientation of Freud[3] with whom Jung began to collaborate in 1907 (Jung 1906–49; 1963: 144–64). His period of involvement with Freud and psychoanalysis (1907–1913) nevertheless enriched Jung's sense that the unconscious could be investigated by scientific means other than experimental, especially by the careful observation of dreams and transference phenomena in individual cases. In separating himself from Freud (1911–12/1952) and developing his own distinctive orientation within depth psychology (Jung 1921; 1912–66), Jung gradually clarified for himself an alternative 'phenomenological' understanding of science. This took the primary data of science as psychic rather than material and recognised that non-rational (fantasy) thinking in addition to rational (directed) thinking could be a valid means of acquiring insight. This approach led to a great extension in the range of subject matter of Jung's psychological investigations: for example, he considered there to be nothing unscientific in examining the phenomena of comparative mythology and religion, Gnosticism, alchemy, and eastern thought (Jung 1911–12/1952; 1928–54; 1944; 1929–54; 1955–6).[4] These areas of interest in turn presented him with coherent and fruitful world-views, such as that of the ancient Chinese, that further threw into relief and relativised for him the embedded assumptions of modern western science (1930: pars. 78–81). Finally, Jung used this vantage-point in conjunction with insights emerging from within western science itself (for example, in quantum physics or the new field of experimental parapsychology) to mount a direct challenge on the very foundations of modern western science through his theory of synchronicity (Jung 1951b; 1952b). In essence, this was a bold attempt to return to the kind of unitary world-view that had prevailed before the emergence of modern science, but to do so through broadening rather than rejecting modern science.[5]

Jung's general analytical psychological critique of science

Jung criticises the dominant science of his day above all for its one-sidedness and its inability to deal with the complexity of individual psychology. This science is one-sided in a number of respects. It is a science of outward things, which neglects the inner nature of human beings (1936b: par. 867; 1947/1954: par. 426). It is materialistic, concerned with 'things that can be seen and touched' and with 'physical and chemical methods of investigation', whereas the object of Jung's interest, the human psyche, is immaterial, 'beyond the brain, beyond the anatomical substrate' (1908/1914: par. 320). Science is intellectual only, incapable of gauging the feeling tones that are so important in forming value judgements (1951a: par. 51). It is based on the causal principle and is therefore reductive, unable to grasp 'the psyche as a creative function' for which 'the constructive standpoint' (elaborating things into something higher and more complicated rather than reducing them into their elements) is required (1914: par. 405). It is a form of directed thinking, which therefore needs to be complemented by the equally important function of fantasy thinking (1911–12/1952: pars. 4–46). It restricts itself to 'the common, the probable, the average', leaving little room for 'the exceptional and extraordinary' (1958b: par. 701). Such science 'imparts an unrealistic, rational picture of the world', marginalising the individual person who, as 'an irrational datum', is 'the true and authentic carrier of reality' (1957: par. 498).

There are two levels within this criticism of science as one-sided. At one level, Jung is criticising materialistic and reductive science. His own broader, phenomenological understanding of science corrects this. However, at another level, he is criticising the scientific approach *per se*. For even phenomenological science is one-sided in that it involves a predominantly rational procedure of observing, classifying, and establishing relations and sequences among data (1976: 567). While feelings, values and meanings can be the objects of such a procedure, they are not part of the procedure itself.[6] Jung's view when he wrote *Psychological Types* was that psychology as a science 'could, and actually does, grasp the processes of feeling, sensation, and fantasy in abstract intellectual form' (1921: par. 84). However, psychology as a practice aims not at abstract intellectual knowledge but at healing and the enhancement of life, and in this capacity is 'no longer science; it is psychology in the wider meaning of the word, a psychological activity of a creative nature in which fantasy is given prior place' (ibid.; cf. 1926/ 1946: pars. 162–3). At this point, where psychology becomes practice rather than theory, we see one of the borders at which psychology's simultaneous affinity with but distinction from science becomes apparent.

Clearly, the criticism of science as one-sided presupposes some of the principles embedded in Jung's psychological model: his emphasis on wholeness and the integration of opposites. Other assumptions of analytical psychology provide the perspective from which he makes further specific criticisms of science. Especially important is Jung's assumption that psychic reality is the only reality of which we have direct experience (1926: par. 623). Such an assumption enhances the epistemological significance of fantasy and images as the primary language of the psyche. Based on this, Jung argues that archetypal images 'even appear in the exact sciences, as the foundation of certain indispensable auxiliary concepts such as energy, ether, and the atom' (1919: par. 278; cf. 1927/1931: par. 342). As a challenge specifically to scientific materialism, he notes that with the concept of 'matter', no genuinely new principle has been introduced but only a 'new hypostasis': 'Whether you call the principle of existence "God", "matter", "energy", or anything else you like, you have created nothing; you have simply changed a symbol' (1939/1954: par. 763). More generally, he asserts that 'it is out of himself and out of his peculiar constitution that man has produced his sciences. They are *symptoms* of his psyche' (1930–1: par. 752; cf. 1927/1931: par. 327).

This has implications for the status of disciplines such as his own: 'Psychology,' he writes, 'as one of the many expressions of psychic life, operates with ideas which in their turn are derived from archetypal structures and thus generate a somewhat more abstract kind of myth' (1940: par. 302). He then extends the insight to science as such: 'Psychology therefore translates the archaic speech of myth into a modern mythologem – not yet, of course, recognized as such – which constitutes one element of the myth "science"' (ibid.). This should not be mistaken for a subordination of science to myth and other forms of fantasy thinking. Jung states that psychology, because it deals with the unconscious, has difficulty extricating itself 'at least so far from the language of metaphor as to reach the level of metaphor used by other sciences' – which implies that not just psychology but other sciences do use metaphors (1921: par. 428). However, his concession is limited, for as he continues, with specific reference to psychology: 'Our science is a language of metaphor too, but in practice it works better than the old mythological hypothesis, which used concretisms as a means of expression, and not, as we do, concepts' (ibid.; see also 1963: 313; 1976: 448–9).

The contribution of synchronicity

Jung's general critique of science provides the context within which he presents his theory of synchronicity. Throughout his principal works on the topic, Jung maintains that synchronicity is an 'empirical concept' (1952b: par. 960) based on 'empirical experiences and experimentation' (1951b: par. 995). 'Although meaningful coincidences are infinitely varied in their phenomenology,' he writes, 'as acausal events they nevertheless form an element that is part of the scientific picture of the world' (ibid.). This is reflected in the emphasis in the works on discussions of physics, experimental parapsychology, descriptive biology, and general issues of scientific methodology and proof. Nevertheless, Jung recognises that contemporary science is unlikely to take seriously either the phenomena to which he is drawing attention or the theory he is proposing to account for them. In large part, his task is to present the phenomena and theory in such a way that their scientific relevance and plausibility become evident. He can do this only to a limited extent within the assumptions of the dominant science of his day or even within the assumptions of his broader notion of phenomenological science. Eventually there comes a point where he has to assert the need for a radical revision of the foundations of science.

Scattered throughout his works on synchronicity, Jung offers his analysis of why most contemporary science is not open to the kind of data and theory he is presenting. This analysis closely reflects the critique outlined above. In sum, he considers the scientific view of his day to be one-sided, 'a psychologically biased partial view' (1952b: par. 821) that 'lack[s] something which played a considerable role in the classical and medieval view' (ibid.: par. 829). Based on a 'method of inquiry' that 'aims at establishing regular events which can be repeated' (ibid.: par. 821) and on the conviction that 'causality alone could be the final principle of explanation' (ibid.: par. 829), contemporary science has indeed been remarkably successful (ibid.: pars. 917, 939). However, 'It produces a merely average picture of natural events, but not a *true* picture of the world as it is' (ibid.: par. 904). It cannot deal adequately with 'remarkable isolated cases' (ibid.: par. 862). Through imposing artificial restrictions, it fails to grasp 'The workings of Nature in her unrestricted wholeness' (ibid.: par. 864), which includes the operations of chance (1950a: par. 967). Above all, Jung faults the science of his day for ignoring 'psychic conditions' (1952b: par. 856). A major aim of his work on synchronicity, therefore, is 'to broaden the basis of our understanding of nature' (ibid.: par. 861).

In a letter to R. F. C. Hull (24 January 1955), Jung reported: 'The latest comment about "Synchronicity" is that it cannot be accepted because it shakes the security of our scientific foundations, as if this were not exactly the goal I am aiming at' (1976: 217). On the same day he wrote to Michael Fordham of 'the impact of synchronicity upon the fanatical one-sidedness of scientific philosophy' (ibid.: 216). Jung's theory of synchronicity is indeed his boldest response to the one-sidedness of science. As we have seen, he believed that the dominant science of his day was materialistic, causal, reductive and excessively rationalistic. The theory of synchronicity, by contrast, emphasises that there can be a psychic and spiritual dimension even to phenomena that are ostensibly material; that objects, events and processes can be connected acausally as well as causally and can be understood not only in terms of their constituent elements but also, no less objectively, in terms of their meaning; and that the irrational is as important a factor to accommodate in our scientific account of reality as is the rational.

Above all, Jung thought that his work on synchronicity demonstrated the need to expand the current conception of science in order to include, in addition to the classical concepts of time, space and causality, a principle of acausal connection through meaning (1952b: pars. 961–63). This, he concluded, would introduce the psychic factor of meaning into our scientific picture of the world, help get rid of 'the incommensurability between the observed and the observer', and make possible a 'whole judgement' (ibid.: par. 961) – that is, a judgement that takes into consideration psychological as well as physical factors (ibid.: par. 964). Jung never made explicit what he thought such a 'scientific picture of the world' would look like. However, we may assume that it would result in an outlook similar or identical to his own: one in which phenomena are observed closely and considered not only from the perspective of all the factual, causal and rationally discernible relations within and among them but also from the perspective of their acausal similarities of form and meaning, especially as these can be related to previously established or intuited universal patterns or archetypes. Judgements resulting from such dual-focused observation and reflection would account not only for the composition and history of phenomena but also for their transpersonal meaning in the present.

We noted that another of Jung's challenges to the one-sidedness of science was to propose that fantasy thinking in terms of archetypal images and myths should be valued no less than directed thinking in terms of rational language and concepts as an instrument for achieving insight into reality. Synchronicity supports this in that 'it makes possible a view which includes the psychoid factor in our description and knowledge of nature – that is, an *a priori* meaning or "equivalence"' (1952b: par. 962). Such a view implies that fundamental reality has a psychic as well as a material aspect, that its nature can manifest in both, and therefore that insights stemming from the inwardly oriented function of creative imagination may be as true to fundamental reality as those stemming from the outwardly oriented function of rational reflection. This clearly has implications for the arts as well as for science and religion.

Empirically, synchronicity emphasises relationships between psyche and matter that are observable and sometimes even measurable. Theoretically, synchronicity suggests the notion of the psychoid unconscious in which psyche and matter unite. In both of these ways, synchronicity relates psychic phenomena, even radically anomalous psychic phenomena, to the physical domain of scientific investigation. Because for Jung the psychological mediates between the physical and the spiritual, to link the physical and psychological in this way entails setting up a potential bridge between the physical and the spiritual, hence between science and religion. This is in no sense an attempt either to reduce science to religion or to conflate science with religion. However, it does deeply implicate the two fields, suggesting that neither can provide a satisfactory picture of reality without at some point invoking the other. As has been noted by Murray Stein (1985),

Jung's characterisation of synchronicity as the 'missing fourth' that needs to be added to the triad of classical science – space, time and causality – is specifically intended to open science to the dimension of religion. 'By including the principle of synchronicity as a fourth principle of science,' Stein writes, 'modern man, whose intellectual commitment is to scientific rationality and empirical method, would have a way of including transcendence and divine activity within a world-view that also paid full recognition to the space–time– causality continuum' (ibid.: 170).

In criticising one-sided science, Jung is also criticising what he saw as its embodiment in Freudian psychoanalysis. For the complementary theory of synchronicity affirms precisely what Freud shunned: the 'occult', the 'mystical', the possibility of transpersonal meaning. Jung does not accuse Freud and modern science for failing to believe in these things but for dismissing them *a priori* and failing to attend to the data that suggest them (1957: par. 530; 1932b: par. 56; 1963: 152). The theory of synchronicity presents data that cannot be readily understood by science based solely on materialistic assumptions. Rather than simply ignore these data, adopt facile *ad hoc* explanations of them, or postulate a multiplicity of new but still causally based mental functions to account for them (telepathy, clairvoyance, psychokinesis, precognition), Jung identified their common denominator in the factor of meaningful coincidence and attempted to find a satisfactory theoretical formulation of that factor (1955–6: par. 662). The formulation he arrived at – of synchronicity as an acausal connecting principle – may disrupt the principles of the dominant materialistic and reductive science but it does not, Jung argues, flinch from the observable data.

Paradoxically, these data, presented as the empirical evidence for synchronicity, both prompted some of Jung's own bolder theoretical speculations and provided him with a resource to temper the speculations of others, especially speculations he encountered in some of the more religious or philosophical sources for his theory. For example, we saw in Chapter 3 that Schopenhauer's philosophical account implied that meaningful coincidences ought to occur 'so regularly and systematically that their verification would be either unnecessary or the simplest thing in the world' (1952b: par. 828). Similarly, Leibniz's account implied that meaningful coincidences would be 'the absolute rule in all cases where an inner event occurs simultaneously with an outside one' (ibid.: par. 938). Though sympathetic to their underlying aspirations, Jung distances himself from these speculations on empirical grounds: Schopenhauer's conclusion 'goes far beyond the bound of what is empirically possible' (ibid.: par. 828), while Leibniz's likewise has to be doubted since 'the synchronistic phenomena that can be verified empirically, far from constituting a rule, are so exceptional that most people doubt their existence' (ibid.: par. 938).

Most grievously, in Jung's view, the one-sidedness of modern science is responsible for its failure adequately to comprehend the complexity of individual psychology. This is epitomised in modern science by its reliance on statistics. The statistical method is able to give an average picture of events but, as Jung repeatedly protests, real life is made up of individuals not averages. Psychology, however, especially psychotherapy, is precisely concerned with individuals and all of their idiosyncrasies (1957: pars. 493–5). Writes Jung:

> The statistical method shows the facts in the light of the ideal average but does not give us a picture of their empirical reality . . . Not to put too fine a point on it, one could say that the real picture consists of nothing but exceptions to the rule, and that, in consequence, absolute reality has predominantly the character of *irregularity*.
>
> (Jung 1957: par. 494)

Synchronicity radically challenges modern science by questioning its reliance on statistics and focusing attention precisely on exceptions to the rule. Jung was certainly interested in attempts, such as those of Rhine, to demonstrate statistically the existence of connections among events that could not be explained in normal causal terms. He even seems to have hoped that his own astrological experiment might be able to provide statistical proof of synchronicity. However, as we noted in Chapter 2, he eventually proposed a more radical way in which statistics could help in the study of synchronicity. On the one hand, as he triumphantly acknowledges, 'synchronicity plays havoc with statistical material' (1958a: par. 1175). On the other hand, synchronicity usefully directs attention to patterns of chance that, from the statistical point of view, are insignificant, yet, from the psychological point of view, can be read as the meaningful expression of archetypes.

Science fails to deal adequately with not only the complexity of individual psychology but also, more generally, the 'workings of Nature in her unrestricted wholeness' (1952b: par. 864). As Jung notes, 'science, whenever possible, proceeds experimentally and in all cases statistically' (ibid.). He continues:

> Experiment, however, consists in asking a definite question which excludes as far as possible anything disturbing and irrelevant. It makes conditions, imposes them on Nature, and in this way forces her to give an answer to a question devised by man. She is prevented from answering out of the fullness of her possibilities since these possibilities are restricted as far as practicable. For this purpose there is created in the laboratory a situation which is artificially restricted to the question and which compels Nature to give an unequivocal answer.
>
> (Jung 1952b: par. 864)

He contrasts this with the approach of traditional Chinese 'science' as embodied in its 'standard text-book' the *I Ching* (1930: par. 80). This is precisely a method for 'grasping the total situation' (1952b: par. 863); it is an 'experiment-with-the-whole' (ibid.: par. 865). The *I Ching* exemplifies the kind of holistic approach Jung wishes to introduce into his expanded conception of modern western science, and the key to doing so is again the notion of synchronicity. For, as Jung notes,

'The science of the *I Ching* is based not on the causality principle but on one which
– hitherto unnamed because not familiar to us – I have tentatively called the
synchronistic principle' (1930: par. 81). With its synchronistic basis in mind, he
grandly characterises the *I Ching* as 'an Archimedean point from which our
Western attitude of mind could be lifted off its foundations' (ibid.: par. 78).

Jung's critique of religion

The theory of synchronicity also plays a role, albeit more covertly, in Jung's
critique of religion. In discussing religion I shall first present Jung's understanding
of the topic, then a summary of his general analytical psychological critique of it,
and finally the specific contribution of synchronicity to this critique.

Jung's understanding of religion

Jung's understanding of religion, like his understanding of science, was many-
sided and developed over the course of his life. Again, a chronological survey
reveals some broadly identifiable phases. In his early years (1875–1900), we
see him awakening to the problem of the relationship between traditional religion
and modern secularity and coming to value personal religious experience
over institutionally sanctioned belief. After an unsatisfying attempt to explain religious phenomena reductively in psychiatric and psychoanalytic terms, he began
increasingly to emphasise the positive, prospective function of religion (1901–12).
In his mature years (1913–37), this strengthened into the conviction that the psyche
is naturally religious and religion of some form is therefore a psychic necessity.
In his later years (1938–63), he moved from this general concern with the value
of religion *per se* to a specific analysis of Christianity as the dominant religious
tradition in western culture, and he provided recommendations for how this tradition might be helped to transform for the better in the light of depth psychological
insights.[7]

The principal distinction throughout Jung's mature work on religion is between
religion as experience and religion as creed:

> A creed gives expression to a definite collective belief, whereas the
> word *religion* expresses a subjective relationship to certain metaphysical,
> extramundane factors. A creed is a confession of faith intended chiefly for
> the world at large and is thus an intramundane affair, while the meaning
> and purpose of religion lie in the relationship of the individual to God
> (Christianity, Judaism, Islam) or to the path of salvation and liberation
> (Buddhism).
>
> (Jung 1957: par. 507)

The definitions of religion that Jung provides all put the accent on experience
rather than belief, ritual or organisation (e.g., 1938/1940: pars. 8, 9, 137). Jung

does also use the term 'religion' to refer to traditions identifiable by their beliefs, practices and institutions – whether mainstream current traditions such as Christianity and Buddhism, defunct traditions such as Mithraism, or little-known indigenous traditions such as that of the Pueblo Indians. However, he is always quick to establish that these doctrinal, ritual and organisational dimensions of religious traditions, with which he was especially concerned in his later writings on Christianity, have their taproot in the dimension of experience.

Jung's general analytical psychological critique of religion

Jung's main dedicated statement of his psychology of religion is contained in the three 'Terry Lectures' on 'Psychology and Religion' that he delivered at Yale University in 1937 (1938/1940). These both sum up his thinking on this subject to date and look forward to his later developments of it.

In the course of the lectures, Jung invokes many of the principal concepts and processes of his psychological model. As we have seen, his most basic assumption is of the primacy of psychic reality: 'the only form of existence of which we have immediate knowledge is psychic' (1938/1940: par. 16). From this, it follows that we cannot know God or any other metaphysical realities in themselves but can know only the psychological experiences and images we have of them. This provides the grounds for Jung's claimed phenomenological and empirical approach to religion: 'Inasmuch as religion has a very important psychological aspect, I deal with it from a purely empirical point of view, that is, I restrict myself to the observation of phenomena and I eschew any philosophical or metaphysical considerations' (ibid.: par. 2). A religious idea, such as the motif of the virgin birth, is 'psychologically true inasmuch as it exists'; what gives such an idea objectivity is that it is 'shared by a society – by a *consensus gentium*' (ibid.: par. 4).

The state of religion that Jung analyses from the perspective of his psychological model is characterised as one in which there is a severe loss of faith (1938/1940: par. 148), one marked by God's death and disappearance (ibid.: par. 149) and by the Church's loss of authority (ibid.: par. 34). Various attempts to reorient in this condition have been attempted – for example, scientific materialism, psychologism (Freud), or atheistic iconoclasm (Nietzsche) – but Jung rejects all of these as inadequate (ibid.: par. 142). His own starting point is to assert the naturalness and importance of immediate religious experience. He provides his broad definition of religion as 'a careful consideration and observation of certain dynamic factors that are conceived as "powers"' (ibid.: par. 8), as 'the attitude peculiar to a consciousness which has been changed by experience of the *numinosum*' (ibid.: par. 9), and as 'a relationship to the highest or most powerful value, be it positive or negative' (ibid.: par. 137). Religious beliefs and dogmas are secondary to this: 'Creeds are codified and dogmatized forms of original religious experience' (ibid.: par. 10). Jung's interpretation of the problem facing modern religions is that their symbols and myths have lost their connection to experience and hence are no longer capable of evoking a living response in the psyches of adherents. Since the psyche has a religious function that cannot be ignored without damage to psychic health, Jung champions a 'psychological approach' as 'probably all that is left us' (ibid.: par. 148). For instance, he argues that 'Revelation is an "unveiling" of the depths of the human soul first and foremost, a "laying bare"; hence it is an essentially psychological event' (ibid.: par. 127). According to his psychological model, and as illustrated by his case study in 'Psychology and Religion', such revelation takes place above all through the medium of dreams and other forms of unconscious fantasy. In making this point, Jung is not unconcerned with traditional forms of religion. Indeed, he acknowledges the value of traditional religious rituals as ways of mediating between consciousness and the unconscious and compares the strengths and weaknesses of Catholicism and Protestantism in this respect (ibid.: pars. 75–80). However, his main concern is with the many people for whom these traditional resources no longer work.

Jung's lectures on 'Psychology and Religion' introduce, mainly through the case study, one of the themes that plays a major role in his subsequent writing in this area. This is the notion that images of God undergo transformation and are currently undergoing one such major transformation, which needs to be recognised and understood. Thus, the quaternity and mandala symbols experienced by the dreamer in Jung's examples spontaneously express a view of divinity that differs markedly from the traditional Trinity through according a place to evil, the feminine and the body. The mandala presents an image of totality rather than perfection, and it is an image at whose centre is the human being rather than a god (1938/1940: pars. 136–9). Jung argues that this is not an idiosyncratic product from the mind of his dreamer but 'the continuation of a process of spiritual development which began in the early Middle Ages [with alchemy], and perhaps even further back [with Gnosticism]' (ibid.: par. 159).

In sum, Jung's analytical psychological critique challenges traditional dogmatic religion in at least the following four ways. First, Jung asserts that the metaphysical claims of religion are epistemologically ungrounded, since psyche is the only reality that can be directly known. Second, he observes that religion based on faith and reason no longer vitally engages many people. Third, he proposes that the experiential element in religion needs to be more emphasised, specifically through attending to numinous psychic events. Fourth, he recommends re-conceiving or re-imagining God as a quaternity rather than Trinity. As we shall now see, the theory of synchronicity partly deepens and partly modifies this critique.

The contribution of synchronicity

Homans rightly notes that Jung's psychology of religion involves 'a double movement of reduction and retrieval of meaning' (1979/1995: 183). The reduction is to challenge dogmatism, reliance on faith, blind adherence to tradition, and the perpetuation of formulations that no longer have psychic validity. The retrieval is to affirm the religious function, the existence of spiritual reality and experiences, and the continuing relevance of religious phenomena when viewed symbolically. The theory of synchronicity contributes primarily to the retrieval of meaning, specifically by providing various reasons for crediting spiritual reality and experience in the face of powerful forces tending towards secularisation.

Synchronicity strongly affirms the experiential approach to religion, even to the extent that Jung on one occasion practically equates religious experience with synchronicity. In an interview with Mircea Eliade that took place in August 1952, he first stated that '[r]eligious experience is *numinous*, as Rudolf Otto calls it, and for me, as a psychologist, this experience differs from all others in the way it transcends the ordinary categories of space, time, and causality' (McGuire and Hull 1978: 230). Then he added, strikingly: 'Recently I have put a great deal of study into synchronicity . . . and I have established that it closely resembles numinous experiences where space, time, and causality are abolished' (ibid.).

We will explore more of the specific connections between synchronicity and religious experience in the next chapter. Here we can note that the general kind of experience synchronicity presents – highly anomalous and baffling, with overtones of the paranormal – is unlikely to be welcomed by traditional institutionalised religions, whose orthodoxy they threaten to disrupt. In this way, while explicitly supporting the experiential approach to religion, synchronicity also implicitly challenges credal religion.

As we have seen, synchronicity denies exclusive validity to the causal emphasis of modern science – its tendency to explain objects, events, and processes reductively in terms of their constituent elements and past history. With the complementary notion of acausality, synchronicity admits the possibility that ostensibly psychic and physical events may also have a spiritual quality. This possibility emerges in a number of ways. In the first place, synchronicity provides evidence that suggests there are dimensions of reality beyond the physical. Thus, Jung points to the 'phenomena of parapsychology' (that is, synchronistic phenomena) with their 'relativization of time and space through psychic factors' as a corrective to the 'overhasty' inference that the psyche is 'a mere epiphenomenon of a biochemical process in the brain' (1957: par. 527). Further, such events suggest a dimension of reality not only beyond the physical but also beyond the psychic. For, as we have seen, the notion of synchronicity entails a broadening of the concept of the archetype, so that it can be seen as not just a psychic factor but a psychophysical one – a formulation that includes the psychic and the physical but also transcends them. In the light of synchronistic experiences, Jung proposes that the 'psychoid' archetype should be seen as 'grounded on an as yet unknown substrate possessing material and at the same time psychic qualities' (1958b: par. 780). The phenomenon of synchronicity, he states, leads to the postulation of 'a unitary aspect of being' at the deepest level of the collective unconscious (1955–6: par. 662) – an aspect that transcends both the physical and the psychic as normally understood.

Again, among the phenomenological characteristics that Jung typically invokes as indicators of the spiritual nature of psychic contents are spontaneity and autonomy. 'The hallmarks of spirit', he writes, 'are, firstly, the principle of spontaneous movement and activity; secondly, the spontaneous capacity to produce images independently of sense perception; and thirdly, the autonomous and sovereign manipulation of these images' (1945/1948b: par. 393). In other words, psychic contents are marked out as spiritual by their having been caused neither physically nor by other psychic contents. Such autonomous and spontaneous yet meaningful activity is an important part of what Jung is trying to theorise with his notion of meaningful acausal connections. Synchronicity thus provides a theoretical framework for appreciating one of the most distinctive and important notions in Jungian psychology: the autonomous psyche.

In observable synchronicities, the spontaneity and autonomy – or acausality – generally take the form of a paralleling of psychic and physical events. In this phenomenon, Jung might have seen a means of firming up his notion of the spiritual or transpersonal nature of the collective unconscious and archetypes. When arguing for this transpersonal viewpoint, Jung generally appealed to 'the repeated observation that, for instance, the myths and fairy tales of world literature contain definite motifs which crop up everywhere', and that '[w]e meet these same motifs in the fantasies, dreams, deliria, and delusions of individuals living today' (1958c: par. 847). He tried to establish that in at least some cases the 'individuals living today' could not possibly have been exposed to any cultural expression of these motifs. Therefore, when the motifs emerged from the unconscious of such individuals, there could be no origin for them in their personal history; they demonstrated the existence of a collective or transpersonal dimension of the unconscious. However, problematically for Jung, in all cases of the emergence of such motifs alternative explanations seem at least as plausible as the hypothesis of a collective unconscious.[8] One alternative explanation is that the motifs do indeed arise independently in each individual but this is because all individuals, *in their personal lives*, are subject to the same basic range of typical experiences (see Palmer 1997: 176–81). Another alternative explanation, this time denying the independent origin of the motifs, is cryptomnesia – the possibility that cultural expressions of the motifs may have been observed but then forgotten (see Noll 1992: 84–5). Similarly, they may have been observed subliminally without ever having entered conscious awareness. At this point, Jung could refer to synchronistic experiences. For in such experiences the same pattern of meaning expresses itself both in the psyche and, without any causal or projective relationship, in the external world. This alone, Jung could argue, is sufficient to demonstrate the transpersonal nature of the unconscious. Whether or not his patient in the incident recounted in Chapter 1 had prior exposure to images of scarabs, and whether or not she could have acquired from her personal experience a disposition to produce symbols of rebirth, the synchronicity suggests that some factor larger than her personal psyche has been involved in the organisation of the events – a factor that encompasses the external world of nature in addition to her inner psychic world.

The same basic argument has been used by Aziz (1990) to defend Jung's overall approach to the psychology of religion against the charge that it is a form of psychological reductionism. Jung may have been well disposed towards religion, and he may have provided a strategy for taking religious phenomena seriously in the face of the reductive claims of materialistic science, but, because his model emphasises the primacy of psychic reality and, on epistemological grounds, denies that anything non-psychic can be directly experienced, it has seemed to many that he is in effect reducing religion to psychology. God as an objective external reality seems to have been replaced by the image of God in a person's mind (ibid.: 46–9). In defence of Jung, Aziz directs attention to synchronistic events. Such events indicate that meanings experienced psychically can also non-projectively be experienced outwardly. Just as the appearance and behaviour of the real scarab beetle demonstrates that the meaning expressing itself in the patient's dream of a scarab is not only internal and subjective but may also involve the external, natural world, so there is no reason to suppose that the meaning expressed in a person's image of God is only internal and subjective. That meaning too could express itself outwardly, neither caused by nor projected from an individual psyche (ibid.: 179–80).

In similar vein, Jung himself appeals to synchronicity in order to counter the charge that in treating religious narratives as myths expressive of archetypal themes he is necessarily denying the historicity of the narrated events. He writes:

> The fact that the life of Christ is largely myth does absolutely nothing to disprove its factual truth – quite the contrary. I would even go so far as to say that the mythical character of a life is just what expresses its universal human validity. It is perfectly possible, psychologically, for the unconscious or an archetype to take complete possession of a man and to determine his fate down to the smallest detail. At the same time objective, non-psychic parallel phenomena can occur which also represent the archetype. It not only seems so, it simply is so, that the archetype fulfils itself not only psychically in the individual, but objectively outside the individual. My own conjecture is that Christ was such a personality.
>
> (Jung 1952a: par. 648)

The notion of synchronicity even provided Jung with a novel way of reading the history of religions. As we saw in Chapter 3 in the section on 'History of Religions and Western Esotericism', Jung was impressed by the coincidences between certain astronomical events as interpreted astrologically and developments within the history of early and medieval Christianity. Similarly, he noted the synchronistic significance of the proliferation of sightings of UFOs from 1947 (1958b) and the promulgation of the Dogma of the Assumption in 1950 (1938/1954: pars. 195–8). The theory of synchronicity enabled Jung to explore the broad significance of these events for the history of human consciousness without having to establish close causal relations among the disparate phenomena that he saw as expressing the emergent pattern of archetypal meaning.

One of the major themes whose emergence Jung identifies by this synchronistic reading of history is the collective transformation of the God image from Trinity to quaternity. Among the ways Jung characterises the fourth element that needs to be incorporated into the image of God is as the body, the instincts, the earth, and the physical domain generally. Just as, from the physical side, synchronicity opens the classical physical triad of space, time and causality to a spiritual dimension (see Stein 1985: 170), so, from the spiritual side, it opens the classical theological Trinity to the dimension of matter. The dual religious and secular character of synchronicity enables it to play this mediating role within Jung's thinking.

In this way, synchronicity contributes to Jung's critique of religion by allowing him to find a balanced, integrative relationship between religion and science. In his *Zofingia Lectures*, he had expressed his extreme dissatisfaction at the attempts of traditional Christianity to accommodate itself to modern science through internalising the rationalism and literalism of science (1896–9: pars. 243–91). Much later, he continued to lament that 'the spiritual content of our Christian Dogma has disappeared in a rationalistic and "enlightened" fog of alarming density' (1943: par. 933). Christianity or any other religion that attempted to grapple with rationalistic science on the latter's terms would forfeit the mystery and symbolic richness that are such vital characteristics of living religion. What was needed for Jung's retrieval of religious meaning in a climate of secular modernity was a means of connecting the religious and scientific spheres in a way that respected both. As argued in the previous chapter, that is precisely what Jung intended the theory of synchronicity to achieve.

Returning to the four elements of Jung's analytical psychological critique mentioned at the end of the previous sub-section (see p. 131), we can see that synchronicity has partly reinforced and partly modified them. On the one hand, the notion of synchronicity supports the experiential approach to religion as opposed to the approach of traditional institutionalised religion based primarily on faith. Indeed, in view of Jung's willingness to equate numinous and synchronistic experiences, the theory of synchronicity arguably articulates the essence of Jung's experiential approach to religion. In addition, the theory plays a major role in Jung's re-conceiving or re-imagining of God as a quaternity. On the other hand, the theory of synchronicity arguably tempers Jung's anti-metaphysical assertion that the only knowable reality is psychic. For it provides a model of how psychic images may be experienced as having transpsychic parallels and referents – that is, the corresponding physical event and the instantiated transcendental meaning of a synchronicity.

Jung's critique of society

In Chapter 4 we argued that Jung's psychology generally, and his theory of synchronicity in particular, emerged largely as a response to the tension between traditional religion and modern science as these existed in the late nineteenth and early twentieth centuries. However, as Homans (1979/1995) has demonstrated, Jung's response to this tension was also bound up with his thinking about society. At the beginning of the present chapter I summarised Homans's account of how Jung's psychology emerged as a response to modernity, including modern social conditions, and I sketched some of the broad outlines of Jung's own view of modernity, including of social conditions. In the remainder of the chapter we will look at Jung's critique of modern society and in particular at the feature of modern society that he most deplored: mass-mindedness.

Jung's understanding of society

Homans shows convincingly that Jung's understanding of modern society was 'identical to that of the theory of mass society' (1979/1995: 178) – a theory which, along with Marxism, is 'the most prevalent and widely known theory of modernity' (ibid.: 174). The modern form of this theory originated in the work of Max Scheler, José Ortega, and Karl Mannheim.[9] Homans surveys their ideas (ibid.: 175–7) and finds 'three major interlocking features that form the core of the theory of the mass society' (ibid.: 177). These are that 'modern man', first, 'has lost contact with the past and thus is uprooted and traditionless'; second, 'has become depersonalized – he has lost his autonomy, separateness, and distinctiveness'; and, third, 'either is isolated and alienated from the social order or else is submissive to its authoritarian political and social structures' (ibid.). As we saw at the beginning of the chapter, Jung's critique of 'modern man' identifies precisely these characteristics.

Jung's general analytical psychological critique of society

By the time he wrote 'The Undiscovered Self' (1957), the language in which Jung articulated his social criticisms was replete with the term 'mass' and its cognates. 'We ought not to underestimate the psychological effect of the statistical world picture', he cautions, for 'it displaces the individual in favour of anonymous units that pile up into mass formations' (ibid.: par. 499). More trenchantly: 'The mass crushes out the insight and reflection that are still possible with the individual' (ibid.: par. 489). Even when the word is not present, the thought is: in modern society 'responsibility is collectivized as much as possible, i.e., is shuffled off by the individual and delegated to a corporate body' (ibid.: par. 504; cf. ibid.: par. 503). The mass formations that result from de-individualisation culminate in the abstract entity of the State (ibid.: par. 499).

The problem of mass-mindedness is compounded for Jung by the probability that large sections of the general population are suffering from latent psychoses. Forming 'a collectively excited group ruled by affective judgments and wish-fantasies' (1957: par. 490), this significant minority can easily infect other, 'so-called normal' people who generally lack the self-knowledge to protect them from unconscious influence. There is then liable to emerge 'a sort of collective possession' which in turn can rapidly develop into a 'psychic epidemic' (ibid.). Especially alarming in these conditions is that the chaotic formlessness of the State tends to be compensated by the appearance of a leader with inflated ego-consciousness (ibid.: 500). The stage is then set for the emergence of the totalitarian state.

Jung is in no doubt about the main source of mass-mindedness: 'one of the chief factors responsible for psychological mass-mindedness', he writes, 'is scientific rationalism, which robs the individual of his foundations and his dignity. As a social unit he has lost his individuality and become a mere abstract number in the bureau of statistics' (1957: par. 501). Jung's critique of mass society therefore entails 'turning a blind eye to scientific knowledge' (ibid.: par. 496) with its 'conformities and regularities' (ibid.: par. 497) and instead aiming to understand the individual as a human being; that is to say, 'as something unique and singular which in the last analysis can be neither known nor compared to anything else' (ibid.: par. 495). Analytical psychology provides a way of achieving such 'individual understanding' (ibid.: par. 497).

The totalitarian states to which, in Jung's analysis, mass-mindedness gives rise derive their power partly from an appropriation of the religious function: 'along with the individual [the totalitarian state] swallows up [the individual's] religious forces. The State takes the place of God' (1957: par. 511). This happens, however unwittingly, for the following reasons. On the one hand, the totalitarian states cannot allow the religious function to find its outlet in actual religion. For '[r]eligion . . . teaches another authority opposed to that of the world' (ibid.: par. 507), it provides 'an extramundane principle capable of relativizing the overpowering influence of external factors' (ibid.: 511), and therefore constitutes a threat to the State and its rulers, who wish to be the sole object of dependency (ibid.: par. 505). Hence, 'all socio-political movements tending in this direction [of totalitarianism] invariably try to cut the ground from under *religion*' (ibid.: par. 505). On the other hand, the religious function, as a natural function, cannot be simply 'disposed of with rationalistic and so-called enlightened criticism' (ibid.: par. 514). Accordingly, '[r]eligion, in the sense of conscientious regard for the irrational factors of the psyche and individual fate, reappears – evilly distorted – in the deification of the State and the dictator' (ibid.). As Jung darkly elaborates, '[t]he State, like the Church, demands enthusiasm, self-sacrifice, and love, and if religion requires or presupposes the "fear of God", then the dictator State takes good care to provide the necessary terror' (ibid.: par. 512). For Jung, therefore, another means of addressing the social crisis represented by mass-mindedness is to promote authentic, experientially based religion as its 'counterbalance'. In the later sections of 'The Undiscovered Self' he elaborates on the role of analytical psychology as a process of self-knowledge that can lead to numinous encounters with the unconscious, 'the only available source of religious experience' (ibid.: par. 565). Only 'religious experience and immediate relation to God', he writes, can provide 'that certainty which will keep me, as an individual, from dissolving in the crowd' (ibid.: par. 564).

The contribution of synchronicity

The theory of synchronicity supports Jung's critique of society above all because it supports his critiques of science and religion. Since scientific rationalism is 'one of the chief factors responsible for psychological mass-mindedness', the challenge that synchronicity presents to the former is simultaneously a challenge to the latter. Indeed, in a letter to Michael Fordham (24 January 1955), Jung states explicitly that he wrote his principal essay on synchronicity in order to address the dangerous *social* implications of scientific rationalism. After expressing his objection to the pernicious influence of statistics and the concomitant failure to attend to exceptions and individual cases, he continues:

> only the individual carries life and consciousness of life, which seems to me rather a significant fact not to be lightly dismissed . . . But wherever a philosophy based upon the sciences prevails . . . , the individual man loses his foothold and becomes 'vermasst', turned into a mass particle, because as an 'exception' he is valueless . . .
> *This is the reason and the motive of my essay.* I am convinced that something ought to be done about this blind and dangerous belief in the security of the scientific Trinity [of time, space and causality].
> (Jung 1976: 216; emphasis added)

As well as undermining the kind of scientific attitude that gives rise to mass-mindedness, synchronicity promotes the kind of religious attitude that Jung sees as the only effective means of opposing or counterbalancing mass-mindedness. This is religion not as a 'creed' or 'definite collective belief' but as a 'subjective relationship to certain metaphysical, extramundane factors' (1957: par. 507). Earlier in the chapter we detailed the principal ways in which synchronicity supports precisely such an attitude (see pp. 131–5).

Jung also appeals to synchronicity when discussing the dangerous social consequences stemming from the split between science and religion or their respective domains of matter and spirit. In the revision of 'Psychological Aspects of the Mother Archetype' (1938/1954) he reflects on the significance of the newly pronounced Dogma of the Assumption of the Blessed Virgin (1950). He notes that its declaration 'comes at a time [the early years of the Cold War] when the achievements of science and technology, combined with a rationalistic and materialistic view of the world, threaten the spiritual and psychic heritage of man with instant annihilation [from the use of nuclear weapons]' (ibid.: par. 195). Viewed from a psychological angle, the dogma of the Assumption – the taking of the Virgin bodily into heaven – can be interpreted as an optimistic sign. For the Virgin can be viewed as an instance of the mother archetype and, states Jung, the relationship to the earth and to matter is one of the inalienable qualities of the mother archetype. So that when a figure that is conditioned by this archetype is represented as having been taken up into heaven, the realm of the spirit, this indicates a union of earth and heaven, or of matter and spirit.

(Jung 1938/1954: par. 195)

Synchronicity is doubly relevant to Jung's analysis here. On the one hand, the declaration of the dogma is synchronistic in the sense that it symbolises the union of matter and spirit, which is precisely what is effected by synchronicity. The taking of the Virgin bodily into heaven symbolises a condition in which '[m]atter . . . would contain the seed of spirit and spirit the seed of matter', writes Jung, adding that '[t]he long-known "synchronistic" phenomena . . . point, to all appearances, in this direction' (ibid.). On the other hand, the declaration of the dogma is synchronistic in the sense that it is timely: 'The dogma of the Assumption, proclaimed in an age suffering from the greatest political schism the world has ever known, is a compensating symptom that reflects the strivings of science for a unifying world picture' (ibid.: 197). This is an instance of Jung's theory of synchronicity providing the basis for an acausal reading of historical and contemporary events. Thus, synchronicity is socially significant here in two senses: first, it is a form of experience that reverses the historical process according to which 'the symbolical unity of spirit and matter fell apart, with the result that modern man finds himself uprooted and alienated in a de-souled world' (ibid.); and second, it provides a framework for understanding the manner in which symbols compensating social crises may emerge into both private and public consciousness.

As well as supporting Jung's critiques of science and religion and contributing to a healing of the split between matter and spirit, synchronicity underpins some of the qualities intrinsic to the kind of individuality that Jung champions against mass-mindedness. For Jung, the character of reality as a whole is not statistical but individual: 'the real picture', he writes, 'consists of nothing but exceptions to the rule, . . . absolute reality has predominantly the character of *irregularity*' (1957: par. 494). The individual person, in particular, is a 'relative exception and an irregular phenomenon' characterised not by the universal but by the unique (ibid.: par. 495). Unequivocally, for Jung, '[t]he individual . . . , as an irrational datum, is the true and authentic carrier of reality' (ibid.: par. 498). Synchronistic events are precisely this: exceptions to the rule, irregular, unique, irrational. In providing a theory that brings such events into view and values them, Jung is implicitly championing the individual as 'the true and authentic carrier of reality' in opposition to the forces of mass-mindedness that threaten to rob the individual of his 'foundations and dignity'. Further qualities threatened by mass-mindedness, but characteristic of the life of the individual, include meaningfulness (ibid.: pars. 501, 503, 587), freedom (ibid.: par. 509; 1958b: par. 718), and autonomy (1957: pars. 509, 529). In a climate where it is all too easy to disbelieve in the reality of these qualities, the theory of synchronicity vigorously affirms them. Writes

Jung: '*Meaning arises not from causality but from freedom, i.e., acausality* [synchronicity]' (1958a: par. 1187; emphasis in original). The related quality of creativity, also much valued by Jung, is similarly affirmed insofar as 'synchronicity represents a *direct act of creation* which manifests itself as chance' (1950–5: par. 1198; emphasis in original).

However, the concept of synchronicity not only valorises the special qualities of the individual but also accounts for how the individual may be connected to society in a way that entails the highest degree of social responsibility. Throughout his mature writings, Jung is consistent in stressing that the only way to bring about genuine and lasting change in society is by bringing about change in the individuals who compose that society. He writes, for example, that '*Resistance to the organized mass can be effected only by the man who is as well organized in his individuality as the mass itself*' (1957: par. 540; emphasis in original). The development and practice of analytical psychology, with its core process of individuation, is the way in which he hoped to foster well-organised individuality and so contribute to genuine change and effective resistance to mass-mindedness. However, the beneficial effect of the individuated person on society does not stem solely from ordinary social and cultural contacts. The means of influence is also subtler and more mysterious than this. Jung attempts to explain it in terms of 'the helpful medieval view that man is a microcosm, a reflection of the great cosmos in miniature' (ibid.). This view, it will be recalled, is also one of the 'forerunners of the idea of synchronicity' discussed by Jung in his 1952 essay. In the present context, he expands as follows:

> Not only is the image of the macrocosm imprinted upon [the individual's] psychic nature, but he also creates this image for himself on an ever-widening scale. He bears this cosmic 'correspondence' within him by virtue of his reflecting consciousness on the one hand, and, on the other, thanks to the hereditary, archetypal nature of his instincts, which bind him to his environment.
>
> (Jung 1957: par. 540)

From this perspective, Jung can write that '[i]ndividuation does not shut one out from the world, but gathers the world to oneself' (1947/1954: par. 432). For 'the collective unconscious is anything but an incapsulated personal system; it is sheer objectivity, as wide as the world and open to all the world' (1954a: par. 46). If, when individuating, one seems at times to be lost in oneself, that is because 'this self is the world, if only a consciousness could see it' (ibid.). In other words, it is part of 'the peculiar nature of the self' that it 'embraces the individual as well as society' (1958b: par. 660). Jung elaborates on this insight and states its important connection with synchronicity:

> As experience shows, the archetypes possess the quality of 'transgressivity'; they can sometimes manifest themselves in such a way that they seem to

belong as much to society as to the individual; they are therefore numinous and contagious in their effects . . . In certain cases this transgressiveness also produces meaningful coincidences, i.e., acausal, synchronistic phenomena, such as the results of Rhine's ESP experiments.

(Jung 1958b: par. 660)

Hence, 'anyone who has insight into his own actions, and has thus found access to the unconscious, involuntarily exercises an influence on his environment' (1957: par. 583).

This outlook has far-reaching ethical implications, for it implies that the psychic states of one person, whether positive or negative, can synchronistically affect the states of others. Jung suggests, for example, that 'the synchronicity factor must be taken into account in considering conscience' (1958c: pars. 849–50). Similarly, Aziz notes that adverse events in the outer world can sometimes be understood as 'synchronistic shadow intrusions' – synchronistic outer manifestations of darker unacknowledged aspects of our psyches. He argues that awareness of this dynamic can act as a check on moral scapegoating (1990: 193–200). Considerations such as these make our responsibility for our psychic states more serious, not just when we are in the company of others but even when in solitude.

Jung pursues the insight even further in a letter to Miguel Serrano (14 September 1960), again with specific reference to pressing social concerns. He expresses the wish for a 'renewed self-understanding of man', which, rather than traditional religion, might provide 'an efficacious answer to the world situation' with its continuing threat of 'mental epidemics and war' (1976: 594). He considers that this renewal 'unavoidably has to begin with the individual' (ibid.) and acknowledges that it would likely take centuries before 'the general mind' underwent any noticeable change. However, he bids the individual take heart:

whoever is capable of such insight, no matter how isolated he is, should be aware of the law of synchronicity. As the old Chinese saying goes: 'The right man sitting in his house and thinking the right thought will be heard 100 miles away.'

Neither propaganda nor exhibitionist confessions are needed. If the archetype, which is universal, i.e., identical with itself always and anywhere, is properly dealt with in one place only, it is influenced as a whole, i.e., simultaneously and everywhere.

(Jung 1976: 595)

Jung's favourite example of this 'law of synchronicity' at work is the story Richard Wilhelm told him about the rainmaker of Kiaochau. Jung recounts the story as 'an example of "being in Tao" and its synchronistic accompaniments' (1955–6: par. 604 n. 211). When Wilhelm was in China there was a great drought where he was living. The locals, having tried unsuccessfully to encourage rain by every kind of prayer and ritual, eventually called for the rainmaker from another province. The rainmaker, a 'dried up old man', duly appeared and sequestered himself in a little house for three days. On the fourth day, there was a heavy, unseasonable snowstorm. When Wilhelm asked the rainmaker how he had made it snow, the old man replied that he had not. In response to Wilhelm's further questioning, he explained what had happened:

> 'I come from another country where things are in order. Here they are out of order, they are not as they should be by the ordinance of heaven. Therefore the whole country is not in Tao, and I also am not in the natural order of things because I am in a disordered country. So I had to wait three days until I was back in Tao and then naturally the rain came.'
> (Jung 1955–6: par. 604 n. 211; cf. 1930–4: 333; 1934–9: 824–5)

As this story vividly suggests, individuation or the process of self-realisation is significant not just for the individual undergoing it but for the society and shared environment in which that individual exists. Nor does an individuating person affect others and the environment only through ordinary social and environmental action. By virtue of the simultaneously individual and social nature of the self and the microcosmic relationship of the individual to the macrocosm of the world, beneficial 'effects' can also come about acausally or synchronistically. This all demands an important qualification to Homans's assertion that 'the collective unconscious . . . is entirely psychical, not social' and that '[t]he end point of individuation is a pure and intensely privatized self, liberated from all obligation imposed from without by the social order' (1979/1995: 143). Although the collective unconscious is not constructed socially, its field of influence inescapably includes society; and although the individuating person's obligations are not imposed directly from the outer, social order, they emerge inwardly partly as a response to and in a form that encompasses the outer, social and indeed environmental order.

It appears that Jung viewed his own life's work in this manner from at least as early as 1914. In *Memories, Dreams, Reflections*, he describes a series of disturbing visions he had between October 1913 and August 1914. He saw monstrous floods across Europe, civilisation reduced to rubble, and thousands of drowned bodies; then the sea turning to blood (1963: 169–70). He had a thrice-repeated dream of the land frozen in summer beneath an Arctic cold wave, though on the third occurrence he saw himself plucking grapes 'full of healing juices' from a tree and giving them to 'a large waiting crowd' (ibid.: 170). At first he suspected that the images related solely to himself and indicated an emerging psychosis (ibid.). However, when the First World War broke out in August 1914, he came to suspect a more collective and social significance: 'Now my task was clear', he writes: 'I had to try to understand what had happened and to what extent my own experience coincided with that of mankind in general. Therefore my first obligation was to probe the depths of my own psyche' (ibid.).

Alien, subversive and prescient

From the preceding account it is clear that an appreciation of synchronicity is essential for understanding not just how Jung theorised about his psychology but also how he applied it. It is clear, too, that he saw synchronicity, for all its redolence of the esoteric and mystical, as profoundly relevant to outer social and cultural concerns. Much recent work in analytical psychology has been concerned with exploring the potential socio-cultural relevance of Jung's legacy of ideas (see, e.g., Samuels 1993, 2001; Adams 1996; Papadopoulos 1997a, 1998; Rowland 1999, 2002; Hauke 2000). Usually, these explorations have involved updating Jung's thought and connecting it with contemporary discourses that enjoy wider acceptance and respect. What the preceding discussion of synchronicity helps to demonstrate is that these kinds of social and cultural application of analytical psychology are wholly consonant with Jung's own aims as pursued even in his seemingly most esoteric texts. At first glance, perhaps none of Jung's psychological concepts seems to promise less for social and cultural thought than does the concept of synchronicity, with its abstruse sources and seemingly regressive claims about the nature of reality. Yet our study has revealed that precisely this alien and subversive character is what fits synchronicity to underpin Jung's radical critique of the scientism, soullessness, and authoritarianism of modern western culture, as he perceived it.

Although our concern has been with describing rather than evaluating Jung's critique, we can briefly note that in some of his criticisms he has arguably been prescient. For example, much of his criticism of scientific rationalism has later been echoed by postmodernists (see Hauke 2000), and his dissatisfaction with the dominance of quantitative scientific methods has been shared by many recent researchers who have therefore turned their attention to developing increasingly sophisticated qualitative methods (see Silverman 1997). Most notably, however, Jung seems to have prefigured the role that experiential religion would come to play in some forms of cultural criticism, as we shall discuss in the following chapter.

Chapter 6

Synchronicity and the spiritual revolution

Having seen that the theory of synchronicity is an integral, even pivotal, part of Jung's critique of science, religion and society we will now look in more detail at some aspects of his critique of religion. Of the three areas previously discussed, this arguably is the one that concerned Jung most intimately. It is also the area that contains most of the positive content of his overall cultural critique. For, while his main task in relation to rationalistic science and mass society was to seek ways to undercut their power, his task in relation to experientially based religion was to seek means of validating it. Experiential religion was for Jung a large part of the antidote to the modern problems spawned by rationalistic science and mass society. Furthermore, Jung's critique of religion, more than his critiques of science and society, continues to have conspicuous relevance in contemporary culture. Above all, both as an influence and as an exemplary or parallel instance, it is relevant to the increasing interest in holistic, alternative, or 'New Age' forms of spirituality.

A widespread shift away from traditional religion towards detraditionalised forms of spirituality has been monitored and discussed by sociologists and historians of religion (York 1995; Heelas 1996, 2002; Hanegraaff 1998, 2002) and has recently been dubbed 'the spiritual revolution' (Heelas 2002; cf. Tacey 2003). This 'spiritual revolution' is not one that threatens to overthrow existing social or even religious structures but, like the counter-cultural movement of the 1960s, is nevertheless significantly affecting mainstream culture in a continual dialectic of challenge and assimilation. The distinction between religion, which people are allegedly turning away from, and spirituality, which they are allegedly turning towards, is explained by Paul Heelas as follows: ' "Religion" can be defined in terms of obedience to a transcendent God and a tradition which mediates his authority; *spirituality* as experience of the divine as immanent in life' (2002: 358). He then characterises the widespread contemporary understanding of both terms:

'Religion' is . . . very much God-centred [and], especially since the 1960s, has increasingly come to be seen as that which is institutionalized: involving prescribed rituals; established ways of believing; the 'official', as regulated and transmitted by religious authorities; that which is enshrined in tradition;

the ethical commandments of sacred texts; the voice of the authority of the transcendent. For many, it has come to be associated with the formal, dogmatic and hierarchical, if not the impersonal or patriarchal.

. . . 'Spirituality' has to do with the personal; that which is interior or immanent; that which is one's experienced relationship with the sacred; and that wisdom or knowledge which derives from such experiences. At heart, spirituality has come to mean 'life' . . . Life, rather than what transcends life, becomes God (thus contemporary spirituality may more precisely be termed 'spirituality of life').[1]

(Heelas 2002: 358–9)

The distinction here between 'religion' and 'spirituality' is practically identical to Jung's distinction between 'creed' and 'religion'. (In the discussions that follow, therefore, we need to be aware that when Jung refers to 'religion' and 'religious', he generally means the same as Heelas would mean by 'spirit' and 'spiritual'. The context should always make this clear.) Heelas suggests that traditional religion is giving way less to secularity than to this kind of spirituality (ibid.). The most conspicuous form of such spirituality is what is popularly known as New Age spirituality, and it is with this that the present chapter will primarily be concerned. However, it should be noted that a turn to spirituality as characterised above is also discernible within some forms of traditional, institutionalised religion, such as Evangelical, Pentecostal, or Charismatic Christianity (ibid.: 366–9). These 'theistic spiritualities of life' (ibid.: 366) retain 'a (relatively) traditionalized Christian frame of reference' but also emphasise 'the immediate and experienced authority of the empowering and life-transforming Holy Spirit, by-passing tradition by virtue of its transmission by way of personal experience' (ibid.: 369). Heelas suggests that it is largely because of their emphasis on spirituality that these religions are thriving (ibid.: 366).[2] Finally, it should also be noted that the emphasis on spirituality is by no means shared by all of the New Religious Movements that have appeared during the same period as the New Age Movement and are often popularly associated with it. Many of these New Religious Movements remain highly traditionalised without any notable turn to spirituality (ibid.: 362).

In the following, we will consider some ways in which Jung's psychological model and theory of synchronicity relate to this spiritual revolution. First, we will look at how the concept of synchronicity can illuminate a range of traditional religious concepts and concerns in a manner that helps to de-traditionalise them. Then, we will look at some of the major connections between Jung's thought and New Age spirituality.

Synchronicity and the illumination of religion

We noted in the previous chapter the general significance of synchronicity as a form of religious or spiritual experience, and can now expand on the particular ways in which this is so. Elsewhere, I have shown connections between synchronicity and traditional spiritual concepts independently of the assumptions of Jung's specific psychological model (Main 2001). Here I will focus on some of the connections that can be found in or readily inferred from Jung's own work. Explicitly, he appealed to synchronicity in addressing such perennial religious concerns as miracles, the possibility of surviving death, and the nature and transformation of conceptions of God. Implicitly, the theory of synchronicity also informed his thinking on mystical unity, self-realisation and the meaning of life.

Miraculousness

Synchronicities could be accounted miracles because the meaningful acausal co-ordination of their component events seems to transgress the usual limitations of what is considered psychophysically possible (see Holland 1967; Polkinghorne 1998: 85). Jung sometimes specifically refers to synchronistic events as miracles, though it is clear that he does so only in a loose way without any expectation of having to provide theological backing for his usage (1952b: par. 848; 1976: 46, 537, 539). Moreover, he is generally quick to re-describe the putative miracle scientifically in terms of either parapsychological findings (1951b: par. 995) or the statistical character of natural law (1976: 540). Occasionally, however, he does address the issue of traditionally designated religious miracles and on these occasions sometimes refers to synchronicity. Thus, speaking of the identity of Christ the 'empirical man' with 'the traditional Son of Man type', he says: 'Wherever such identities occur, characteristic archetypal effects appear, that is *numinosity* and *synchronistic phenomena*, hence tales of miracles are inseparable from the Christ figure' (ibid.: 21; cf. 1952a: par. 648). At other times he invokes synchronicity to help account for miracle cures that cannot be satisfactorily explained in other ways (1976: 498–500). Other times again, he suggests that explanations for apparent miracles, such as the case of Brother Klaus living twenty years without material sustenance, should be sought more specifically in the realm of parapsychology and mediumistic phenomena (1950/1951: pars. 1497–8). Even here, however, the implication is that the sustained paranormal phenomena constituting the miracle are synchronistic archetypal 'effects' rendered possible by the maintaining of a numinous religious attitude (cf. Jung 1976: 576).

Mystical unity

The intimate non-causal connection that can be experienced between the outer physical world and one's inner subjectivity implies that the separateness usually experienced between inner and outer, psychic and physical, or self and world can to a significant degree be dissolved. Further, the sense of unity can be experienced as existing not just between the psychic and the physical but between the psychophysical as a whole and a transcendent, spiritual, or divine aspect of reality.

Thus, Jung's visionary experiences of union, which attended his near-fatal illness in 1944, though they do not involve outer physical events and so do not fit Jung's commonest definition of synchronicity, nonetheless can be understood in the light of synchronicity. These experiences are recalled in detail in *Memories, Dreams, Reflections* (1963: 270–7). A shorter account, written just a few months after the experiences, appears in a letter to Kristine Mann (1 February 1945):

> I found myself 15,000 km. from the earth and I saw it as an immense globe resplendent in an inexpressibly beautiful blue light. I was on a point exactly above the southern end of India, which shone in a bluish silvery light with Ceylon like a shimmering opal in the deep blue sea. I was in the universe, where there was a big solitary rock containing a temple. I saw its entrance illuminated by a thousand small flames of coconut oil. I knew I was to enter the temple and I would reach full knowledge. But at this moment a messenger from the world (which by then was a very insignificant corner of the universe) arrived and said that I was not allowed to depart and at this moment the whole vision collapsed completely. But from then on for three weeks I slept, and was wakeful each night in the universe and experienced the complete vision. Not I was united with somebody or something – *it* was united, *it* was the *hierosgamos*, the mystic Agnus. It was a silent invisible festival permeated by an incomparable, indescribable feeling of eternal bliss, such as I never could have imagined as being within reach of human experience.
>
> (Jung 1973: 357–8)

In his fuller account of the vision, Jung characterises it in terms of 'a quality of absolute objectivity' and of 'a non-temporal state in which present, past, and future are one' (1963: 275). This characterisation clearly reflects the 'absolute knowledge' and 'space–time relativity' involved in synchronicities. Further, his sense of his visions as representing a kind of mystic marriage between self and world – the *hierosgamos* or *mysterium coniunctionis* (ibid.: 274–5) – suggests that they may constitute an experiential realisation of the unitary dimension of existence (the *unus mundus*) towards which he considered the more familiar forms of synchronicity to be pointing (see 1955–6: pars. 662, 767–9). It recalls his earlier characterisation of 'The realization of Tao' with its quality of 'being in a sort of synchronistic relation with everything else; . . . that is the general mystical experience, the coincidence of the individual condition with the universe, so that the two become indistinguishable' (1930–4: 608).

Self-realisation/transformation

As discussed in Chapter 1, Jung's understanding of the meaning of synchronicity is bound up with his overall understanding of the process of psychological transformation. Synchronistic experiences are meaningful largely because they promote individuation and increased realisation of the self. Since for Jung the archetype of the self is functionally equivalent to the archetype of God, at least in terms of its expressions in consciousness, it is clear that individuation is envisaged as a fundamentally religious or spiritual process. Therefore, insofar as synchronicity promotes individuation, it also is part of a process of spiritual transformation and self-realisation.

Life after death

Jung considered that synchronicity has implications for the question of possible life after death. For epistemological reasons, he does not think one can actually prove that there is survival of death, but he considers it significant that the unconscious psyches of people approaching death generally present dreams and other spontaneous imagery which imply an expected continuity (1934b: pars. 809–10; 1963: 278–80). The hint provided by this is supported by two different aspects of synchronicity. On a general level, Jung argues that the space–time relativisation involved in synchronicity implies that the psyche 'touches on a form of existence outside time and space' (1934b: par. 814; cf. 1976: 561; 1963: 282–3). Although we do not know in detail what 'existence outside time and space' is like, we can at least infer that it is 'outside change' (1976: 561) and 'partakes of what is inadequately and symbolically described as "eternity"' (1934b: par. 815) – grounds for supposing that it may not end with the death of the body. More concretely, Jung considers that certain synchronistic phenomena that occur in relation to death – veridical dreams and apparitions, for instance – can express the idea of survival also in terms of their content (1963: 289–92; see also von Franz 1987). His own most striking example occurred after the death of a friend. During the night after the funeral, Jung was lying awake thinking of his friend when suddenly he had the sense that his friend was in the room and was beckoning Jung to follow him. Although questioning the reality of what he was experiencing, Jung decided to give the apparition the benefit of the doubt and followed it in his imagination. He was led out of his own house, along the street, and into his friend's house, where, in the study, his friend indicated to him the second of five books with red bindings that stood on the second shelf from the top. Intrigued, Jung visited his friend's widow the following day and asked if he could look up something in the study. There, in the same high place as in the dream, he saw the book that had been indicated to him. The title was not legible without climbing up on a stool. When he did, he saw that the book was a translation of a novel by Émile Zola: *The Legacy of the Dead* (1963: 289–90).

Images of God

Jung devoted a considerable amount of research and reflection to the question of why, how, and when traditional images of God undergo transformation (Jung 1938/1940, 1942/1948, 1951a, 1952a). His notion of synchronicity played a part in this in at least two important ways. First, Jung maintained that any major transformation of the culturally dominant God image, such as he believed had occurred at the beginning of the Christian era and in the late Middle Ages and was again occurring at the present time, was expressive of a shift in the arche-types dominant in the collective unconscious. Such an archetypal shift could be accompanied by synchronistic events on a collective scale. Thus, he noted the coincidence of religious innovations and transformations in widely separated geographical areas, the concurrence of these with the emergence of specific cultural symbols, and the paralleling of these symbols with seemingly independent astrological events (1951a: pars. 140, 233, 287; 1963: 210). Second, Jung pre-sented the emergence of the theory of synchronicity itself as part of a move towards a more integral relationship between the spiritual and material domains. Thus, synchronicity supplies the missing fourth to the incomplete triad of classical physical concepts (space, time and causality) and thereby connects matter with the realm of psyche and spirit (Stein 1985: 170). This can be understood as the complement of the process whereby matter, evil, or the feminine provides the missing fourth to the incomplete Trinity of traditional Christian religion and thereby, among other things, connects spirit to the realm of matter (Jung 1942/ 1948, 1951a).

Jung's proposal concerning transformations of the God-image has provoked some of the most vigorous criticism of his psychology of religion from theolo-gians. It is therefore worth noting some interesting parallels between Jung's notion of synchronicity and a recent attempt to reconceptualise God by the Harvard theologian Gordon Kaufman. Kaufman argues (2001a, 2001b) that traditional conceptions of God as creator, lord and father are no longer intelligible in the light of contemporary scientific understandings in cosmology and evolutionary theory. For instance, since the conditions necessary for the emergence of persons are a very late evolutionary development, it becomes implausible to think of a personal being as the agent of creation (2001a: 411). Kaufman proposes instead that we think of God as 'serendipitous creativity'. Creativity, 'the coming into being through time of the previously non-existent, the new, the novel' (ibid.), is, for Kaufman, 'very close to being a synonym of the concept of mystery' (ibid.: 412). Unlike the notion of a creator, creativity does not presuppose the existence of a force or agent responsible for what comes into being: 'Creativity *happens*: this is an absolutely amazing mystery' (ibid.). Unlike personality, creativity, in the sense understood by Kaufman, must have existed throughout the cosmological and evolutionary development of the universe. Such creativity is serendipitous both in that 'more [happens] than one would have expected, given previously prevailing circumstances, indeed, more than might have seemed possible' (ibid.: 412, quoting from Kaufman's own earlier work) and in that it is beneficial for us, at least within 'the specific *trajectory* . . . of the cosmic evolutionary process that produced us humans' (ibid.: 414–15).

Kaufman presents a plausible account of how thinking of God as serendipitous creativity still enables one to address such traditional theological themes as the problem of evil and 'God is love' (2001a: 416–21). He notes that it implies a '*decisive qualitative distinction* (though not an ontological separation) between God and the created order' (ibid.: 423), a less immediate relation of humans to God (ibid.: 422), and greater human responsibility (ibid.: 422–3). It also, he suggests, provides possibilities for greater dialogue between western and East Asian religious traditions (ibid.: 414). Thinking of God as serendipitous creativity is, in other words, a notion that can claim a serious place in current theological debates.

The parallels between Kaufman's notion and Jung's concept of synchronicity are suggestive. Kaufman's insistence that creativity should be conceived in such a way that no force, not even an impersonal force, is assumed to be responsible for it (2001a: 412) resembles Jung's insistence that synchronicity is truly acausal: synchronistic events, like creative events, mysteriously just happen. Kaufman's characterisation of serendipity as implying that more happens than would have been expected or seemed possible reflects Jung's characterisation of synchronistic events as being both improbable (unexpected) and acausal (seemingly impossible). When Kaufman elaborates that creativity is also serendipitous in the sense that it is beneficial for us, though not necessarily for our self-centred aims, we are put in mind of Jung's characterisation of synchronistic events as meaningful in the sense of promoting individuation, a process that furthers the aims of the self rather than of the ego. Again, when Kaufman asserts that the mystery of God as creativity should not be compromised by claims to special experiences or revelations of God, there is a parallel with Jung's assertion that the archetypes manifesting within synchronistic events are themselves utterly unknowable. Finally, not the least important similarity between Kaufman's conception and Jung's is that both have evidently emerged as attempts to rethink religion in the face of challenges from contemporary science.

The meaning of life

Synchronicity also played a pivotal role in some of Jung's speculations concerning the ultimate meaning of human life. That meaning, according to Jung's 'explanatory myth' (1963: 371), consists in the task of increasing consciousness. This in turn entails reconciling, in the unity and wholeness of the self, the unavoidable internal contradictions in the image of the Creator-god (ibid.). 'That is the goal,' he writes in the chapter in *Memories, Dreams, Reflections* entitled 'Late Thoughts', 'or one goal, which fits man meaningfully into the scheme of creation, and at the same time confers meaning upon it' (ibid.). As noted in the previous sub-section, synchronicity is not only one of the processes by which greater unity of the God-image comes about – through disclosing reconciling symbols both intrapsychically and outwardly – but itself is also, as a 'world-constituting factor' (1952b: par. 964) that has not yet been integrated into the dominant western world-view, one of the contradictory elements that needs to be reconciled.

Reflecting on the slow process of biological development, Jung considers it improbable that the 'extremely indirect methods of creation, which squander millions of years upon the development of countless species and creatures, are the outcome of purposeful intention' (1963: 371). However, the situation changes with the emergence of the human mind: 'Here the miracle of reflecting consciousness intervenes – the second cosmogony' (ibid.). He continues:

> The importance of consciousness is so great that one cannot help suspecting the element of *meaning* to be concealed somewhere within all the monstrous, apparently senseless biological turmoil, and that the road to its manifestation was ultimately found on the level of warm-blooded vertebrates possessed of a differentiated brain – found as if by chance, unintended and unforeseen, and yet somehow sensed, felt and groped for out of some dark urge.
>
> (Jung 1963: 371–2)

In a letter to Erich Neumann (10 March) 1959, Jung elaborates on how this 'miracle of reflecting consciousness' may have come about:

> It staggers the mind even to begin to imagine the accidents and hazards that, over millions of years, transformed a lemurlike tree-dweller into a man. In this chaos of chance, synchronistic phenomena were probably at work, operating both with and against the known laws of nature to produce, in archetypal moments, syntheses which appear to us miraculous. Causality and teleology fail us here, because synchronistic phenomena manifest themselves as pure chance. The essential thing about these phenomena is that an objective event coincides meaningfully with a psychic process: that is to say, a physical event and an endopsychic one have a common meaning. This presupposes not only an all-pervading, latent meaning which can be recognized by consciousness, but, during that preconscious time, a psychoid process with which a physical event meaningfully coincides.
>
> (Jung 1976: 494–5; cf. Kaufman 2001a: 412)

Most forthrightly and grandly, Jung states that '[s]ince a creation without the reflecting consciousness of man has no discernible meaning, the hypothesis of a latent meaning endows man with a cosmogonic significance, a true *raison d'être*' (1976: 495). The importance of synchronistic experiences here is that '[t]hey point to a latent meaning which is independent of consciousness' (ibid.). In doing this, synchronistic experiences themselves point towards humanity's cosmogonic significance and *raison d'être*.

De-traditionalised spirituality

The above examples indicate how the notion of synchronicity contributed, sometimes explicitly and sometimes implicitly, to Jung's thinking about a range of traditional religious concepts and themes. Because it does so with reference to experiences rather than beliefs and dogmas, the concepts and themes are largely disembedded from traditional contexts. It becomes possible to think of miracles, mystical unity, spiritual transformation, life after death, images of God, and the meaning of life in a manner less dependent on traditional assumptions. Synchronicity thus supports the trend of the spiritual revolution towards an increasing de-traditionalisation of religion. This said, it does not necessitate de-traditionalisation, and traditional religions could readily co-opt the Jungian evidence and insights to support their own positions. However, in doing so, they would be reaching into an experiential space that is equally accessible to other religious traditions as well as to non-religious orientations – a relatively neutral ground that might be conducive to inter-religious relations and dialogues between religion and science. Providing this resource is another of the ways in which synchronicity may be able to contribute to the transformation of contemporary religion.

Synchronicity and New Age spirituality

Analytical psychology has been related to many forms of non-institutional, de-traditionalised, and implicit spirituality (see, e.g., Corbett 1996; Shorter 1996; Sandner and Wong 1997; Smith 1997; Casement 1998: 11; Young-Eisendrath and Miller 2000; Schlamm 2000, 2001; Samuels 2001: 122–34; Tacey 2001). However, the connections between analytical psychology and the spiritual revolution, and especially between synchronicity and the spiritual revolution, are clearest in the case of New Age spirituality. We can approach these connections by illustrating the extent to which New Age spirituality, like analytical psychology and the theory of synchronicity, emerged as a response to tensions between traditional religion and modern science.

Religion, science and the New Age

In Chapter 4 we noted that the complex interactions between religion and science provide one of the major contexts within which we can understand late twentieth-century and early twenty-first-century manifestations of religion. Most of the implications that we mentioned there concerned the more public, institutionalised forms of religion. However, the interactions between religion and science are no less important for the more private, often non-affiliated forms of contemporary spirituality, which for convenience I am calling 'New Age spirituality'. There is a great deal of controversy about the use of the phrase 'New Age'. Many of those to whose beliefs and practices it is applied repudiate it, insisting that the New Age needs to be clearly distinguished from Wicca, neo-paganism, and other new or revived religious movements with which it tends to be conflated. Others who formerly embraced the label 'New Age' now prefer such alternative descriptions as 'holistic spirituality' (e.g., Bloom 2003). Again, it is possible to distinguish between a strict sense and a wider sense of the phrase 'New Age' – the former referring to 'the movement born in the context of the post-Second World War UFO cults and flowering in the spiritual utopianism of the 1960s and 1970s', the latter to 'the general "cultic milieu" of alternative religion which flourished after the 1970s and has become increasingly "mainstream" since' (Hanegraaff 2002: 261). In the following discussion I use the phrase in the wider sense as an umbrella term that includes neo-paganism, Wicca and other differentiated categories within contemporary alternative spirituality. When the need arises later in the chapter I will introduce and discuss a more precise and detailed definition.

First, in order to bring this topic into focus as well as to prepare the ground for the comparison with Jung's theories later in the chapter, we will look at a number of salient features of New Age spirituality and consider how they may relate to interactions between traditional religion and modern science. To anticipate, we will find that many features of the New Age stem from the same kind of tension between religion and science as gave rise to synchronicity. In other words, in at least some important respects, synchronicity and the New Age arose from similar historical and cultural contexts. The list of features that we will discuss is not meant to be either definitive or exhaustive but simply useful for the purposes of this study.

Ambivalence towards science

Overall, the New Age is ambivalent towards modern science. On the one hand, there is sharp criticism of the rationalising and reductive tendencies of modern science and a corresponding celebration of whatever promotes a more intuitive and spiritually uplifting outlook. As Heelas observes: 'the New Age is largely opposed to the rational outlook of the philosopher and the verificationist approach of the scientist, rejecting "the head" in favour of "the heart" and relying on "intuition" or "inner wisdom"' (1996: 5). On the other hand, there are scientists who have been specially adopted by the New Age because the emphasis of their work seems to support some of the underlying holistic assumptions of New Age spirituality: Fritjof Capra (1976), David Bohm (1980) and Rupert Sheldrake (1981) are prominent examples. We could formulate this ambivalence by saying that, in general, *New Agers react against the reductive tendencies of modern science while at the same time selectively appropriating ideas from modern science*. Sometimes, as in the cases of Bohm and Sheldrake, the New Age-friendly features of their work reflect or build on areas of genuine uncertainty and ambivalence within science itself. At other times, images of the development and present state of religion, science, and their relationship are elaborated with little regard for the realities and complexities of history. The historians of science John Brooke and Geoffrey Cantor have taken Capra to task on this point in their essay 'Against the Self-Images of the New Age' (1998: 75–105). Even more commonly, New Agers speak and write about science, whether drawing on or denigrating it, with very little understanding of actual scientific theories or methodologies (York 1995: 52).

Psycho-spiritual transformation

Another salient feature of the New Age is its *interest in psycho-spiritual trans-formation*. Michael York goes so far as to suggest that 'What unites all New Agers ... is the vision of radical mystical transformation on both the personal and collective levels' (1995: 39). This interest in transformation may relate to interactions between religion and science in several ways. For instance, the transformation is often promoted by application of spiritual techniques that, as Robert Wuthnow notes, 'bear the distinctive imprint of the prevailing technological worldview' (1985: 46). As well as providing the means of psycho-spiritual transformation (or at least the rhetoric for enhancing the attractiveness of these means), science ironically has also been largely responsible for the mindset from which New Agers seek transformative liberation. Heelas characterises the transformation that New Agers seek as an attempt to liberate the Self through letting go of 'ego-attachments' (1996: 20). These ego-attachments include the ways in which a person internalises and conforms to social standards, but they may also more specifically refer to the kind of rational modes of thought involved in science (ibid.: 36). Again, New Age interest in psycho-spiritual transformation may, in some cases, be an attempt to claim for personal spirituality a potential for the kind of 'progress' and 'evolution' vaunted by science (Wilber 1998). Observes Heelas: 'Modernity, in many respects, has to do with evolutionary notions of perfectibility . . . . The New Age belongs to modernity in that it is progressivistic . . . . [O]ne can go on *events*, to change for the *better*' (1996: 169).

Modernisation, secularisation and globalisation

At a general level, we can see New Age spirituality, like other twentieth-century manifestations of religion, as *a response (or set of responses) to modernisation, secularisation and globalisation*. There is much debate about the range and kind of influence these processes have had on contemporary religion as well as about the connections among them (see Berger 2002; Lehmann 2002), and it would certainly be problematic to claim that modern science has straightforwardly caused the processes. For instance, as Brooke notes with reference to secularisation:

> The replacement of spiritual by material values would seem to owe more to the security of modern medicine, to the seduction of urban comforts and economic prosperity than to any scientific imperative. And insofar as the social functions once performed by religion have been taken over by secular groups and institutions, it is to their social and political origins one must look for insights into the redistribution of power.
>
> (Brooke 1991: 340)

Nevertheless, as we shall see, modernisation, secularisation and globalisation undoubtedly have contributed enormously to the milieu in which contemporary religions, and especially New Age spirituality, exist in the West, and the processes would be extremely unlikely to have occurred without modern science.

Primarily, the New Age has responded to – indeed has defined itself in relation to – these tendencies by resisting them. As Heelas notes, 'The New Age . . . runs counter to many of the great canons and assumptions of modernity', including 'the faith that has been placed in obtaining progress by way of scientific expertise' (1996: 135–6). Rather than secularisation, Heelas argues, the New Age promotes the reverse process of sacralisation ('making sacred') (ibid.: 106). Michael York concurs that the New Age provides a counterbalance to the rationalism and scientific methodology of modernity (1995: 14). However, Heelas's analysis explores ways in which the New Age not only breaks with but also continues many of the cultural trajectories of modernity (1996: 153–77). He refers to 'those processes – the "fall of public man", the construction of the expressivist self, the internalisation of religion, and so on – which have been completed by the [New Age] Movement' (ibid.: 154). In other words, we need to recognise romantic as well as rationalist currents as constitutive of modernity. While opposing the rationalist currents, the New Age in many ways furthers the romantic currents. As we shall discuss more fully later, Wouter Hanegraaff stresses the complex relationship of the New Age to secularisation throughout his study, as indicated by its subtitle: *New Age Religion and Western Culture: Esotericism in the Mirror of Secular Thought* (1998).

Again, consider globalisation – the increasing worldwide link-up of political, economic and cultural systems. This has accelerated under the impact of scientific and technological developments, particularly in the areas of transport and communications. Globalisation has had various frequently noted effects on traditional religions. In some cases, it has arguably strengthened fundamentalist attitudes as religious groups entrench themselves in an attempt to preserve their beleaguered identities. In other cases, increasing exposure to alternative world-views has resulted in a liberalisation of attitudes and the growth of tolerance, interfaith dialogue, and, for some, a more perennialist outlook (e.g., Wilber 1998). However, globalisation also provides the context for understanding some specific features of the New Age movement. David Spangler, co-director in the 1970s of the New Age community at Findhorn, Scotland, remarked that 'The New Age deals with issues of planetization and the emergence of an awareness that we are all one people living on one world that shares a common destiny' (in York 1995: 35). Other representatives of the New Age express the same sentiment: Marilyn Ferguson speaks of the 'global consciousness' to which the New Age aspires (in ibid.; see Ferguson 1982) and William Bloom notes that one of the major fields comprising the New Age is ecology, which, as York puts it, 'through interdependence and interpenetration, accepts responsibility for the planetary state' (1995: 89).

Non-western, pre-modern and esoteric traditions

Another significant feature of the New Age is *eclectic engagement with non-western, pre-modern and esoteric traditions*. According to York, 'New Age is a blend of pagan religions, Eastern philosophies, and occult-psychic phenomena' (1995: 34). According to Heelas, 'From the detraditionalized stance of the New Age what matters is the "arcane", the "esoteric", the "hidden wisdom", the "inner or secret tradition", the "ageless wisdom"' (1996: 27). These traditions – including Yoga, Taoism, Gnosticism, divination, magic, alchemy and much else – may appeal partly because in them the problematic relationship between religion and science is assumed not to exist as it does in the modern western mainstream. The traditions operate before (pre-modern), distant from (non-western), or in secrecy from (esoteric) the rise of modern science. Accordingly, so it can be argued, they have been able to avoid the catastrophic splitting off of the emotional and intuitive functions that took place in modern western consciousness. We can therefore turn to these traditions in order to reconnect with a more holistic outlook. Here, then, modern science and traditional religion have influenced the New Age by presenting a picture of problematic relations in contrast to which other traditions seem, often unrealistically, more attractive.

Myth

A further, closely related feature is that *New Agers often frame contemporary experience in terms of myth*. Of course, there is a mythical dimension to most if not all religions, traditional and modern (Smart 1997: 10, 130–64). I refer here to the particular salience of myth in New Age spirituality. This is especially the case with neo-paganism. Beliefs and stories about Egyptian, Graeco-Roman and northern European gods and goddesses, among many others, play a major role in neo-pagan rituals and world-views. Above all, the myth of the Great Goddess is invoked both to interpret and to encourage further the rise of feminine consciousness and spirituality, as in Starhawk [Miriam Simos]'s *The Spiral Dance: A Rebirth of the Ancient Religion of the Great Goddess* (1979). New Age uses of myth presuppose that it is not a primitive form of explanation of the physical world now superseded by science. Rather, it is a valid alternative form of cognition, with a different subject matter (the psycho-spiritual rather than the physical world) and a different function (to disclose spiritual meaning rather than to explain physical processes). This revived appeal of myth can be partly accounted for if we consider that myth, because it does not make the same claims to explanatory adequacy as religious doctrines traditionally have, is less vulnerable to direct criticism from science and so can survive better as a container of spiritual meaning (Segal 1999b: 21–35).

Personal experience

Even more salient is that *New Agers generally prioritise personal experience over institutionalised beliefs*. As York observes, 'New Age is a decentralized movement – one built around not doctrines or particular belief systems but an experiential vision' (1995: 39). New Agers would mostly agree with Carl Rogers when he says, 'Experience for me is the highest authority' (1967: 24). New Age appeals to experience may partly be an attempt to appropriate some of the charisma of science, for it is possible to see a loose analogy between experiencing and experimenting, inasmuch as both involve testing things for oneself rather than accepting traditionally sanctioned pronouncements. In any case, the tendency among New Agers is to move beyond socialised beliefs to the authenticity of the inner realm (Heelas 1996: 19). Indeed, New Agers actively work to achieve liberation from social conditioning (ibid.: 25). Largely, this shift from the external and social to the inner and individual can be accounted for in terms of various institutional failures:

> The institutional fabric, whose basic function has always been to provide meaning and stability for the individual, has become incohesive, fragmented and thus progressively deprived of plausibility. Institutions then confront the individual as fluid and unreliable, in the extreme case as unreal. Inevitably, the individual is thrown back upon himself, on his own subjectivity, from which he must dredge up the meaning that he requires to exist.
>
> (Berger *et al.* 1974: 85)

More specifically, many women have felt that the authoritarian and patriarchal structure of the Church is irredeemably obstructive to them; people seeking healing have felt that conventional allotropic medicine fails to respect the wholeness of their personality; and political activists, disillusioned about significantly changing the outer structures of society, have retreated to working at inner change (Heelas 1996: 141–2). This suspicion of and disillusionment with institutions may also stem from an increased awareness of the actual workings of institutions fostered by historical and social scientific analyses.

Authority of the self

Finally, and perhaps most important of all, *New Agers tend to locate spiritual and ethical authority within the individual self*. The prominent New Age teacher Sir George Trevelyan advises his listeners: 'Only accept what rings true to your Inner Self' (reported in Heelas 1996: 21). Starhawk likewise emphasises 'self-responsibility and the individual as final arbiter for the meaning and direction of life' (York 1995: 113). Indeed, Heelas identifies 'Self-spirituality' as *the* defining and unifying feature of the New Age. 'Self-spirituality' involves 'the monistic assumption that the Self itself is sacred' (1996: 2) and an outlook where '[t]he "individual" serves as his or her own source of guidance' (ibid.: 23). According to Heelas, this notion is responsible for a 'remarkable consistency' beneath 'much of the heterogeneity' of the New Age (ibid.: 2). He even proposes that '[t]he New Age shows what "religion" looks like when it is organised in terms of what is taken to be the authority of the Self' (ibid.: 221). This is not to deny that New Agers sometimes recognise other sources of authority besides the inner spiritual self – e.g., more traditional teachers and external systems of thought (ibid.: 34–5) – or that there is a strong social current within the New Age – e.g., in its association with the Green movement (York 1995: 22). However, as Heelas again summarises: 'Overall, the New Age has become more detraditionalized; the shift in emphasis has been from cosmologies to experiences; from beliefs to spiritual technologies; from heeding Mahatmas to heeding the Self' (1996: 67). The influence on this of interactions between religion and science can probably be detected among several of the considerations that have already been mentioned. For emphasis on the self is likely to be encouraged by institutional failure, by the loose equation of experience with experiment, by concern with spiritual meaning rather than physical explanation, by retreat to a domain not so dominated by science (a domain where human subjectivity can better flourish), and by the goal of psycho-spiritual transformation.

Jung and the New Age

Although Jung died before the New Age movement emerged as a distinctive socio-cultural force and, in any case, arguably would have repudiated much of what goes under the New Age banner (Tacey 1999), there are several good reasons for studying his work in relation to New Age spirituality.

Affinities between Jung and the New Age

If we scan the shelves of a New Age or Mind/Body/Spirit section in any major bookshop, we are likely to find not only many books by and on Jung himself but also books on a wide range of subject matter that closely reflects the scope of Jung's interests. We will probably find books on western esotericism, including magic and alchemy; divination, including astrology and the *I Ching*; eastern religions from India and China; indigenous religions of Africa and North America; myths from all over the world; and reinterpretations of Christianity from a mythic or perennialist point of view. There will be books on holistic science and on healing by creative visualisation, by connecting with one's higher self, and by various other kinds of spiritually oriented therapy. Other books will be about paranormal phenomena, including hauntings, communications supposedly channelled from discarnate spirits, and UFOs. Jung, more perhaps than any other twentieth-century thinker, engaged seriously with all these subjects. Such close parallels suggest either influence or common origins and concerns.

In fact, there can be little doubt that in many cases the parallels do represent actual influences. In a survey conducted in the late 1970s, Marilyn Ferguson asked her New Age-inclined subjects to name those who had most influenced them. Among the 185 responses, Jung's name was the second most frequently cited (Ferguson 1982). In a more recent 1994 survey of subscribers to *Kindred Spirit*, the largest-selling New Age magazine in Britain, Stuart Rose asked the same question. Among over 900 responses Jung's name was again the second most frequently cited (Rose 1997). Indeed, Jung's name was the only one to appear among the top ten in both surveys (Heelas 1996: 126). This finding is supported by indications from many other sources. To name a few: the parallels between Jung and the New Age have been considered worthy of special comment by Jungians themselves, such as David Tacey (1999, 2001) who worries that the similarities between Jung and the New Age may obscure their important differences; by biographers such as Frank McLynn (1996) who entitled the penultimate chapter of his life of Jung 'New Age Guru'; by scholars of religion such as Paul Heelas who considers Jung one of '[t]hree key figures' (along with Helena Blavatsky and George Gurdjieff) for understanding the development of the New Age movement (1996: 46–7); and by New Age practitioners such as the Wiccan Vivianne Crowley (1989), who, herself a Jungian-oriented psychotherapist, observes that traditional pagan notions of gods, goddesses and magic can be and frequently are recast as Jungian notions of archetypes and synchronicity.

Again, although Jung rarely, perhaps only once, used the phrase 'New Age' (1973: 285), he frequently drew attention to the inauguration of a new era with the imminent precession of the spring equinox from Pisces into Aquarius. The phrase 'Age of Aquarius' represented in the 1960s and early 1970s much of what later came to be represented by the phrase 'New Age' (see Ferguson 1982). Writing in the late 1950s about the numerous reported sightings of flying saucers, Jung interprets them as signs of 'coming events which are in accord with the end of an era' (1958b: par. 589). He explains:

> As we know from ancient Egyptian history, they [i.e., these coming events] are manifestations of psychic changes which always appear at the end of one Platonic month [i.e., an astronomically determined period of approximately 2,000 years] and at the beginning of another. Apparently they are changes in the constellation of psychic dominants, of the archetypes, or 'gods' as they used to be called, which bring about, or accompany, long-lasting transformations of the collective psyche. This transformation started in the historical era and left its traces first in the passing of the aeon of Taurus into that of Aries, and then of Aries into Pisces, whose beginning coincides with the rise of Christianity. We are now nearing that great change which may be expected when the spring point enters Aquarius.
>
> (Jung 1958b: par. 589)

Finally, we may add several deeper affinities of underlying orientation and principle to these outer affinities between Jung and the New Age. Specifically, each of the characteristic features of New Age spirituality that we identified in the previous sub-section is also a major emphasis within Jung's psychology. Like New Agers, Jung reacts against the reductive tendencies of modern science while at the same time selectively appropriating ideas from modern science; accords a central place to the notion of psycho-spiritual transformation; has an ambivalent but largely oppositional relationship to secular modernity; engages eclectically with non-western, pre-modern and esoteric traditions; frames contemporary experience in terms of myth; prioritises personal experience over institutionalised beliefs; and locates authority in the individual self.

Differences between Jung and the New Age

In spite of these evident affinities and influences, some writers have preferred to place the accent on the differences between Jung and the New Age. The most extensive treatment so far published of Jung's relationship to the New Age is David Tacey's *Jung and the New Age* (2001). Writing as a Jungian-oriented cultural critic, Tacey considers that both Jung and the New Age are right to criticise traditional western religion (patriarchal monotheism) for its setting aside or forcible repression of various vital contents and forces:

> the 'forbidden' realm of polytheistic experience and the plurality of the Gods; the 'banned' realm of eros, sexuality and the body; the 'immoral' realm of the shadow and evil; the 'suppressed' domain of women and the archetypal feminine; and the 'pagan' field of nature and the animated earth.
>
> (Tacey 2001: 8)

These repressed contents, Tacey argues, are at present spontaneously resurfacing through a process of unconscious archetypal compensation at a collective level, and it is their shared responsiveness to this, over and above any direct influence, that accounts for many of the similarities between Jungian psychology and the New Age. However, where the New Age tends to identify with and champion the emerging compensatory forces, thereby promoting a one-sided outlook no better than the one-sidedness of the traditional outlook it criticises, Jungian psychology, at least in principle, advocates the careful avoidance of identification with any archetypal forces and the maintaining of a difficult middle path in which the opposites are held in creative tension. Many New Age writers, Tacey argues, appropriate Jungian ideas but distort them through failing to appreciate that Jung is critical of identification with any archetype and emphasises how such identi-fication leads to the disastrous condition of psychic inflation. Worse, many Jungian writers 'defect' to the New Age position in order to cash in on the immense popularity that can be won through promoting a bowdlerised, anodyne version of Jungian ideas. Tacey acknowledges the partial validity of the New Age outlook but considers that what is needed is 'a new synthesis' in which the New Age will supply the challenging new ideas about the individual experience of spirit, the feminine face of God, and the resacralisation of nature and the earth, while the mainstream Western religious traditions – Christian, Jewish, Islamic – will contribute historical, moral and ethical counterpoints to the new rush toward personal and unhistorical experience of the sacred.

(Tacey 2001: 5)

Jungian psychology, he believes, can point us towards this new synthesis and in part already represents its achievement.

Tacey's highlighting of the differences between Jung and the New Age appears most starkly in an earlier article entitled 'Why Jung would doubt the New Age', where he singles out two major points on which he considers them to differ (1999: 36–42). One is their attitude towards the feminine. While he acknowledges that both Jung and the New Age attach greater importance to the feminine than has traditional patriarchal European culture, he argues that their attitudes to the feminine also contrast in an important respect. The New Age, according to Tacey, tends to identify with the emergence of feminine values and swings over to a celebration of these values that is no less one-sided than was the previous commitment to patriarchal values. Jung, by contrast, recognised and described the phenomena associated with the ascendancy of the feminine but did not naïvely celebrate this collectively occurring process. Rather, he recommended integrating the new collective values with the old, identifying with neither but maintaining a stance of critical individuality.[3]

A second point of difference for Tacey concerns attitudes towards suffering. He considers that the New Age naïvely elevates bliss over suffering, whereas Jung is closer to traditional Christianity in his emphasis on the redemptive significance of suffering. New Agers, according to Tacey, aim to experience the spirit as a further form of gratification for the ego. Jung, by contrast, recognises that spiritual development (that is, individuation) is 'an heroic and often tragic task, the most difficult of all, it involves a suffering, a passion of the ego' (Jung 1942/1948: par. 233, quoted in Tacey 1999: 40).

In regard both to the feminine and to suffering, Tacey is undoubtedly putting his finger on differences that do exist in many instances. However, the differences are far from absolute. The New Age is an expansive movement in which people participate in varying ways and at varying levels of sophistication. For many, the feminine is valued in much the way Tacey attributes to Jung: as a compensatory force to be brought into balanced relationship with the masculine. For example, York notes the following difference between the thinking of two prominent Wiccans, one representing the attitude Tacey criticises, the other the attitude he favours:

Unlike Starhawk's almost exclusively feminist brand of Wicca – one in which the male god is seen as a subordinate emanation of the Goddess – [Vivianne] Crowley's Alexandrian persuasion clearly emphasizes the male and female balance necessary within its image of the divine. To focus on either the Goddess or God alone, Crowley contends, produces both social and individual spiritual imbalance.

(York 1995: 121)

Suffering, too, is not always treated as lightly within the New Age as Tacey implies. Heelas, for example, on the one hand can describe the New Age as 'a highly optimistic, celebratory, utopian and spiritual form of humanism' (1996: 28), while on the other hand he registers the Caucasian mystic Gurdjieff as one of the '[t]hree key figures' to have influenced the development of the New Age (ibid.: 47). Gurdjieff's system presents a very grim picture of the human condition: transformation is possible but only through 'conscious effort and intentional suffering' (Hinnells 1997: 198). Furthermore, even if Tacey is largely right in identifying one-sided attitudes towards the feminine and suffering within much of the New Age, this need not constitute a definitive indictment. There is in principle no reason why the New Age, while retaining its basic character, should not become more balanced precisely in the ways indicated by Tacey.

Overall, in spite of some noteworthy but still debatable differences, the relationship between Jung's psychology and New Age thought seems sufficiently close for the study of one to provide illuminating perspectives on the other. On this basis, we will now look at New Age thinking in the light of the theory of synchronicity.

New Age thinking in the light of synchronicity

The notion of synchronicity directly figures in the New Age in a number of ways. For instance, some neo-pagans explain the alleged efficacy of their magical practices in terms of synchronicity rather than, as formerly, in terms of 'corre-spondences' (York 1995: 120). Synchronicity also features as part of the general New Age concern with the paranormal and 'psi' experiences. Of the over 900 respondents to Stuart Rose's survey of subscribers to the New Age magazine *Kindred Spirit*, 40 per cent reported having experienced synchronicity (Rose 1997). Again, New Agers for whom external religious forms have lost their authority and who therefore look to their inner self for guidance sometimes also appeal to chance outer events as signs or omens. These chance events may be deliberately generated by means of a method of divination such as the *I Ching* or they may occur spontaneously. In either case they are treated as synchronistic events: chance but meaningful. This use of synchronicity as a form of spiritual guidance is epitomised in James Redfield's *The Celestine Prophecy* (1994). This popular New Age adventure story involves the sequential discovery by its protagonist of a series of nine key insights, the first of which is that 'coincidences are real, synchronistic events, and once you become sensitive to them they will lead to your individual spiritual truth' (Beaumont 1994–1995: 18; see Redfield 1994: 11–51). Synchronicity therefore accords with New Age sensibilities in being a form of direct personal experience and in looking towards the inner individual rather than towards external institutionalised authorities.

There are also many less direct parallels between synchronicity and the New Age. For instance, we have seen that synchronicity can promote psycho-spiritual transformation in its Jungian form of individuation. Again, not only does synchronicity engage with non-western, pre-modern, and esoteric traditions, it derives directly from them and, by Jung's own account, is largely a translation of them into modern idiom (1951b: par. 995). Further, as Jung's example of the scarab beetle indicated, the content of synchronistic events is often mythic. This is not surprising if we bear in mind that, for Jung, synchronistic events are based on the activation of archetypes and myths are the narrative elaboration of archetypal motifs.

Most significantly, however, synchronicity shares with the New Age a profoundly ambivalent attitude towards science. Like the New Age, the theory of synchronicity represents both a reaction against the reductive tendencies of modern science and a selective appropriation of ideas from modern science. Synchronicity expresses the same valuation of holism as does the New Age and similarly aspires towards an integration of the material and spiritual realms. Indeed, the theory of synchronicity attempts what may also be a deeper aspiration of the New Age: to bring about a major revision of our understanding of both religion and science as well as of their relationship.

In the following discussion we shall pursue some of these connections in more detail. The aim is to exemplify how patterns of thought implicit in Jung's theory have also surfaced in a contemporary socio-cultural movement. Studying Jung's theory alongside this movement may help to illuminate both. In particular, it may suggest how Jung's theory, as well as having directly and indirectly influenced New Age thinking, can provide a helpful perspective for understanding some of the principal contexts, tenets and aspirations of the New Age.

Defining the New Age

For the purposes of this more detailed discussion I shall take my bearings from the following widely respected definition of the New Age movement distilled by Wouter Hanegraaff from his compendious examination of New Age sources:

> The New Age movement is the cultic milieu having become conscious of itself, in the later 1970s, as constituting a more or less unified "movement". All manifestations of this movement are characterized by a popular western culture criticism expressed in terms of a secularized esotericism.
>
> (Hanegraaff 1998: 522)

We will focus primarily on the second half of this definition, since our concern here is with the underlying patterns of thought of the New Age movement.

However, a number of issues need to be briefly clarified. First, I should state that what I find most relevant about Hanegraaff's definition is its precise identification and characterisation of a socio-cultural movement and set of ideas. Whether the movement and ideas so identified and characterised are named 'New Age' or something else, such as 'alternative spirituality' or 'holistic spirituality', is of less importance. Second, the term 'cultic milieu' requires a short explanation. It was coined by the sociologist Colin Campbell (1972) and refers to 'the cultural underground of society', including 'all deviant belief systems and their associated practices ... unorthodox science, alien and heretical religion, deviant medicine, ... the collectivities, institutions, individuals and media of communication associated with these beliefs' (ibid.: 122, in York 1995: 252). In spite of its diversity and diffuseness, Campbell suggests that the cultic milieu is 'a single entity' that, in York's words, 'is a more viable focus of sociological inquiry than the individual cult itself' (York 1995: 252; see also Hanegraaff 2002: 251–2). Third, it is worth noting that Hanegraaff distinguishes between the New Age movement, originating in 'the later 1970s', and New Age religion ('the general type of culture criticism based on a foundation of secularized esotericism'), which, he argues, 'was born in the 19th century and had reached maturity not later than the beginning of the 20th' (1998: 521–2). It is thus possible that, while Jung certainly influenced the New Age movement, he may himself have been influenced by New Age religion, understood in Hanegraaff's sense, or can even be considered one of its representatives.

New Age religion, as Hanegraaff sees it, typically consists of the following five elements: this-worldliness, holism, evolutionism, the psychologisation of religion and sacralisation of psychology, and expectations of a coming new age (1998: 514). Each of these is also an element in Jung's outlook. By 'this-worldliness' Hanegraaff means an orientation that seeks its goals in the actual world we live in rather than in another, transcendent world. He distinguishes between strong this-worldliness, which accepts this world as it is in the present, and weak this-worldliness, which looks to this world as it will be in the future (this world but better). Most, though not all, New Age religion is this-worldly in the weak sense (ibid.: 113–19). Jung's thought, too, with its focus on the phenomenal world of experience and its aim of promoting individuation in the actual conditions of life, is clearly a this-worldly perspective – strong in his insistence that self-realisation should be sought in the individual's current life situation, weak in his belief that, collectively, conditions could become more conducive to the pursuit of individuation than they are at present (Jung 1976: 595).

Holism we shall discuss below (see also Hanegraaff 1998: 119–58). Evolutionism refers to the view that human consciousness, in individuals and in humanity as a whole, is developing or can develop into higher forms (ibid.: 158–68). Jung clearly shares this view, with his belief that different stages of development, both collectively and in the individual, are characterised by different relationships between consciousness and the unconscious: non-differentiation in primitives; projection of the unconscious as gods in traditional cultures; withdrawal of projections and loss of contact with the unconscious in moderns; and a differentiated reconnection with the unconscious in people pursuing the Jungian path of individuation or an equivalent (see Segal 1992: 11–18).

The psychologisation of religion and sacralisation of psychology refer to precisely the kind of process exemplified by Jungian psychology, where on the one hand psychology is employed to explain religious phenomena but on the other hand a religious attitude informs some of the central assumptions of the psychology (Hannegraaff 1998: 224–9). The psychology of William James and the transpersonal psychology movement are two further examples (see Barnard 2001).

Expectations of a coming New Age usually relate to the astronomical precession of the spring equinox into the constellation of Aquarius and the astrological mythology associated with that event. Views on precisely what the 'New Age' will consist of and how quickly its presence will be felt vary among authors (Hanegraaff 1998: 331–56). As we have seen, Jung shared this expectation that a great change – a long-lasting transformation of the collective psyche – would occur with the advent of the Age of Aquarius. However, he does not appear to have assumed that the new age would necessarily be better than the old one. It might simply be very different, with new conditions, new challenges and new problems.

The two most interesting elements in Hanegraaff's characterisation of the New Age are his assertions that it is a form of 'popular western culture criticism' and that it is 'based on a secularized esotericism'. As Hanegraaff sees it, the New Age movement exhibits 'a common pattern of criticism directed against dominant cultural trends' (1998: 515). Examples of these trends are philosophical dualism and reductionism, excessive rationalism and religious authoritarianism – all themes against which Jung too directed his critiques. The usual pattern of New Age criticism is not to challenge these perceived negative trends directly by means of intellectual argument – that would be to succumb to the very thing criticised – but to move away from the negative trends by promoting and celebrating their contraries: holism, emotional expressivism and spiritual autonomy.

Hanegraaff's characterisation of New Age religion as a 'western' phenomenon may initially seem surprising in view of the extensive role played in the New Age by eastern religions and philosophies, such as those of Hinduism, Buddhism and Taoism. However, Hanegraaff's point is that in New Age religion these eastern sources are mostly drawn on by westerners for the purpose of criticising western cultural trends. Jung similarly appeals to eastern religions and philosophies primarily in order to gain a critical perspective on western European culture (see Clarke 1994).

That New Age religion should be characterised as a popular movement is uncontroversial. More surprising is that Jungian psychology, and in particular the difficult theory of synchronicity, should be aligned with this popular movement. However, it becomes less surprising when the religious implications of Jung's theories are kept in mind and the theory is viewed in the light of some of Homans's observations in the essay he added to the second edition of *Jung in Context*: 'Reading the Depth Psychologies at Century's End: Review and Prospects'. In that essay, Homans reviews two books that have been enormously popular in contemporary America: M. Scott Peck's *The Road Less Travelled* (1978) and Clarissa Pinkola Estes's *Women Who Run with the Wolves* (1992). Peck's book is about mental growth and for the most part is presented in classic Freudian psychoanalytic terms. However, towards the end Peck introduces Jungian, religious interpretations of the unconscious as 'a source of wisdom, insight, and hidden truths' and of becoming conscious as a process of 'spiritual growth' (Homans 1979/1995: xli–xlii). Estes's book is an exploration of the new archetype of the Wild Woman that she claims to have identified. It consists throughout of folktales, myths and Jungian psychological commentary, and is clearly religious in the Jungian sense. Homans attributes the success of these books precisely to their religious tone, for, in his view, 'popular psychology is most popular when it is blended with religion' (ibid.: xl). The alliance between New Age spirituality and Jungian psychology, including the theory of synchronicity, is a prime example of this blending of psychology with religion, and in Homans's view is the kind of result that Jung intended:

> Jungian psychology slips quietly, effortlessly, and unmolested into the registers of popular culture. It can become part of our culture's belief system without distortion. That is because this is exactly what Jung wanted it to do, and he wrote it the way he did for this reason. Jung sought to revitalize contemporary culture, which – he believed – had lost its anchorage in the past, by re-linking that culture to its past (especially the mythic past) with the assistance of depth psychology, and he worked within the assumptive world of Christian humanism.
>
> (Homans 1979/1995: xliii)

Arguably, Hanegraaff's most interesting finding of all is that New Age culture criticism is based on a secularised esotericism. He understands esotericism largely in the sense defined by Antoine Faivre. For Faivre, there are four essential and two non-essential characteristics of esotericism. The four essential characteristics are: a world-view based on correspondences; an account of nature as living; the importance of imagination and mediations between a seen and an unseen world; and the experience of transmutation. The two non-essential characteristics are 'the praxis of concordance' – that is, establishing connections between different traditions and fields of knowledge – and transmission – the passing on of knowledge from teacher to disciple, often by means of initiations (summarised in Hanegraaff 1998: 398–400; see also 2002: 255–6). However, Hanegraaff suggests that by the end of the nineteenth century traditional esotericism had been transformed by its reflection in what he calls the 'four "mirrors of secular thought": the new worldview of "causality", the new study of religions, the new evolutionism, and the new psychologies' (1998: 518; see also 2002: 257–8). In a later publication, Hanegraaff suggests that to these four mirrors 'perhaps a fifth one may be added that became dominant only after the Second World War, and is fully characteristic of the New Age movement of the 1980s and 1990s: the impact of the capitalist market economy on the domain of spirituality' (2002: 258).

That New Age culture criticism should base itself on secularised esotericism provides a further warrant for our comparison of New Age thinking with Jungian psychology, especially his theory of synchronicity. Not only did Jung clearly align his psychology with traditional esotericism, alchemy above all, but it is also not difficult to discover Jungian parallels for every one of the essential, non-essential and secularised characteristics of esotericism mentioned by Faivre and Hanegraaff. Regarding the essential characteristics, we need only think of Jung's concerns with synchronicity (correspondences), vitalism (living nature), symbols and myths (imagination and mediations) and individuation (experience of transmutation). Regarding the non-essential characteristics, we can refer to amplification and the comparative method (praxis of concordance) and the process of analysis and analytic training (transmission). Finally, Jung's thought, including his theory of synchronicity, is deeply shaped by each of Hanegraaff's secularising tendencies: by the world-view of causality, not least in the lengths to which he has to go to assert the complementary view of acausality; by the study of religions, which provided him with much of his comparative material, including knowledge of the *I Ching* as a system based on the principle of synchronicity; by evolutionism, in his model of the development of consciousness both historically and in the individual – synchronicity, as we have seen, playing a part in both; and, clearly, by the new psychologies, of which his own model, into which the theory of synchronicity fits, is an eminent instance. Hanegraaff dates the emergence of his fifth mirror – the impact of the capitalist market economy – to a period by which Jung had already mostly developed his theories into their mature forms. Nevertheless, it would be interesting, though beyond our scope here, to explore the impact of the fifth mirror on the subsequent development of analytical psychological theory and practice.

From the preceding discussion it is clear that Jung's psychological model and theory of synchronicity bear close comparison with even a precisely formulated understanding of New Age spirituality. We will now explore some ways in which these similarities may provide a helpful perspective for both scholars and practitioners to deepen their understanding of New Age spirituality.

The relationship between religion and science

As our discussion earlier in the chapter indicated, one dominant theme in New Age thinking is the attempt to integrate religion and science. Usually the attempt involves promoting certain kinds or aspects of religion and science over others – for example, promoting esoteric or mystical religion over traditional institutionalised religion, or promoting speculative, holistic theories in physics over the mechanistic theories that dominate the field. The same overall aim of integrating religion and science, and the same strategy of selective engagement with religion and science, is evident in Jung's work – most notably in his theory of synchronicity. As we have seen, when presenting this theory Jung drew for support on both religious and scientific sources, as well as explicitly esoteric ones in which religion and science have not yet been clearly separated. In the light of this parallel, a close examination of the influence of the interaction between religion and science on Jung's theory of synchronicity, where it is clearly documented, could help elucidate the similar influence on the origins of New Age thinking.

Correspondences

New Age thinking, especially among those involved in revived practices of magic, astrology and other forms of divination, attaches considerable importance to the notion of correspondences (Hanegraaff 1998: 398). Explicitly or implicitly, such practitioners accept that non-causal relationships exist between different levels or domains of reality simply by virtue of inner affinities. For example, the planet Venus, the metal copper, the colour green, and the emotion of love are all considered to be inwardly related, as are all copper things, all green things, and all erotic things among themselves, even where there is no plausibility of causal connections among the objects or events. In Jung's classic example, this style of thinking is evident in the *acausal* connection between the dream of the scarab and the appearance of the real scarab. Indeed, we can recall Jung's explicit description of synchronicity as 'a modern differentiation of the obsolete concept of correspondence, sympathy, and harmony' (1951b: par. 996). As we have noted, some New Agers follow this hint and substitute the concept of synchronicity for that of correspondences when explaining the philosophy underlying magical practices (York 1995: 120).

However, there may be a richer potential in Jung's concept than New Agers have generally realised. In his discussion of this issue, Hanegraaff distinguishes between two forms of secularised esotericism. Both try to update esotericism in order to make it appear scientific and therefore acceptable within an increasingly secularised culture, but they do so in different ways. One way tries to incorporate the principle of causality, perceived to be the key to the successes of science. The principle of correspondences is retained, but in a form blended with casual thinking. A prime example is theosophy, which attaches special importance to the notion of *karma* because this notion on the one hand applies across all domains of reality, including the spiritual, and on the other hand translates into western terms as a principle of cause and effect. Other examples include spiritualism and the occultism of such organisations as the Hermetic Order of the Golden Dawn. The other way of updating esotericism, adopted by Jung, draws implicitly on German romantic *Naturphilosophie*. In this the notion of correspondences is retained without attempting to synthesise it with the principle of causality. Hanegraaff writes:

The significance of [Jung's] approach to esotericism is that it enabled him to appear 'scientific' while *avoiding* the necessity of compromising with the worldview of 'causality.' It is by building his psychology on a concept of science derived from Romantic *Naturphilosophie* (and opposed to modern 'causality') that Jung may have succeeded in finding a way to 'update' traditional esotericism without disrupting its inner consistency. From the perspective of the historical study of esotericism, this makes him a unique figure.

(Hanegraaff 1998: 505)

If Hanegraaff's distinction is correct, Jung's theory of synchronicity provides an intellectual framework for understanding how esoteric practices can be revived without having to be distorted in an attempt at accommodation with mainstream causal science. This could enable New Age thinking to liberate itself from some of its pseudo-scientific modes of self-representation. There are, indeed, indications of this move away from causal thinking in some recent work on astrology and other forms of divination specifically influenced by Jung's theories (see Hyde 1992; Cornelius 1994; Karcher 2003).

Holism and interconnection

Another major theme in New Age thinking is a concern with holism and interconnection. As Hanegraaff observes, holism in the New Age context implies not so much a positive doctrine as a general 'quest for "wholeness" at all levels of existence' and a widely shared opposition to dualism and reductionism (1998: 119; cf. Heelas 1996: 33–4). Jung's overall psychology strongly supports this concern, with its emphasis on individuation as a process of psychological development involving the continual integration of psychic opposites, most generally of consciousness and the unconscious, in order to forge the 'self' as an entity of greater psychic wholeness. However, with his theory of synchronicity Jung can take this integrative tendency even further. For synchronistic events show that the psyche can be integrated not only within itself but also with the external world. When inner psychic events meaningfully but acausally connect with outer physical events, one can infer, as does Jung, that 'all reality [may be] grounded on an as yet unknown substrate possessing material and at the same time psychic qualities' (1958b: par. 780). The synchronistic principle, says Jung, 'suggests that there is an interconnection or unity of causally unrelated events, and thus postulates a unitary aspect of being which can very well be described as the *unus mundus* ['one world']' (1955–6: par. 662). With this formulation Jung avoids both dualism, since psyche and matter prove to be aspects of the same substrate, and reductionism, since the unity is achieved not by suggesting that psyche is an epiphenomenon of matter or matter is an emanation of psyche but by postulating a more fundamental unitive dimension that involves but transcends both psyche and matter.

Among New Age writers, support for the perspective of holism typically comes from references to developments in systems theory and physics (including relativity theory, quantum mechanics, and the process of holography), where there is an emphasis on the interconnected and web-like nature of social and physical reality (Hanegraaff 1998: 128–51). Jung's notion of synchronicity adds support from the realm of psychological experience, where the emphasis is on the crucial connection between the psychic and physical domains of reality. It is true that one of the findings of modern physics – that how subatomic entities present themselves, as particles or waves, depends on the manner in which they are observed – does provide some connection between the psychic domain (the observer or operator of the observing instrument) and the physical domain. However, the connection in this case is very tenuous. With synchronistic experiences, the connection is much stronger, indeed is one of the identifying and defining features of such experiences. The evidence for a holistic outlook is brought more firmly into the domain of available experience.

Re-enchantment

One of the consequences of the development of scientific and secular outlooks was the so-called 'disenchantment' of the world, the removal of the sense that we inhabit a world filled with meaning and mystery (see Jung 1938/1940: pars. 140–1; Hanegraaff 1998: 409, 421, 423). New Agers seek to reverse this trend by 're-enchanting the world' (see Berman 1983). Synchronicity could serve here by providing not just a theoretical assumption but also an experiential indication that the natural world is not, after all, entirely alienated from human purposes but can be intimately involved with them. Thus, the real scarab beetle in Jung's example behaved in a way that seemed mysteriously connected with the patient's inner psychic world. As Jung remarked to a correspondent: 'at the moment my patient was telling me her dream a real "scarab" tried to get into the room, as if it had understood that it must play its mythological role as a symbol of rebirth' (1976: 541). Jung goes further: 'Even inanimate objects', he writes, 'behave occasionally in the same way – meteorological phenomena, for instance' (ibid.). However, Jung's theory does not necessarily entail that all natural phenomena always exhibit meaning and mystery, only that any natural (or indeed cultural) phenomenon sometimes might exhibit such meaning and mystery.

Ironically, the development of depth psychology partly contributed to the disenchantment of the world, for its central notion of projection implies that the meanings we perceive in the world are not there in reality but are being foisted onto the world from the human mind, albeit the unconscious mind. In Jung's psychological model, even after his development of the notion of synchronicity, projection remains a concept of central importance. However, what his later, synchronistic psychology implies is that meaning relevant to humans can indeed, at least sometimes, exist in the world independently of, that is, not projected by, the human mind yet discernible by it. In this way, the world again becomes filled with objective meaning and mystery.

The cosmogonic significance of consciousness

Much New Age thinking attributes to human consciousness the power to create reality. Sometimes this means only that our particular experience of reality depends on our state of mind, so that by changing our states of mind we can change the way in which we experience reality, in that sense creating a new reality for us. Mostly, however, the claim is grander than this. In a section of his study entitled 'Creating Our Own Reality' Hanegraaff summarises the view in one influential New Age source: the 'Seth Material' channelled by Jane Roberts. According to this source there is a 'general "natural law" underlying all manifestation', by which '[w]e live our lives in "dreams" of our own making, which reflect our unconscious beliefs. By changing our beliefs, we automatically change our reality' (1998: 230). At other times the cosmogonic claim is grander still. Appeal is made to the finding of quantum physics that the way the subatomic components of physical reality manifest – as particles or waves – depends on how they are observed. Until the 'quantum wave function' is collapsed by an observing consciousness, it is argued, physical reality does not yet have manifest existence. From this it is inferred that consciousness creates, or at least co-creates, not just our particular circumstances but the very substance of physical reality. As Hanegraaff points out, this kind of thinking, in both its grander and its more modest variants, risks leading to solipsistic and narcissistic conclusions (ibid.: 230–3).

Jung too, in speculative moments, writes of the cosmogonic significance of human consciousness. In 'The Undiscovered Self' he describes consciousness as 'one of the two indispensable conditions for existence as such'. He continues:

> Without consciousness there would, practically speaking, be no world, for the world exists for us only in so far as it is consciously reflected by a psyche. *Consciousness is a precondition of being.* Thus the psyche is endowed with the dignity of a cosmic principle, which philosophically and in fact gives it a position co-equal with the principle of physical being.
>
> (Jung 1957: par. 528)

Earlier in this chapter, when discussing Jung's myth of the meaning of human life, we saw the important role played by synchronicity in his account of the cosmogonic significance of consciousness. That involvement of synchronicity helps protect Jung's account from the charges of solipsism and narcissism that have been levelled against the New Age accounts. In the first place, he does not credit consciousness with the creation of the substance of reality; what consciousness discovers or co-creates, in its 'second cosmogony', is meaning. In the second place, although the consciousness in question is 'the reflecting consciousness of man', it is not a quality with which humans can possessively identify. For consciousness itself emerged out of a 'psychoid process' that already existed at an early stage in biological evolution during the 'preconscious time' (1976: 495).

It is possible to construe the philosophical position underlying Jung's psychology as an idealist one (see Nagy 1991: 265). Synchronicity can even be co-opted in support of an idealist philosophy on the grounds that synchronistic connections show mind and matter to be not distinct things but different modalities of the same fundamental stuff – mind or psyche (see Mansfield 1995: 185–203). Jung does indeed many times state that he considers psyche to be the only immediately experienced reality. However, in making this claim, he does not deny that matter and spirit are also real; he only insists that their reality is always mediated in the form of psychic images. Jung's account of psychic reality risks being tautologous in that, when he says only psyche can be immediately experienced, he seems to be equating the psychic with the experienceable, so that anything experienced *ipso facto* is psychic. Nevertheless, within the field of the experienceable, Jung clearly differentiated different kinds of phenomena: material phenomena such as tables and trees; psychic phenomena such as thoughts and fantasies; and spiritual phenomena such as moments of insight and creativity or senses of numinous presence. Calling these all psychic in the broader sense does not, for Jung, collapse the differences among them. When he writes of synchronicities as connecting psychic events with physical ones and then marvels at how this connection can be, he is affirming rather than denying the ontological difference between the experienced events.

Spiritual experience

As we have seen, another central feature of New Age thinking is not to be satisfied with the pronouncements of others about the spirit but to aspire to experience spirit for oneself, and synchronicity is one of the modes of spiritual experience explicitly acknowledged by many New Agers. Some of the specific ways in which synchronicity can be seen as a form of spiritual experience have been discussed above (see also Main 2001). Considering the central role that Jung accords to numinosity in religious/spiritual experience (1938/1940: par. 6) and his equation of synchronicity with numinous experience (McGuire and Hull 1978: 230), one could even argue that he sees synchronicity as constituting the essence of religious/ spiritual experience. This might help account for why synchronicity can be readily related to so many traditional spiritual concepts and concerns, making it an especially attractive notion to New Agers who are often in search of the perennial core within traditional religions (Hanegraaff 1998: 327–30). Another attraction of synchronicity as a form of spiritual experience could be that it seemingly does not require arduous preparation but happens spontaneously and frequently to almost anyone, as surveys testify. For example, in a 1987 study into the incidence of various kinds of religious experience in Britain (based on volunteered reports and not specifically targeting New Agers), 'synchronicity and patterning of events' was the most frequently reported category (see Hay 1990: 41–3, 83–4).

Authority of the spiritual self

Earlier we saw that an especially prominent, arguably a defining feature of the New Age is the tendency to locate spiritual and ethical authority within the individual self. This clearly accords with Jung's general psychological model based on individuation. However, the Jungian understanding of this issue is given an additional twist by the theory of synchronicity. In Jung's model, synchronistic experiences promote individuation – that is, realisation of the transpersonal centre of the psyche that Jung designates by the term 'self'. This self, as the telos or goal towards which the psyche is striving, functions as an implicit source of guidance for the psychologically developing individual. However, as a manifestation of the self, synchronicity is distinctive in that it takes a form involving not only images and intuitions and other senses of inner direction but also events in the external world. This could be taken as an additional check on the kind of subjectivism to which appeals to exclusively inner sources of direction are prone. An inner image or intuition could all too easily be a purely subjective phenomenon, a projection of the previously internalised voice of another, and thus no alternative to external, perhaps parental or institutional, authorities but only a displaced and disguised version of them. The way in which synchronistic manifestations of the self involve the outer world at least suggests that they are not wholly subjective phenomena but transcend the purely personal sphere. Of course, they suggest rather than prove this; for it will always remain possible that the meaning or directive perceived in a synchronicity is subjective, even if the objective occurrence of an unlikely coincidence is acknowledged. Nevertheless, the case for the transpersonal nature of the self and its guidance is strengthened by synchronicity.

Objective symbolism and mystery

In the closing pages of *New Age Religion and Western Culture*, Hanegraaff raises the question of 'what has been lost in the course of the processes by which modern movements and individuals [in this case the New Age movement and its participants] have attempted to preserve the "wisdom of the past"' (1998: 523). Following the scholar of Jewish mysticism Gershom Scholem, he identifies two such losses: the loss of a world of objective, obligating symbols, this having been replaced by worlds of private symbolism; and the loss of, in Scholem's words, 'the feeling that there is mystery – a secret – in the world' (in ibid.: 524). Writes Hanegraaff in his penultimate sentence:

> The New Age movement tends to make each private individual into the center of his or her symbolic world; and it tends to seek salvation in universal explanatory systems which will leave no single question of human existence unanswered, and will replace mystery by the certainty of perfect knowledge.
>
> (Hanegraaff 1998: 524)

If Hanegraaff is correct in his identification of what is in danger of being lost in New Age thinking, then Jung's psychological model in general and theory of synchronicity in particular could provide some possible strategies or perspectives that New Agers could adopt to avoid these losses. For these two factors – objective symbolism and mystery – are precisely what Jung was attempting to preserve. As a psychotherapist daily working with the dreams and fantasies of his patients, Jung was no stranger to worlds of private symbolism. However, the emphasis of his therapeutic technique was on finding within his patients' subjective and personal imagery archetypal motifs that transcend the merely personal and reflect universal human experiences and dispositions. These motifs, in Jung's view, are the expression of innate forms that are transpersonal and objective. Insofar as such images manifest as fantasies within the human mind, there will always be the suspicion that they do not after all represent anything transpersonal. However, Jung's theory of synchronicity supports their objective, transpersonal nature by showing that they can be as much physical as psychic, involving the outer world of nature as well as the human mind.

Jung's theory also preserves the feeling of mystery. The very concept of the unconscious as an inalienable feature of the human psyche ensures that 'the certainty of perfect knowledge' is unattainable. This is especially the case with Jung's model of the unconscious, whose basic elements, the archetypes, he insists are essentially unknowable. Indeed, Jung even asserts that mystery and numinosity constitute the true healing factor in psychotherapy. As he wrote to P. W. Martin (20 August 1945): 'the approach to the numinous is the real therapy and inasmuch as you attain to the numinous experiences you are released from the curse of pathology' (1973: 377).

The theory of synchronicity supports this focus on the mysterious and numinous in Jungian psychology. Indeed, one of the arguments of this book has been that Jung developed his theory of synchronicity precisely in order to shore up his general psychological theory against the threat of its being collapsed into a purely personal and naturalistic model. Prominent among the features of synchronicity that contribute to its preservation of mystery are the baffling notion of acausality, the transgression of the boundaries of the psychic and physical, the relativisation of time and space that can occur in precognitive and clairvoyant synchronicities, and, not least, the above-mentioned indications of a dimension of objective meaning.

Conclusion
The rupture of time

This book has aimed to clarify what Jung really meant by synchronicity, why the idea was so important to him, and how it informed his thinking about modern western culture. The book has focused on Jung's own writings and statements, examining, first, various theoretical aspects of synchronicity, above all its relation to analytical psychology; second, the personal, intellectual and social contexts out of which the idea developed; and third, the principal socio-cultural fields in which Jung applied the idea. My hope is that the book may have illuminated some long-standing difficulties with Jung's writings on synchronicity, opened some previously unsuspected lines of inquiry, and in general have provided both a resource and a stimulus for future researchers. In this conclusion I shall summarise and briefly discuss the overall argument and findings and suggest some possible directions for future work.

The theory of synchronicity is an integral part of Jung's overall psychological model (Chapter 1). The theory meshes with all the major concepts of analytical psychology that had been developed before Jung began to theorise about meaningful coincidences and especially requires the framework of analytical psychology in order to account adequately for the meaning that can adhere to such events. Within the framework of analytical psychology the theory of synchronicity can provide a coherent explanation of coincidences as well as a way of working with them either therapeutically or for spiritual self-development. Moreover, Jung's reflections on synchronicity prompted him to some far-reaching revisions or developments of analytical psychology, especially concerning the psychoid unconscious and the psychic relativisation of space and time – revisions that consolidate and extend the transpersonal implications of analytical psychology. It is therefore not possible fully to understand Jung's mature psychological model without considering the role that synchronicity plays within it. With its basis in analytical psychology, synchronicity provides an explanation of coincidences that, compared with other explanations that have been proposed, is distinctive because of its combination of empirical grounding, depth psychological sophistication and openness to the dimension of spirit.

Nevertheless, viewed with a critical eye, the theory of synchronicity turns out to be fraught with difficulties in its definition, characterisation and core concepts

(Chapter 2). Some of these difficulties can be resolved through applying a subtler understanding of analytical psychology, introducing updated knowledge in some of the fields on which Jung drew, or viewing the theory in the light of different phases of his work. Some of the difficulties indicate conscious uncertainties in Jung's thinking, while others suggest unconscious confusion. Overall, however, there is a sense that in his writing on synchronicity Jung is pushing at the limits of his knowledge and discipline. With his notions of the psychoid unconscious and the psychic relativisation of space and time, he expanded analytical psychological theory into territory that even many of his followers would prefer not to enter. In his discussions of physics and parapsychology, and in his prefiguration of qualitative psychological methods, he was engaging with the science of his day at some of its frontiers. His work on synchronicity makes radical philosophical suggestions regarding the nature of space, time and causality; boldly engages with the thought-worlds of historically and geographically remote cultures; and, above all, tries to find a formulation that will encompass events 'infinitely varied in their phenomenology' (1951b: par. 995). In all these ways we get a sense that Jung is trying to push his theory to grasp something that, in the last resort, may not be graspable in terms of the rational frameworks of knowledge dominating his culture. Jung clearly believes in the reality and significance of synchronicity, even if he often seems defeated in his attempts to communicate his belief and understanding in a satisfactory way. Nevertheless, from each defeat something valuable is gained. For in pushing at the limits of the rationally graspable, Jung succeeds in making synchronicity, or at least the zone in which it operates, more visible. In this sense, synchronicity can be seen as a special, vivid instance of what it is to engage with the unconscious generally. It can be seen as a symbol of mystery and the limits of reason. The apparent ungraspability of synchronicity should not forestall further inquiry, but any discussion of the phenomenon would do well to bear this feature in mind.

Jung drew on an exceptionally wide range of sources and influences when developing his theory of synchronicity (Chapter 3). On the one hand, this diversity of sources and influences helps account for the extraordinary richness of the theory, as it provided Jung with perspectives, insights and encouragement from many different angles. On the other hand, the diversity also helps account for some of the difficulties in the theory, since Jung was faced with an overwhelming task of integrating disparate material. If he had drawn on a narrower range of sources his task of arriving at a coherent formulation of synchronicity might have been simpler. However, the formulation arrived at would doubtless have been correspondingly narrower and more partial, and it is to Jung's credit that he did not shun the riskier task of aiming for a more comprehensive and integrative account.

The complex situation resulting from the diversity of Jung's sources and influences was turned to account by finding in it a clue to his deeper aim in developing the theory of synchronicity (Chapter 4). For his wide-ranging researches can be viewed as an attempt to reintegrate spheres of knowledge that had become dissociated from one another with the rise of modernity. The theory of synchronicity appears as the culmination of Jung's lifelong struggle to resolve the tension he experienced, both in himself and in his culture, between the claims of science and religion. More specifically, the theory can be seen as an attempt to strengthen the religious aspect of analytical psychology. The purpose is not to present analytical psychology as a form of religion but, in the face of pressures threatening to collapse analytical psychology into a purely secular discipline, to preserve its integrating and mediating status between the sacred and secular domains. Hence, Jung drew on both scientific and religious sources, as well as on esoteric sources in which the scientific and religious had either not yet been separated or had already been recombined. In the light of this broad socio-cultural context many of the major characteristics of Jung's theory of synchronicity, including its difficulties and weaknesses, become more comprehensible.

However, synchronicity not only stems from attempts to resolve the tension between religion and science but also provides a perspective from which religion and science can be criticised in their turn (Chapter 5). Indeed, synchronicity emerges as a major component of Jung's overall critique of modern western culture. First, synchronicity is central to Jung's criticism of scientific rationalism, the one-sidedness of which it aims to compensate. Synchronicity champions a holistic and vitalistic view of science that leaves room for teleology as well as causes. It supports qualitative approaches, such as have been increasingly adopted in psychology, sociology and other social sciences. Again, synchronicity challenges existing models of science by suggesting that matter may have a psychic aspect that needs to be taken into consideration in the investigation of physical reality. Furthermore, because for Jung the psyche is partly spiritual, the connection of the psychic and physical in synchronicity may also provide the basis for a partial integration of religion and science. Second, synchronicity has a crucial contribution to make to Jung's critique of traditional dogmatic religion, in contrast to which it promotes experiential spirituality. The notion of synchronicity provides deep empirical and theoretical support for the religious attitude within analytical psychology; strengthens the case for acknowledging transpsychic reality; and helps with Jung's attempt to re-imagine God as a quaternity in which God's traditional spiritual attributes are linked to matter. Third, synchronicity plays an important role in Jung's critique of mass-minded society, the field in which the negative consequences of one-sided science and moribund religion are played out most conspicuously and perilously. Synchronicity suggests a way of under-standing social phenomena that recognises the possibility of acausal patterns of events. This provides an additional, complementary way of reading the social and political worlds. Furthermore, synchronicity suggests that the individual citizen can be viewed, in at least some respects, as a microcosm of society, which implies that the social effectiveness of individual action can be acknowledged even in contexts where any direct causal influence seems implausible. Synchronicity therefore supports an ethic of the highest individual responsibility. In sum, the theory of synchronicity is not just of theoretical or psychotherapeutic interest, nor is it only relevant to the introverted and esoteric aspects of analytical psychology. It is also highly relevant to the engagement of analytical psychology with the outer social and cultural worlds.

Further examination of some of the implications of the theory of synchronicity for the field of religion (Chapter 6) reveals that synchronicity can illuminate many traditional religious notions in a de-traditionalising manner that promotes or provides a basis for inter-religious relations and dialogues between religion and science. Furthermore, on many points analytical psychology and the theory of synchronicity bear close comparison with contemporary alternative (New Age or holistic) spirituality. Based on these parallels, there are various ways in which the theory of synchronicity might provide a resource both for better understanding New Age spirituality and for deepening or modifying it in directions already implicit in its underlying assumptions. From its connections with New Age thinking, the theory of synchronicity emerges even more clearly as a form of cultural criticism – one that reaches back deeply into the intellectual history of the West at the same time as it permeates widely through contemporary popular culture.

In sum, we have found that a detailed study of Jung's writings and statements on synchronicity advances understanding not only of synchronicity itself but also of the theoretical coherence and implications of his overall psychological model, the multiple contexts that gave rise to that model, and the possibilities of applying the model to illuminate social and cultural issues. The claims embedded in the concept of synchronicity – that there are uncaused events, that matter has a psychic aspect, that the psyche can relativise space and time, and that there is a dimension of objective meaning – are not inherently absurd. Indeed, these ideas have been implicitly if not explicitly believed in by much, perhaps most, of humanity throughout history. Even if Jung's theory of synchronicity were ultimately disproved, it would still have alerted people to an important set of phenomena and mode of thinking, disclosed much of their character, and rehearsed some of the intellectual moves needed adequately to engage with them.

There remain many questions about synchronicity that this study has not been able to address. One ambitious question that must enter the mind of anyone examining the area is whether Jung's theory of synchronicity is true. However, like many theories, the theory of synchronicity is of a speculative kind whose truth or falsity it may not be possible to demonstrate decisively. The question of truth therefore converts into such alternative questions as whether synchronicity is in any way amenable to experimental testing or whether it provides an accurate, or at least the best available, account of the psychodynamics of meaningful coincidence. Regarding experimental testing, we considered in Chapter 2 some of the difficulties encountered by Jung in his attempt to investigate synchronicity by means of his astrological experiment. Elsewhere Jung alludes to other attempts made with his analytical psychological colleagues in Zurich to investigate synchronicity experimentally using a range of divinatory techniques, though he says the experiments were cut short because of a lack of resources (1976: 538; cf. von Franz 1992: 260–1). A few subsequent researchers have obtained suggestive results using *I Ching* data (Rubin and Honorton 1971; Thalbourne *et al.* 1992–3). However, definitional problems remain about whether experiments such as these are investigating acausal (synchronistic) or causal (parapsychological) phenomena (Mansfield *et al.* 1998), and Mansfield is one well-informed, thoughtful and sympathetic commentator who has questioned whether the nature of synchronicity allows for experimental investigation even in principle (2002: 161–79). Nonetheless, the issue is far from settled.

Regarding the psychodynamics of synchronicity, while we have closely examined Jung's account we have not attempted to evaluate whether synchronicity does in fact relate to human psychology in the way he describes. Do synchronicities compensate the attitude of consciousness? Do they involve a withdrawal of psychic energy from consciousness and a corresponding accumulation of it around an archetypal theme in the unconscious? Do they promote individuation? Do they do these things always, some of the time, or never? To begin to answer these questions, we would need to examine a great number of detailed cases of coincidence. Several studies do include substantial collections of anecdotes: for example, Johnson (1899), Kammerer (1919), Hardy *et al.* (1973), Bolen (1979), Vaughan (1979), Aziz (1990), Inglis (1990), Mansfield (1995), Cousineau (1997), Hopcke (1997) and Plaskett (2000). However, while some of these studies helpfully categorise the events, very few provide not only a description and summary analysis of the coincidence events themselves but also sufficient background information to facilitate a deeper psychological and sociological exploration of the phenomenon and its implications. The studies that do provide more background information, such as those by Bolen, Aziz, Mansfield and Hopcke, already assume the validity of the Jungian psychodynamic framework. A greater number of phenomenologically richer accounts of meaningful coincidence need to be collected by researchers from a wider variety of theoretical orientations.[1] This material might then provide the basis for a comparison of different theoretical models, whether on the adequacy of their psychodynamic explanations or on other points.

Jung's definitions and characterisations of synchronicity repeatedly refer to the ideas of time, acausality, meaning and probability. Yet, as we have seen, he makes no sustained attempt to explain how far his understanding of these ideas conforms to the ways they are understood in wider philosophical and psychological discourses. Each of the ideas has been scrutinised in pertinent ways by later writers: von Franz has looked at time (1992: 63–143, 293–323), Mansfield at acausality (1995: 72–83), Mathers at meaning (2000) and Combs and Holland at probability (1994: 155–9; see also Fordham 1957; Diaconis and Mosteller 1989; McCusker and Sutherland 1991). Nevertheless, further systematic studies comparing Jung's use of these ideas with the ways they are used in historical and contemporary discussions in philosophy and psychology would greatly help in evaluating Jung's theory.

With a few exceptions, this study has focused primarily on Jung's own writings and has not extensively addressed post-Jungian work either on synchronicity or on the theory, contexts and applications of analytical psychology. While this focus has been deliberate, it does leave unanswered questions about the extent to which post-Jungian work might allow for or even necessitate a modified understanding of synchronicity. Many post-Jungians writing on synchronicity closely follow Jung's own classical formulations and framework (for example, Jaffé 1979; Meier 1963; von Franz 1992; also Aziz 1990; Mansfield 1995). However, others comment from a developmental perspective, with closer attention to transference issues and other clinical dynamics (for example, Fordham 1957; Gordon 1983; Williams 1957). Others again offer insights from an archetypal perspective, focusing more on the 'gods' and other images that might inform the concept of synchronicity and questioning the assumed relation of the phenomenon to the dynamics of compensation and individuation (for example, Hillman 1972: lvi–lix; 1979: 63–4). A careful assessment of the implications of these variations in emphasis would certainly be worth while. In this spirit, James Hall (2000) has proposed to explore the relative incidence of reports of synchronistic events and the various styles of working with them among analysts oriented towards the different schools classified by Samuels (1985: 1–22). However, this suggestion has yet to be successfully implemented.

Another question that has been largely untouched by this study is how reliably Jung uses his sources. The question could be asked of any of his sources, but particularly valuable would be a consideration of the extent to which the pre-modern, non-western and esoteric bodies of thought that he invokes really are based, as he suggests, on modes of thought that could be characterised as synchronistic. An indication of the need for such work concerns Jung's characterisation of the way of thinking of the Chinese who produced the *I Ching*. Their mind, he writes, 'seems to be exclusively preoccupied with the chance aspect of events' so that 'what we worship as causality passes almost unnoticed' (1950a: par. 968). However, the Sinologist Willard Peterson has presented evidence for a much more complicated situation. He has shown that, during the period when the *I Ching* was crystallising into its present form (from *c*. 400 BCE to *c*. 200 CE), the Chinese conceived of the connections among events in a wide variety of ways, including in terms of causality (Peterson 1988). Furthermore, the kind of 'correlative thinking' that did exist among the Chinese (see Needham 1962: 279–91) may not perfectly equate with what Jung means by synchronicity, for at least two reasons. First, the Chinese view is primarily cosmological, whereas Jung's is primarily psychological (see Main 1997a: 41); second, the Chinese view presupposes correlations among all phenomena, whereas for Jung synchronistic connections are notable exceptions. Similar questions arise in relation to Jung's statements about medieval and Renaissance theories of magical and astrological correspondences. I would not conclude that such discrepancies are irresolvable, but they do indicate areas where further historical research on Jung's theory of synchronicity would be desirable.

While this book has had much to say about the explicit and implicit ways in which Jung's work on synchronicity informed his critique of modern western culture it has not attempted to evaluate that critique itself, or the role of synchronicity within it, beyond showing their continued relevance for certain topics in the study of religion. This leaves unaddressed the question as to whether Jung's socio-cultural critique, including its underpinnings in the theory of synchronicity, is sufficiently plausible and relevant to deserve a hearing in current social and cultural debates more broadly. As we have noted elsewhere in this study, considerable energy has recently been expended to bring analytical psychology into dialogue with academic discourses on such topics as postmodernism (Hauke 2000), feminism (Rowland 2002), multiculturalism (Adams 1996) and politics (Samuels 1993, 2001), among others. Can the involvement of the idea of synchronicity in Jung's socio-cultural thinking assist these efforts, or is it more likely to hamper them as soon as the idea's radical and academically dubious implications about the nature of reality become visible?

Before suggesting that Jung's socio-critical thinking needs to be purged of its connections with synchronicity it is worth noting that the idea of synchronicity has already been found relevant for discussions of science, religion and society beyond the specifically Jungian framework to which this study has mostly confined itself. In the realm of science, the implications of synchronicity for an understanding of the relationship between mind and matter have been explored in a manner more aligned to the physics theory of David Bohm than the psychological theory of Jung (see Peat 1987). In the study of religion, the category of synchronicity, understood as the meaningful patterning of events, has proven informative in research into spiritual experiences reported by people who mostly could not be expected to have deep knowledge of Jungian psychology (see Hay 1990: 41–3, 83–4). In social anthropology, the notion of synchronicity has been found useful for understanding the interaction of simultaneity and causal sequencing in the creation of social meaning (see Parkin 1991: 174–5). If the idea of synchronicity has been found valuable in socio-cultural thinking that is not primarily Jungian it would seem rash not to continue exploring its relevance for socio-cultural thinking that avowedly is Jungian.

The rupture of time

In conclusion, I would like to return to the statement Jung made in his interview with Mircea Eliade in 1952:

> Religious experience is *numinous*, as Rudolf Otto calls it, and for me, as a psychologist, this experience differs from all others in the way it transcends the ordinary categories of space, time, and causality. Recently I have put a great deal of study into synchronicity (briefly, the 'rupture of time'), and I have established that it closely resembles numinous experiences where space, time, and causality are abolished.
>
> (McGuire and Hull 1978: 230)

In this statement, religious experience is characterised as numinous, and what is distinctive about numinous experiences is said to be that they transcend the ordinary categories of space, time and causality. Synchronicity, as the technical term that Jung developed to articulate this transcendence of space, time and causality, thus implicitly describes what for Jung is the kernel of numinous or religious experience. His view of the social and cultural significance of this emerges from an assertion he made later in the same interview: 'The modern world', he states, 'is desacralized, that is why it is in a crisis. Modern man must rediscover a deeper source of his own spiritual life' (ibid.). Jung's work on synchronicity can therefore be seen as part of his strategy for rediscovering a deeper source of spirituality in order to re-sacralise the modern world and thereby address the crisis of modernity.

In the course of presenting the above ideas, Jung defines synchronicity – briefly, parenthetically, and in scare quotes – as 'the rupture of time' (McGuire and Hull 1978: 230). This definition is poetic rather than formal. It may also owe something to the context in which it was uttered, since a major argument in the work of Jung's interviewer, Eliade, is that religious myths and rituals are essentially attempts to commemorate and return to a sacred timeless realm of origins, the *illud tempus*, through the abolition of profane time and history (see Hinnells 1997: 151). Further, when Jung states that religious or numinous experience 'differs from all others' we are reminded of Eliade's theory that religious experience is *sui generis* and cannot be explained away in psychological or sociological terms (ibid.).[2] However, whether or not influenced by its context of utterance, Jung's definition of synchronicity as the rupture of time conveys the richness, power and significance of his concept singularly well. For the definition gathers several senses in which, as we have seen in the preceding pages, synchronicity does indeed radically challenge our notions and experience of time.[3]

Synchronicity flagrantly transgresses the normal ways in which time is understood to operate. When synchronicity is conceived in terms of the simultaneity of coinciding events, the simultaneity implies that there has been no time for a causal influence to be transmitted from one of the events to the other. The meaningful connection between the events leads us to expect a temporal sequence, but the simultaneity (assuming, too, that there is no discernible common source) disrupts and defeats that expectation. When, alternatively, synchronicity involves not simultaneity but precognition, or occasionally retrocognition, what is overcome is the power of time to render future or past events inaccessible to consciousness. Time in this case is relativised or abolished, so that the timeless unconscious irrupts into time, thereby making present both the past, including ancient wisdom and mythology, and the future, including anticipated psychological and cosmic wholeness. In these ways, synchronicity disrupts our tendency to think in a manner oriented either towards the past, in terms of causality, or towards the future, in terms of teleology, focusing our attention instead on patterns of meaning disclosed in the present. In synchronicity, uniformly unfolding clock time is interrupted with moments of extraordinary timeliness, which in turn can open our eyes to a sense of present time as qualitative, filled with varying landscapes of meaning. Thereby, according to Jung, one can gain a deeper appreciation of the very nature of reality. With synchronicity, he remarks, 'one discovers an entirely different world . . . ; instead of looking at the causes that brought about certain conditions, one can look just as well at the actual being together of things' (1930–4: 334). One should then begin to 'realize what life is':

> Small things, which were formerly just banal and self-evident, should now have a real value, they should mean something and have a life of their own. For then one can take care of things properly – value things. One becomes considerate, and if it is a deep realization, one begins to pay attention to the things that simply happen. One never says, 'this is nothing', but one says, 'this is'. And then one understands what the transversal connection, the synchronistic connection, really is . . .
>
> (Jung 1930–4: 340)

As well as rupturing our individual notions and experience of time, synchronicity arguably plays a role in the rupture of time on a collective and historical scale. One of the influences on Jung's thinking about synchronicity was his investigation of astrology, from which he drew the idea that humanity is currently living in a period of transition between the two astrological aeons of Pisces and Aquarius. In the idiom of analytical psychology, such transitions symbolise 'changes in the constellation of psychic dominants, of the archetypes, . . . which bring about, or accompany, long-lasting transformations of the collective psyche' (1958b: par. 589). Jung certainly anticipated a significant rupture between the quality of psychological and social experience before the present time of transition and their quality after it.

If we prefer to leave aside such astrological speculation, the theory of synchronicity can still be seen, historically, to have emerged during a period of the rupture of time. In Chapter 5 we noted that not just Jung but many other commentators have characterised modernity in terms of a major break with tradition and the past. Jung and his analysands and contemporary readers lived in the midst of the rootlessness, alienation and depersonalisation generated by this rupture with the past. As we have seen, Jung's psychological work, especially on synchronicity, was largely an attempt to reorient within this condition through finding a mode of thought that could mediate between modernity and tradition. However, the theory of synchronicity not only is a response to a historical rupture of time that has taken place but also attempts to effect a further such rupture of its own. For modernity, in its close alignment with the achievements and aspirations of science, deeply embeds a belief in development and progress which, because it fosters domineering and distorting attitudes, itself arguably needs to be ruptured. Some of the strategies of postmodernism have been concerned with this, and the theory of synchronicity can be seen as a contribution to the same overall cultural critique (see Hauke 2000: 236–63). In these ways, the emergence of the theory of synchronicity can itself be seen as synchronistic – as the timely appearance of a way of understanding and orienting within a period of the rupture of time.

Notes

Introduction

1 Mainstream acceptance of Jung's ideas, especially within the academy, has been further obstructed by the widespread perception of them as essentialist, patriarchal, racist, mystical, and lacking in social awareness. Recent work has addressed these concerns, with fruitful connections established between Jungian thought and postmodernism (Hauke 2000), feminism (Rowland 2002), multiculturalism (Adams 1996), contemporary trends in religion (Young-Eisendrath and Miller 2000; Tacey 2001), politics (Samuels 1993, 2001), and other areas.

2 On Jung's relationship with Pauli, see the section on 'Physics' in Chapter 3 of the present work (see pp. 86–88). On Jung's involvement in the yearly Eranos conferences, which began in 1933, see Kirsch (2000: 6–7).

3 I use the term 'theory' simply to refer to the total body of related principles and ideas that Jung presented about synchronicity and do not imply that I consider, or that Jung considered, synchronicity a confirmed hypothesis. Jung himself refers to synchronicity variously as a concept, idea, principle, factor, hypothesis, thesis or model (1952b: pars. 852, 916, 947, 961; 1976: 109, 437) .

1 Synchronicity and analytical psychology

1 There is an important non-simultaneous aspect even to Jung's paradigm case of the scarab. For the patient's dream, rather than her decision to tell the dream, preceded the actual appearance of the scarab by several hours. Yet, Jung would doubtless have considered the coincidence between the dream and the actual appearance synchronistic even if the patient had not decided to tell the dream at just that moment.

2 Jung carefully distinguishes individuation from individualism: 'Individualism means deliberately stressing and giving prominence to some supposed peculiarity rather than to collective considerations and obligations. But individuation means precisely the better and more complete fulfilment of the collective qualities of the human being, since adequate consideration of the peculiarity of the individual is more conducive to a better social performance than when peculiarity is neglected or suppressed' (1928: par. 267).

3 As Watt points out, some serious criticisms have been levelled against the principal literature emphasising the biases that can enter the picture when one uses cognitive heuristics. For example, criticisms have been made of the way value-laden language has been used to convey a negative message about subjects' cognitive abilities; of the undeclared fact that the statistical assumptions behind the probability problems used to establish the biases in cognitive heuristics come from a school of reasoning that is held

by only a minority of statisticians, there being in fact no normative probability theory; of how certain errors and biases in judgement can be made to disappear if different experimental methodologies are applied; and finally, of the fact that cognitive heuristics, rather than being explanatory theories with predictive potential, are 'hardly more than re-descriptions of the phenomena seen in judgement under uncertainty' (1990–1: 72–4). On there being no normative probability theory, see also Combs and Holland (1994: 158). While considering that a good deal of work still needs to be done, Watt nevertheless concludes positively that 'cognitive heuristics can potentially identify the processes underlying decision-making, and can potentially suggest how to solve decision-making problems and improve judgement. For these reasons, they may be useful in evaluating coincidences' (1990–1: 75–6).

4 Zusne and Jones make the interesting observation that all acts of conjuring fall into the two main categories of alleged paranormal phenomena: 'mental magic, or the manipulation of "thoughts", and physical magic, or the manipulation of objects' (1989: 151–2).

5 Reasons for not preferring Faber's psychoanalytic model might include the failure of his reductive approach to account adequately for the reported phenomenology of religious experience, especially its cognitive and moral aspects (see, e.g., James 1902: 370–420). He also fails to engage with the mass of parapsychological research which overwhelmingly demonstrates that chance alone is not a satisfactory explanation for the occurrence of many anomalous events (see, e.g., Jahn and Dunne 1988; Radin 1997). Jung's approach, by contrast, both deeply respects the phenomenology of religious experience and engages seriously with the most advanced parapsychological research of his day (see Chapter 3).

2 Intellectual difficulties

1 Deirdre Bair writes that Jung heard the sounds of festivity 'in his head' (2004: 323). However, she doesn't explain why the experience should be interpreted solely intraphysically.

2 Victor Mansfield has pointed out that the particular quantum phenomena singled out by Jung and, following him, von Franz are mostly inappropriate (1995: 30). Nevertheless, he considers that 'Jung and von Franz are quite right to appeal to quantum mechanics', since 'Innumerable quantum phenomena are acausal in the strict sense' (ibid.: 32). With appropriate examples substituted for the inappropriate ones, Jung's argument can be followed as it stands.

3 For the influence of paranormal events on Jung's formulation of synchronicity, see the section 'Psychical Research and Parapsychology' in the following chapter.

3 Sources and influences

1 Most of the texts recounting the experiences related in this section are collected in Main (1997b).

2 In this approach, as in the format of his dissertation generally, Jung was following the model of the seminal study of a medium by Théodore Flournoy, *From India to the Planet Mars* (1899).

3 Freud was influenced in this by the Hungarian psychoanalyst Sandor Ferenczi (Charet 1993: 196–7). He is also known to have conducted informal experiments in telepathy with his daughter, Anna (see Gay 1988: 445).

4 For a full account of the conflict between Freud and Jung over spiritualistic phenomena, see Charet (1993: 171–227). For a collection of the writings that Freud eventually published on telepathy and occultism, as well as other psychoanalytic writings on these

subjects up to the year 1951, see Devereux (1953); see also Freud (1919, 1921a, 1921b, 1925, 1933).

5   This appears to be the view of Stefanie Zumstein-Preiswerk, a blood relation of both Jung and his medium (1975: 110). Hillman, however, thinks the relationship should be understood more in terms of transference and *participation mystique* (1976: 131–3).

6   Rudi Schneider's mediumship is, as John Beloff remarks, 'rightly considered among the best authenticated in the literature' (1993: 107).

7   For an interesting account of Schlag and the fate of his 'sample of ectoplasm', see Mulacz (1995).

8   The relationship of this episode to synchronicity is discussed more fully in Chapter 6.

9   For fuller detail on Jung's engagement with eastern thought, see Clarke (1994).

10 The active, almost shamanistic, role Jung assumed in the scarab incident – catching the insect as it flew in and dramatically presenting it to the patient with the words 'Here is your scarab' – has raised the eyebrows of several analysts with whom I have discussed the episode. Many contemporary analysts in Jung's position would, it seems, focus on their countertransference feelings about the tapping on the window and would not follow through with the dramatic enactment of the patient's dream. Especially critical is the psychoanalyst Mel Faber who describes Jung's response as an instance of 'therapeutic manipulation and authoritarianism' (1998: 135).

11 The principal topics were analytical psychology (1925), dream analysis (1928–30), interpretations of visions (1930–4), Kundalini yoga (1932a), and Nietzsche's *Thus Spoke Zarathustra* (1934–9).

12 However, Jung's earliest published reference to Kammerer seems to be in a letter to Pascual Jordan, dated 10 November 1934 (Jung 1973: 178).

13 For a lucid overview of Rhine's work, see Beloff (1993: 125–51). Though Rhine's work is no longer considered as unimpeachable as when it first appeared, equally challenging parapsychological results, meeting the more rigorous experimental standards that critics demand, have recently been produced by other researchers (see, e.g., Jahn and Dunne 1988; Radin 1997).

14 Jung also applied the notion of complementarity to the relationship between consciousness and the unconscious and between physics and psychology (Jung 1947/ 1954: par. 440).

15 It can be noted, too, that Pauli himself was prone to experiencing synchronicities, especially of the psychokinetic variety (see, e.g., Meier 2001: xviii; Hardy *et al.* 1973: 177–80).

16 For example, John Kerr suggests that Jung's notion of synchronicity owes much to his reading of E. T. A. Hoffmann's tale *The Devil's Elixirs* with its 'tangled web of fate and chance' (1988, in Bishop 1999: 138). Gottfried Heuer quotes a summary of the work of Otto Gross, which suggests that no later than the early 1920s Gross believed that 'even fate and coincidence become a symbol whose overarching conditions we can pursue analytically' (in Heuer 2003: 139; cf. Stanton 1992: 200–8). Again, probable influences on the theory of synchronicity could doubtless be traced within Jung's extensive, detailed engagement with Nietzsche's philosophy (see Burniston 1994; Bishop 1995).

4 Religion, science and synchronicity

1   To be sure, actual positions on the issue were subtler and more varied than these titles suggest, and there was a notable counter-trend that presented religion and science as fundamentally consistent with and supportive of each other. For example, Freud, when he was a student, came close to losing his lack of faith, so impressed was he by the

persuasive arguments of the philosopher Franz Brentano, an ex-priest who 'believed in God and respected Darwin at the same time' (Gay 1988: 29). The dominant rhetoric, however, was of titanic conflict. For fuller discussions, see Brooke (1991).

2 Indeed, the pressure on Jung of his commitment to both the religious and the scientific viewpoints undoubtedly contributed to the development of this theory, inasmuch as one of his requirements of a satisfactory psychological theory would have been its compatibility with both of these commitments.

3 'Concerning spirit (pneuma) I want to say that spirit and matter are a pair of opposite concepts which designate only the bipolar aspect of observation in time and space. Of their substance we know nothing. Spirit is just as ideal as matter. They are mere postulates of reason. Therefore I speak of psychic contents that are labelled "pneumatic" and others "material"' (Jung 1973: 421).

5 Synchronicity and Jung's critique of science, religion and society

1 For an excellent historical discussion of Jung's psychology and science see Shamdasani (2003).

2 The understanding of science as the systematic study of a field had existed at least since Aristotle.

3 Freud, however, did not believe in any easy reduction of the psychological to the physical, as his abandonment of his early 'Project for a Scientific Psychology' indicates.

4 For Jung the narrowness of the method of the science of his day and the narrowness of its subject matter went together and were equally to be criticised.

5 In spite of these developments, Jung at the end of his life maintained that he had always proceeded in a way consistent with 'scientific method' (1976: 567). He also suggested that part of the confusion regarding the scientific status of his work stemmed from differences in the Anglo-Saxon understanding of the term 'science', where it generally refers to the natural sciences, and the continental understanding, where 'science' can refer to any systematic approach to knowledge and therefore might include the social sciences and even such humanities subjects as history (ibid.).

6 This said, it should be noted that judgements of feeling, value and meaning do enter into some of Jung's procedures for gathering and interpreting data, such as dream interpretation, amplification, active imagination, and attention to the transference and countertransference.

7 For fuller discussion, see Main (2004).

8 See the section 'Alternative Theoretical Perspectives' (Chapter 1, pp. 27–35).

9 It is not clear how familiar Jung may have been with the work of these thinkers. His library contains two works by Scheler: *Mensch und Geschichte* [*Man and History*] (1929) and *Die Stellung des Menschen im Kosmos* [*The Place of Men in the Cosmos*] (1928) (*C. G. Jung Bibliothek: Katalog*, Küsnacht-Zürich, 1967: 65). In a letter to Count Hermann Keyserling (21 May 1927) Jung refers to Scheler disapprovingly as someone who has 'a predominantly intellectual attitude' (1973: 46). There are no references to Scheler in any of Jung's works dealing with social issues and, to the best of my knowledge, no references anywhere to Ortega or Mannheim.

6 Synchronicity and the spiritual revolution

1 For a fuller depiction and discussion of the new spirituality, see Tacey (2003).

2 The revitalisation of Christianity through focusing on personal spiritual experience was one of Jung's chief concerns in the field of religion, and an interesting project for

future research might be to explore connections between analytical psychology and those forms of Christianity that seemingly have transformed in this direction.

3 It should be noted that this characterisation of Jung's theoretical position regarding the feminine, though accurate, side-steps issues such as Jung's personal attitudes towards women and his gender essentialism that many contemporary commentators have found problematic (see, e.g., Wehr 1987; Young-Eisendrath 1997).

Conclusion: the rupture of time

1 The difficulties of gathering the kind of data that would be needed for a more systematic study emerged recently from a survey undertaken by The Synchronicity Committee, an international group of Jungian analysts, parapsychologists, physicists and other researchers and academics (see Hall *et al.* 1998). In spite of sending a questionnaire inviting accounts of synchronicities to every Jungian analyst and trainee in the United Kingdom and every member of the International Association for Analytical Psychology, only a handful of responses was received (with no returns at all in the United Kingdom).

2 Of course, the reverse is also possible: Eliade's formulations could have been shaped by his familiarity with Jung's work.

3 Synchronicity does not just rupture time. As Jung repeatedly notes, it ruptures space and causality as well as time. However, of these three concepts, time seems to be the most potently symbolised for Jung, as evinced by his symbolic identification with the Mithraic deity Aion (see Jung 1925; Noll 1992) and by his book named after the deity (1951a), to say nothing of his decision to adopt for his theory of meaningful coincidences a term embedding the idea of time.

References

Adams, M. V. (1996) *The Multicultural Imagination: 'Race', Colour and the Unconscious*, London and New York: Routledge.

Anderson, K. (1995) *Coincidences: Chance or Fate?*, London: Blandford.

Aziz, R. (1990) *C. G. Jung's Psychology of Religion and Synchronicity*, Albany, N.Y.: State University of New York Press.

Bair, D. (2004) *Jung: A Biography*, New York: Little Brown & Company.

Barbour, I. (1998) *Religion and Science: Historical and Contemporary Issues*, London: SCM Press.

Barnard, G. W. (2001) 'Diving into the Depths: Reflections on Psychology as a Religion', in D. Jonte-Pace and W. Parsons (eds) *Religion and Psychology: Mapping the Terrain. Contemporary dialogues, future prospects*, London and New York: Routledge.

Baumann-Jung, G. (1975) 'Some Reflections on the Horoscope of C. G. Jung', *Spring: An Annual of Archetypal Psychology and Jungian Thought*: 35–55.

Beaumont, R. (1994–5) 'What Value a Vision?', Interview with James Redfield, *Kindred Spirit* 3, no. 5: 16–20.

Beloff, J. (1977) 'Psi Phenomena: Causal versus Acausal Interpretation', *Journal of the Society for Psychical Research* 49: 573–82.

Beloff, J. (1993) *Parapsychology: A Concise History*, London: The Athlone Press.

Berger, P. (2002) 'Secularization and De-secularization', in L. Woodhead, P. Fletcher, H. Kawanami and D. Smith (eds) *Religions in the Modern World*, London and New York: Routledge.

Berger, P., Berger, B. and Kellner, H. (1974) *The Homeless Mind*, Harmondsworth: Penguin.

Berman, M. (1983) *All That Is Solid Melts Into Air: The Experience of Modernity*, London: Verso.

Bishop, P. (1995) *The Dionysian Self: C. G. Jung's Reception of Nietzsche*, Berlin: Walter de Gruyter.

Bishop, P. (2000) *Synchronicity and Intellectual Intuition in Kant, Swedenborg, and Jung*, Lampeter: The Edwin Mellen Press.

Bishop, P. (2002) *Jung's Answer to Job: A Commentary*, Hove and New York: Brunner-Routledge.

Bishop, P. (ed.) (1999) *Jung in Contexts: A Reader*, London and New York: Routledge.

Bloom, W. (2003) 'A Changing Perspective on the New Age Movement: From Marginal Flakiness to an Intelligent Religion for Mature People', Paper delivered at the

Alternative Spiritualities and New Age Studies Conference, 30 May to 1 June, The Open University, Milton Keynes, UK.

Bohm, D. (1980) *Wholeness and the Implicate Order*, London: Routledge & Kegan Paul.

Bohm, D. (1990) 'A New Theory of the Relationship of Mind and Matter', *Philosophical Psychology* 3, no. 2: 271–86.

Bolen, J. S. (1979) *The Tao of Psychology: Synchronicity and the Self*, New York: Harper & Row.

Bright, G. (1997) 'Synchronicity as a Basis of Analytic Attitude', *Journal of Analytical Psychology* 42, no. 4: 613–35.

Brooke, J. (1991) *Science and Religion: Some Historical Perspectives*, Cambridge: Cambridge University Press.

Brooke, J. and Cantor, G. (1998) *Reconstructing Nature: The Engagement of Science and Religion*, Edinburgh: T & T Clark.

Brooke, R. (1997) 'Jung in the Academy: A Response to David Tacey', *Journal of Analytical Psychology* 42, no. 2: 285–96.

Burniston, A. (1994) 'Synchronicity: A Dionysian Perspective', *Harvest: Journal for Jungian Studies* 40: 118–27.

Campbell, C. (1972) 'The Cult, the Cultic Milieu and Secularization', *A Sociological Yearbook of Religion in Britain* 5: 119–36.

Capra, F. (1976) *The Tao of Physics*, London: Fontana, 1983.

Casement, A. (1998) *Post-Jungians Today: Key Papers in Contemporary Analytical Psychology*, London and New York: Routledge.

Charet, F. X. (1993) *Spiritualism and the Foundations of C. G. Jung's Psychology*, Albany, N.Y.: State University of New York Press.

Clarke, J. J. (1992) *In Search of Jung: Historical and Philosophical Enquiries*, London and New York: Routledge.

Clarke, J. J. (1994) *Jung and Eastern Thought: A Dialogue with the Orient*, London: Routledge.

Combs, A. and Holland, M. (1994) *Synchronicity: Science, Myth and the Trickster*, Edinburgh: Floris Books; originally published New York: Paragon House, 1990.

Corbett, L. (1996) *The Religious Function of the Psyche*, London and New York: Routledge.

Cornelius, G. (1994) *The Moment of Astrology: Origins in Divination*, London: Penguin Arkana.

Cousineau, P. (1997) *Soul Moments: Marvelous Stories of Synchronicity – Meaningful Coincidences from a Seemingly Random World*, Berkeley, Calif.: Conari Press.

Crowley, V. (1989) *Wicca: The Old Religion in the New Age*, Wellingborough: Aquarian Press.

Devereux, G. (ed.) (1953) *Psychoanalysis and the Occult*, London: Souvenir Press, 1974; originally published New York: International Universities Press.

Diaconis, P. and Mosteller, F. (1989) 'Methods for Studying Coincidences', *Journal of the American Statistical Association* 84, no. 408: 853–61.

Dieckmann, H. (1976) 'Transference and Counter Transference: Results of a Berlin Research Group', *Journal of Analytical Psychology* 21, no. 1: 25–35.

Douglas, C. (1997) 'The Historical Context of Analytical Psychology', in P. Young-Eisendrath and T. Dawson (eds) *The Cambridge Companion to Jung*, Cambridge: Cambridge University Press, 17–34.

Draper, J. W. (1875) *History of the Conflict between Religion and Science*, London.

Eisenbud, J. (1983) *Parapsychology and the Unconscious*, Berkeley, Calif.: North Atlantic Books.

Eisenbud, J. (1990) 'Of Mice and Mind, or The Sorcerer's Apprentice: A Cautionary Tale', *Journal of the American Society for Psychical Research* 84: 345–64.

Ellenberger, H. (1970) *The Discovery of the Unconscious: The History and Evolution of Dynamic Psychiatry*, London: Allen Lane/The Penguin Press.

Erkelens, H. van (1991) 'Wolfgang Pauli's Dialogue with the Spirit of Matter', *Psychological Perspectives* 24: 34–53.

Erkelens, H. van (1999) 'Wolfgang Pauli and the Chinese Anima Figure', *Eranos Yearbook* 68: 21–45.

Estes, C. P. (1992) *Women Who Run with the Wolves: Myths and Stories of the Wild Woman Archetype*, New York: Random House.

Faber, M. (1998) *Synchronicity: C. G. Jung, Psychoanalysis, and Religion*, Westport, Conn.: Praeger.

Ferguson, M. (1982) *The Aquarian Conspiracy: Personal and Social Transformation in the 1980s*, London, Granada.

Flew, A. (1953) 'Coincidence and Synchronicity', *Journal of the Society for Psychical Research* 37, no. 677: 198–201.

Flournoy, T. (1899) *From India to the Planet Mars: A Case of Multiple Personality with Imaginary Languages*, ed. S. Shamdasani, with foreword by C. G. Jung and commentary by Mireille Cifali, tr. D. Vermilye, Princeton, N.J.: Princeton University Press.

Fordham, M. (1957) 'Reflections on the Archetypes and Synchronicity', in *New Developments in Analytical Psychology*, London: Routledge & Kegan Paul.

Fordham, M. (1962) 'An Interpretation of Jung's Thesis about Synchronicity', *British Journal of Medical Psychology* 35: 205–10.

Fordham, M. (1993) *The Making of an Analyst: A Memoir*, London: Free Association Books.

Freud, S. (1919) 'The Uncanny', in *The Standard Edition of the Complete Psychological Works of Sigmund Freud*, trans. and ed. J. Strachey, vol. 17, London: The Hogarth Press.

Freud, S. (1921a) 'Dreams and Telepathy', in *The Standard Edition of the Complete Psychological Works of Sigmund Freud*, trans. and ed. J. Strachey, vol. 18, London: The Hogarth Press.

Freud, S. (1921b) 'Psycho-analysis and Telepathy', in *The Standard Edition of the Complete Psychological Works of Sigmund Freud*, trans. and ed. J. Strachey, vol. 18, London: The Hogarth Press.

Freud, S. (1925) 'The Occult Significance of Dreams', in *The Standard Edition of the Complete Psychological Works of Sigmund Freud*, trans. and ed. J. Strachey, vol. 19, London: The Hogarth Press.

Freud, S. (1927) 'The Future of an Illusion', in *The Standard Edition of the Complete Psychological Works of Sigmund Freud*, trans. and ed. James Strachey, vol. 21, London: The Hogarth Press.

Freud, S. (1933) 'Dreams and Occultism', in *The Standard Edition of the Complete Psychological Works of Sigmund Freud*, trans. and ed. J. Strachey, vol. 22, London: The Hogarth Press.

Gammon, M. (1973) '"Window into Eternity": Archetype and Relativity', *Journal of Analytical Psychology* 18, no. 1: 11–24.

Gay, P. (1988) *Freud: A Life for Our Time*, London: Dent.

Giegerich, W. (1987) 'The Rescue of the World: Jung, Hegel, and the Subjective Universe', *Spring: Journal of Archetype and Culture* 48: 107–14.

Gordon, R. (1983) 'Reflections on Jung's Concept of Synchronicity', in *In the Wake of Jung: A Selection from 'Harvest'*, ed. M. Tuby, London: Coventure.

Grattan-Guinness, I. (1978) 'What are Coincidences?', *Journal of the Society for Psychical Research* 49: 949–55.

Grattan-Guinness, I. (1983) 'Coincidences as Spontaneous Psychical Phenomena', *Journal of the Society for Psychical Research* 52: 59–71.

Hall, J. (2000) Personal communications to the author.

Hall, J., Main, R. and Marlan, J. (1998) 'Synchronicity in Jungian Analysis', *The Umbrella Group Newsletter* 3 (Spring/Summer): 17–18, 38–9; partly reprinted in the *International Association for Analytical Psychology Newsletter* 18 (1998): 146–9.

Hanegraaff, W. (1998) *New Age Religion and Western Culture: Esotericism in the Mirror of Secular Thought*, Albany, N.Y.: State University of New York Press; Leiden: E. J. Brill, 1996.

Hanegraaff, W. (2002) 'New Age Religion', in L. Woodhead, P. Fletcher, H. Kawanami and D. Smith (eds) *Religions in the Modern World*, London and New York: Routledge.

Hannah, B. (1977) *C. G. Jung: His Life and Work – A Biographical Memoir*, London: Michael Joseph.

Hardy, A., Harvie, R. and Koestler, A. (1973) *The Challenge of Chance: Experiments and Speculations*, London: Hutchinson.

Hauke, C. (2000) *Jung and the Postmodern: The Interpretation of Realities*, London and New York: Routledge.

Hay, D. (1990) *Religious Experience Today: Studying the Facts*, London: Mowbray.

Heelas, P. (1996) *The New Age Movement: The Celebration of the Self and the Sacralization of Modernity*, Oxford: Blackwell.

Heelas, P. (2002) 'The Spiritual Revolution: From "Religion" to "Spirituality"', in L. Woodhead, P. Fletcher, H. Kawanami and D. Smith (eds) *Religions in the Modern World*, London and New York: Routledge.

Heisig, J. (1972) 'The *VII Sermones*: Play and Theory', *Spring: An Annual of Archetypal Psychology and Jungian Thought*: 206–18.

Henry, J. (1993) 'Coincidence Experience Survey', *Journal of the Society for Psychical Research* 59, no. 831: 97–108.

Heuer, G. (2003) 'The Devil Underneath the Couch: The Secret Story of Jung's Twin Brother', *Harvest: International Journal for Jungian Studies* 49, no. 2: 130–45.

Hillman, J. (1972) 'An Essay on Pan', in W. H. Roscher and J. Hillman, *Pan and the Nightmare*, Zürich: Spring Publications.

Hillman, J. (1976) 'Some Early Background to Jung's Ideas: Notes on *C. G. Jung's Medium* by Stephanie Zumstein-Preiswerk', *Spring: An Annual of Archetypal Psychology and Jungian Thought*: 123–36.

Hillman, J. (1979) 'Peaks and Vales', in J. Hillman, H. Murray, T. Moore, J. Baird, T. Cowan and R. Severson, *Puer Papers*, Dallas, Tex.: Spring Publications.

Hinnells, J. (ed.) (1997) *The Penguin Dictionary of Religions*, London: Penguin.

Holland, R. F. (1967) 'The Miraculous', in D. Z. Phillips (ed.) *Religion and Understanding*, Oxford: Basil Blackwell.

Homans, P. (1979/1995) *Jung in Context: Modernity and the Making of a Psychology*, Chicago, Ill.: The University of Chicago Press.

Honner, J. (1987) *The Description of Nature: Niels Bohr and the Philosophy of Quantum Physics*, Oxford: Clarendon Press.

Hook, D. (1973) *The I Ching and You*, London: Routledge & Kegan Paul.

Hopcke, R. (1990) 'The Barker: A Synchronistic Even in Analysis', *Journal of Analytical Psychology* 35, no. 4: 459–73.

Hopcke, R. (1997) *There Are No Accidents: Synchronicity and the Stories of Our Lives*, London: Macmillan.

Hyde, M. (1992) *Jung and Astrology*, London: Aquarian Press.

Inglis, B. (1990) *Coincidence: A Matter of Chance – or Synchronicity?*, London: Hutchinson.

Jaffé, A. (1967) 'C. G. Jung and Parapsychology', in J. R. Smythies (ed.), *Science and ESP*, London: Routledge & Kegan Paul, 263–80.

Jaffé, A. (1971) *From the Life and Work of C. G. Jung*, London: Hodder & Stoughton.

Jaffé, A. (1979) 'Synchronistic Phenomena', in *Apparitions: An Archetypal Approach to Death, Dreams and Ghosts*, Irving, Tex.: Spring Publications.

Jaffé, A. (1984) 'Details about C. G. Jung's Family', *Spring*: Journal of Archetype and Culture 45: 35–43.

Jahn, R. G. and Dunne, B. J. (1988) *Margins of Reality*, San Diego, Calif.: Harcourt Brace Jovanovich.

James, W. (1890) *The Principles of Psychology*, 2 vols, New York: Dover, 1950.

James, W. (1902) *The Varieties of Religious Experience*, 2nd edn, New York: Longman Green.

Jarrett, J. (1981) 'Schopenhauer and Jung', *Spring: Journal of Archetype and Culture*: 193–204.

Johnson, A. (1899) 'Coincidences', *Proceedings of the Society for Psychical Research* 14: 158–330.

Jung, C. G. (1896–9) *The Collected Works of C. G. Jung*, eds Sir Herbert Read, Michael Fordham and Gerhard Adler, executive editor William McGuire, trans. R. F. C. Hull [hereafter *Collected Works*], vol. A, *The Zofingia Lectures*, Princeton, N.J.: Princeton University Press, 1983.

Jung, C. G. (1902)'On the Psychology and Pathology of So-Called Occult Phenomena', in *Collected Works*, vol. 1, *Psychiatric Studies*, London: Routledge & Kegan Paul, 1957.

Jung, C. G. (1904–37) *Collected Works*, vol. 2, *Experimental Researches*, London: Routledge & Kegan Paul, 1973.

Jung, C. G. (1905) 'On Spiritualistic Phenomena', in *Collected Works*, vol. 18, *The Symbolic Life*, London: Routledge & Kegan Paul, 1977.

Jung, C. G. (1906–49) *Collected Works*, vol. 4, *Freud and Psychoanalysis*, London: Routledge & Kegan Paul, 1963.

Jung, C. G. (1908/1914) 'The Content of the Psychoses', in *Collected Works*, vol. 3, *The Psychogenesis of Mental Disease*, London: Routledge & Kegan Paul, 1960.

Jung, C. G. (1911–12) *Psychology of the Unconscious*, London: Kegan Paul, Trench, Trubner & Co., 1919.

Jung, C. G. (1911–12/1952) *Collected Works*, vol. 5, *Symbols of Transformation*, 2nd edn, London: Routledge & Kegan Paul, 1967.

Jung, C. G. (1912) 'New Paths in Psychology' in *Collected Works*, vol. 7, *Two Essays on Analytical Psychology*, 2nd edn, London: Routledge & Kegan Paul, 1966.

Jung, C. G. (1912–66) *Collected Works*, vol. 7, *Two Essays on Analytical Psychology*, 2nd edn, London: Routledge & Kegan Paul, 1966.

Jung, C. G. (1914) 'On Psychological Understanding', in *Collected Works*, vol. 3, *The Psychogenesis of Mental Disease*, London: Routledge & Kegan Paul, 1960.

Jung, C. G. (1916) 'The Structure of the Unconscious', in *Collected Works*, vol. 7, *Two Essays on Analytical Psychology*, 2nd edn, London: Routledge & Kegan Paul, 1966.

Jung, C. G. (1916/1948) 'General Aspects of Dream Psychology', in *Collected Works*, vol. 8, *The Structure and Dynamics of the Psyche*, 2nd edn, London: Routledge & Kegan Paul, 1969.

Jung, C. G. (1916/1957) 'The Transcendent Function', in *Collected Works*, vol. 8, *The Structure and Dynamics of the Psyche*, 2nd edn, London: Routledge & Kegan Paul, 1969.

Jung, C. G. (1919) 'Instinct and the Unconscious', in *Collected Works*, vol. 8, *The Structure and Dynamics of the Psyche*, 2nd edn, London: Routledge & Kegan Paul, 1969.

Jung, C. G. (1920/1948) 'The Psychological Foundations of Belief in Spirits', in *Collected Works*, vol. 8, *The Structure and Dynamics of the Psyche*, 2nd edn, London: Routledge & Kegan Paul, 1969.

Jung, C. G. (1921) *Collected Works*, vol. 6, *Psychological Types*, London: Routledge & Kegan Paul, 1971.

Jung, C. G. (1925) *Analytical Psychology: Notes of the Seminar Given in 1925*, ed. William McGuire, London: Routledge, 1990.

Jung, C. G. (1926) 'Spirit and Life', in *Collected Works*, vol. 8, *The Structure and Dynamics of the Psyche*, 2nd edn, London: Routledge & Kegan Paul, 1969.

Jung, C. G. (1926/1946) 'Analytical Psychology and Education: Three Lectures', in *Collected Works*, vol. 17, *The Development of Personality*, London: Routledge & Kegan Paul, 1954.

Jung, C. G. (1927/1931) 'The Structure of the Psyche', in *Collected Works*, vol. 8, *The Structure and Dynamics of the Psyche*, 2nd edn, London: Routledge & Kegan Paul, 1969.

Jung, C. G. (1928) 'The Relations Between the Ego and the Unconscious' in *Collected Works*, vol. 7, *Two Essays on Analytical Psychology*, 2nd edn, London: Routledge & Kegan Paul, 1966.

Jung, C. G. (1928–30) *Dream Analysis: Notes of the Seminar Given in 1928–1930*, ed. W. McGuire, London, Melbourne and Henley: Routledge & Kegan Paul, 1984.

Jung, C. G. (1928/1931) 'The Spiritual Problem of Modern Man', in *Collected Works*, vol. 10, *Civilization in Transition*, 2nd edn, London: Routledge & Kegan Paul, 1970.

Jung, C. G. (1928–54) *Collected Works*, vol. 11, *Psychology and Religion: West and East*, 2nd edn, London: Routledge & Kegan Paul, 1969.

Jung, C. G. (1929) 'Problems of Modern Psychotherapy', in *Collected Works*, vol. 16, *The Practice of Psychotherapy*, 2nd edn, London: Routledge & Kegan Paul, 1966.

Jung, C. G. (1929–54) *Collected Works*, vol. 13, *Alchemical Studies*, London: Routledge & Kegan Paul, 1968.

Jung, C. G. (1930) 'Richard Wilhelm: In Memoriam', in *Collected Works*, vol. 15, *The Spirit in Man, Art and Literature*, London: Routledge & Kegan Paul, 1966.

Jung, C. G. (1930–1) 'The Stages of Life', in *Collected Works*, vol. 8, *The Structure and Dynamics of the Psyche*, 2nd edn, London: Routledge & Kegan Paul, 1969.

Jung, C. G. (1930–4) *Visions: Notes of the Seminar Given in 1930–1934 by C. G. Jung*, ed. C. Douglas, 2 vols, London: Routledge, 1998.

Jung, C. G. (1932a) *The Psychology of Kundalini Yoga: Notes of the Seminar given in 1932*, ed. S. Shamdasani, Princeton, N.J.: Princeton University Press; London: Routledge, 1996.

Jung, C. G. (1932b) 'Sigmund Freud in His Historical Setting', in *Collected Works*, vol. 15, *The Spirit in Man, Art and Literature*, London: Routledge & Kegan Paul, 1966.

Jung, C. G. (1933/1934) 'The Meaning of Psychology for Modern Man', in *Collected Works*, vol. 10, *Civilization in Transition*, 2nd edn, London: Routledge & Kegan Paul, 1970.

Jung, C. G. (1934a) 'A Review of the Complex Theory', in *Collected Works*, vol. 8, *The Structure and Dynamics of the Psyche*, 2nd edn, London: Routledge & Kegan Paul, 1969.

Jung, C. G. (1934b) 'The Soul and Death', in *Collected Works*, vol. 8, *The Structure and Dynamics of the Psyche*, 2nd edn, London: Routledge & Kegan Paul, 1969.

Jung, C. G. (1934–9) *Nietzsche's 'Zarathustra': Notes of the Seminar Given in 1934–1939*, 2 vols, ed. J. L. Jarrett, London: Routledge, 1989.

Jung, C. G. (1934/1950) 'A Study in the Process of Individuation', in *Collected Works*, vol. 9i, *The Archetypes and the Collective Unconscious*, 2nd edn, London: Routledge & Kegan Paul, 1968.

Jung, C. G. (1935) 'The Tavistock Lectures', in *Collected Works*, vol. 18, *The Symbolic Life*, London: Routledge & Kegan Paul, 1977.

Jung, C. G. (1936a) 'The Concept of the Collective Unconscious', in *Collected Works*, vol. 9i, *The Archetypes and the Collective Unconscious*, 2nd edn, London: Routledge & Kegan Paul, 1968.

Jung, C. G. (1936b) 'Yoga and the West', in *Collected Works*, vol. 11, *Psychology and Religion: West and East*, 2nd edn, London: Routledge & Kegan Paul, 1969.

Jung, C. G. (1938/1940) 'Psychology and Religion', in *Collected Works*, vol. 11, *Psychology and Religion: West and East*, 2nd edn, London: Routledge & Kegan Paul, 1969.

Jung, C. G. (1938/1954) 'Psychological Aspects of the Mother Archetype', in *Collected Works*, vol. 9i, *The Archetypes and the Collective Unconscious*, 2nd edn, London: Routledge & Kegan Paul, 1968.

Jung, C. G. (1939) 'The Symbolic Life', in *Collected Works*, vol. 18, *The Symbolic Life*, London: Routledge & Kegan Paul, 1976.

Jung, C. G. (1939/1954) 'The Tibetan Book of the Great Liberation', in *Collected Works*, vol. 11, *Psychology and Religion: West and East*, 2nd edn, London: Routledge & Kegan Paul, 1969.

Jung, C. G. (1940) 'The Psychology of the Child Archetype', in *Collected Works*, vol. 9i, *The Archetypes and the Collective Unconscious*, 2nd edn, London: Routledge & Kegan Paul, 1968.

Jung, C. G. (1942/1948) 'A Psychological Approach to the Dogma of the Trinity', in *Collected Works*, vol. 11, *Psychology and Religion: West and East*, 2nd edn, London: Routledge & Kegan Paul, 1969.

Jung, C. G. (1943) 'The Psychology of Eastern Meditation', in *Collected Works*, vol. 11, *Psychology and Religion: West and East*, 2nd edn, London: Routledge & Kegan Paul, 1969.

Jung, C. G. (1944) *Collected Works*, vol. 12, *Psychology and Alchemy*, 2nd edn, London: Routledge & Kegan Paul, 1968.

Jung, C. G. (1945) 'Marginalia on Contemporary Events', in *Collected Works*, vol. 18, *The Symbolic Life*, London: Routledge & Kegan Paul, 1976.

Jung, C. G. (1945/1948a) 'On the Nature of Dreams', in *Collected Works*, vol. 8, *The Structure and Dynamics of the Psyche*, 2nd edn, London: Routledge & Kegan Paul, 1969.

Jung, C. G. (1945/1948b) 'The Phenomenology of the Spirit in Fairytales', in *Collected Works*, vol. 9i, *The Archetypes and the Collective Unconscious*, 2nd edn, London: Routledge & Kegan Paul, 1968.

Jung, C. G. (1946) 'The Psychology of the Transference', in *Collected Works*, vol. 16, *The Practice of Psychotherapy*, 2nd edn, London: Routledge & Kegan Paul, 1966.

Jung, C. G. (1947/1954) 'On the Nature of the Psyche', in *Collected Works*, vol. 8, *The Structure and Dynamics of the Psyche*, 2nd edn, London: Routledge & Kegan Paul, 1969.

Jung, C. G. (1949) 'Foreword to Abegg: *Ostasien denkt anders*', in *Collected Works*, vol. 18, *The Symbolic Life*, London: Routledge & Kegan Paul, 1976.

Jung, C. G. (1950a) 'Foreword to the "I Ching"', in *Collected Works*, vol. 11, *Psychology and Religion: West and East*, 2nd edn, London: Routledge & Kegan Paul, 1969.

Jung, C. G. (1950b) 'Foreword to Moser: "Spuk: Irrglaube oder Wahrglaube?"', in *Collected Works*, vol. 18, *The Symbolic Life*, London: Routledge & Kegan Paul, 1976.

Jung, C. G. (1950/1951) 'The Miraculous Fast of Brother Klaus', in *Collected Works*, vol. 18, *The Symbolic Life*, London: Routledge & Kegan Paul, 1976.

Jung, C. G. (1950–5) 'Letters on Synchronicity', in *Collected Works*, vol. 18, *The Symbolic Life*, London: Routledge & Kegan Paul, 1976.

Jung, C. G. (1951a) *Collected Works*, vol. 9ii, *Aion*, 2nd edn, London: Routledge & Kegan Paul, 1968.

Jung, C. G. (1951b) 'On Synchronicity', in *Collected Works*, vol. 8, *The Structure and Dynamics of the Psyche*, 2nd edn, London: Routledge & Kegan Paul, 1969.

Jung, C. G. (1952a) 'Answer to Job', in *Collected Works*, vol. 11, *Psychology and Religion: West and East*, 2nd edn, London: Routledge & Kegan Paul, 1969.

Jung, C. G. (1952b) 'Synchronicity: An Acausal Connecting Principle', in *Collected Works*, vol. 8, *The Structure and Dynamics of the Psyche*, 2nd edn, London: Routledge & Kegan Paul, 1969.

Jung, C. G. (1954a) 'Archetypes of the Collective Unconscious', in *Collected Works*, vol. 9i, *The Archetypes and the Collective Unconscious*, 2nd edn, London: Routledge & Kegan Paul, 1968.

Jung, C. G. (1954b) 'Letter to Père Lachat', in *Collected Works*, vol. 18, *The Symbolic Life*, London: Routledge & Kegan Paul, 1977.

Jung, C. G. (1954c) 'On the Psychology of the Trickster-Figure', in *Collected Works*, vol. 9i, *The Archetypes and the Collective Unconscious*, 2nd edn, London: Routledge & Kegan Paul, 1968.

Jung, C. G. (1954d) 'On Resurrection', in *Collected Works*, vol. 18, *The Symbolic Life*, London: Routledge & Kegan Paul, 1977.

Jung, C. G. (1955) *Synchronicity: An Acausal Connecting Principle*, London: Ark Paperbacks, 1987.

Jung, C. G. (1955–6) *Collected Works*, vol. 14, *Mysterium Coniunctionis: An Inquiry into the Separation and Synthesis of Psychic Opposites in Alchemy*, London: Routledge & Kegan Paul, 1963.

Jung, C. G. (1957) 'The Undiscovered Self (Present and Future)', in *Collected Works*, vol. 10, *Civilization in Transition*, 2nd edn, London: Routledge & Kegan Paul, 1970.

Jung, C. G. (1958a) 'An Astrological Experiment', in *Collected Works*, vol. 18, *The Symbolic Life*, London: Routledge & Kegan Paul, 1977.

Jung, C. G. (1958b) 'Flying Saucers: A Modern Myth of Things Seen in the Skies', in *Collected Works*, vol. 10, *Civilization in Transition*, 2nd edn, London: Routledge & Kegan Paul, 1970.

Jung, C. G. (1958c) 'A Psychological View of Conscience', in *Collected Works*, vol. 10, *Civilization in Transition*, 2nd edn, London: Routledge & Kegan Paul, 1970.

Jung, C. G. (1963) *Memories, Dreams, Reflections*, recorded and edited by A. Jaffé, trans. R. and C. Winston, London: Collins and Routledge & Kegan Paul, 1963.

Jung, C. G. (1973) *Letters 1: 1906–1950*, selected and edited by G. Adler in collaboration with A. Jaffé, trans. R. F. C. Hull, London: Routledge & Kegan Paul.

Jung, C. G. (1976) *Letters 2: 1951–1963*, selected and edited by G. Adler in collaboration with A. Jaffé, trans. R. F. C. Hull, London: Routledge & Kegan Paul.

Jung, C. G. and Pauli, W. (1955) *The Interpretation of Nature and the Psyche*, trans. R. F. C. Hull, London: Routledge & Kegan Paul.

Kalupahana, D. J. (1975) *Causality: The Central Philosophy of Buddhism*, Honolulu: The University Press of Hawaii.

Kammerer, P. (1919) *Das Gesetz der Serie*, Stuttgart and Berlin: Deutches Verlags-Anstalt.

Karcher, S. (2003) *Total I Ching: Myths for Change*, London: TimeWarner Books.

Kaufman, G. (2001a) 'On Thinking of God as Serendipitous Creativity', *Journal of the American Academy of Religion* 69, no. 2: 409–25.

Kaufman, G. (2001b) 'Re-conceiving God and Humanity in Light of Today's Evolutionary-Ecological Consciousness', *Zygon* 36, no. 2: 335–48.

Kelly, S. (1993) 'A Trip through Lower Town: Reflections on a Case of Double Synchronicity', *Journal of Analytical Psychology* 38, no. 2: 191–8.

Kerr, J. (1988) '*The Devil's Elixirs*, Jung's "theology" and the dissolution of Freud's "poisoning complex"', in P. Bishop (ed.) *Jung in Contexts: A Reader*, London and New York: Routledge, 1999.

Keutzer, C. S. (1982) 'Archetypes, Synchronicity and the Theory of Formative Causation', *Journal of Analytical Psychology* 27, no. 3: 255–62.

Keutzer, C. S. (1984) 'The Power of Meaning: From Quantum Mechanics to Synchronicity', *Journal of Humanistic Psychology* 24, no. 1: 80–94.

Kirsch, T. (2000) *The Jungians: A Comparative and Historical Perspective*, London and Philadelphia (Pa.): Routledge.

Koestler, A. (1972) *The Roots of Coincidence*, London: Hutchinson.

Koestler, A. (1975) *The Case of the Midwife Toad*, London: Picador.

Legge, J. (trans.) (1882) *The Yi King*, in M. Müller (ed.) *The Sacred Books of the East*, vol. 16, Oxford: The Clarendon Press; reprint, Delhi, Varanasi, Patna: Motilal Banarsidass, 1966.

Lehmann, D. (2002) 'Religion and Globalization', in L. Woodhead, P. Fletcher, H. Kawanami and D. Smith (eds) *Religions in the Modern World*, London and New York: Routledge.

Lindorff, D. (1995a) 'One Thousand Dreams: The Spiritual Awakening of Wolfgang Pauli', *Journal of Analytical Psychology* 40, no. 4: 555–69.

Lindorff, D. (1995b) 'Psyche, Matter and Synchronicity: A Collaboration Between C. G. Jung and Wolfgang Pauli', *Journal of Analytical Psychology* 40, no. 4: 571–86.

McCusker, B. and Sutherland, C. (1991) 'Probability and the Psyche I: A Reproducible

Experiment using Tarot, and the Theory of Probability', *Journal of the Society for Psychical Research* 57, no. 822: 344–53.

McGuire, W. (ed.) (1974) *The Freud/Jung Letters: The Correspondence between Sigmund Freud and C. G. Jung*, trans. R. Manheim and R. F. C. Hull, Princeton, N.J.: Princeton University Press.

McGuire, W. and Hull, R. F. C. (eds) (1978) *C. G. Jung Speaking: Interviews and Encounters*, London: Thames & Hudson.

McLynn, F. (1996) *Carl Gustav Jung*, New York: Bantam Press.

Main, R. (1997a) 'Synchronicity and the *I Ching*: Clarifying the Connections', *Harvest: Journal for Jungian Studies* 43, no. 1: 31–44.

Main, R. (ed.) (1997b) *Jung on Synchronicity and the Paranormal*, London: Routledge; Princeton, N.J.: Princeton University Press.

Main, R. (2000) 'Religion, Science, and Synchronicity', *Harvest: Journal for Jungian Studies* 46, no. 2: 89–107.

Main, R. (2001) 'Putting the Sinn Back into Synchronicity: Some Spiritual Implications of Synchronistic Experiences', 2nd Series Occasional Paper 28, Lampeter: Religious Experience Research Centre.

Main, R. (2004) 'Religion', in R. Papadopoulos (ed.) *The Handbook of Jungian Psychology: Theory, Practice and Applications*, Hove and Philadelphia (Pa.): Brunner-Routledge.

Mansfield, V. (1995) *Synchronicity, Science, and Soul-Making: Understanding Jungian Synchronicity through Physics, Buddhism, and Philosophy*, Chicago and La Salle, Ill.: Open Court.

Mansfield, V. (2002) *Head and Heart: A Personal Exploration of Science and the Sacred*, Wheaton, Ill.: Quest Books.

Mansfield, V., Rhine-Feather, S. and Hall, J. (1998) 'The Rhine–Jung Letters: Distinguishing Synchronicity from Parapsychological Phenomena', *Journal of Parapsychology* 62, no. 1: 3–25.

Mathers, D. (2000) *An Introduction to Meaning and Purpose in Analytical Psychology*, London and Philadelphia (Pa.): Routledge.

Meier, C. A. (1963) 'Psychosomatic Medicine from the Jungian Point of View', *Journal of Analytical Psychology* 8, no. 2: 103–21.

Meier, C. A. (ed.) (2001) *Atom and Archetype: The Pauli/Jung letters 1932–1958*, London: Routledge.

Mulacz, W. P. (1995) 'Oscar R. Schlag', *Journal of the Society for Psychical Research* 60: 263–7.

Nagy, M. (1991) *Philosophical Issues in the Psychology of C. G. Jung*, Albany, N.Y.: State University of New York Press.

Needham, J. (1962) *Science and Civilisation in China*, vol. 2, Cambridge: Cambridge University Press.

Noll, R. (1992) 'Jung the *Leontocephalus*', in P. Bishop (ed.) *Jung in Contexts: A Reader*, London and New York: Routledge, 1999.

Noll, R. (1994) *The Jung Cult: The Origins of a Charismatic Movement*, Princeton, N.J.: Princeton University Press.

Noll, R. (1997) *The Aryan Christ: The Secret Life of Carl Jung*, New York: Random House.

Odin, S. (1982) *Process Metaphysics and Hua-Yen Buddhism*, Albany, N.Y.: State University of New York Press.

Oeri, A. (1970) 'Some Youthful Memories of C. G. Jung', *Spring: An Annual of Archetypal Psychology and Jungian Thought*, 182–9.

Palmer, M. (1997) *Freud and Jung on Religion*, London and New York: Routledge.

Papadopoulos, R. (1984) 'Jung and the Concept of the Other', in R. Papadopoulos and G. Saayaman (eds) *Jung in Modern Perspective: The Master and His Legacy*, Bridport: Prism Press, 1991, 54–88.

Papadopoulos, R. (1997a) 'Individual Identity and Collective Narratives of Conflict', *Harvest: Journal for Jungian Studies* 43, no. 2: 7–26.

Papadopoulos, R. (1997b) 'Is Teaching Jung Within the University Possible?: A Response to David Tacey', *Journal of Analytical Psychology* 42, no. 2: 297–301.

Papadopoulos, R. K. (1998) 'Destructiveness, Atrocities and Healing: Epistemological and Clinical Reflections', *Journal of Analytical Psychology* 43, no. 4: 455–77.

Papadopoulos, R. K. (ed.) (1992) *Carl Gustav Jung: Critical Assessments*, 4 vols, London and New York: Routledge

Papadopoulos, R. K. and Saayaman, G. S. (eds) (1984) *Jung in Modern Perspective: The Master and His Legacy*, Bridport: Prism Press, 1991.

Parkin, D. (1991) 'Simultaneity and Sequencing in the Oracular Speech of Kenyan Diviners', in P. Peek (ed.) *African Divination Systems: Ways of Knowing*, Bloomington and Indianapolis: Indiana University Press.

Pauli, W. (1955) 'The Influence of Archetypal Ideas on the Scientific Theories of Kepler', in C. G. Jung and W. Pauli, *The Interpretation of Nature and the Psyche*, trans. R. F. C. Hull, London: Routledge & Kegan Paul.

Peat, F. D. (1987) *Synchronicity: The Bridge Between Matter and Mind*, New York: Bantam.

Peck, M. S. (1978) *The Road Less Travelled*, New York: Simon & Schuster.

Peterson, W. (1988) 'Some Connective Concepts in China in the Fourth to Second Centuries BCE', *Eranos Yearbook* 57: 201–34.

Plaskett, J. (2000) *Coincidences*, Hastings: Tamworth Press.

Polkinghorne, J. (1998) *Science and Theology: An Introduction*, London: SPCK.

Price, H. H. (1953) Review of C. G. Jung and W. Pauli, *Naturerklärung und Psyche*, in *Journal of the Society for Psychical Research* 37: 26–35.

Progoff, I. (1973) *Jung, Synchronicity, and Human Destiny*, New York: Julian Press.

Radin, D. (1997) *The Conscious Universe: The Scientific Truth of Psychic Phenomena*, New York: HarperCollins.

Redfield, J. (1994) *The Celestine Prophecy*, London: Bantam.

Ritsema, R. and Karcher, S. (trans.) (1994) *I Ching: The Classic Chinese Oracle of Change*, Shaftesbury: Element.

Rogers, C. (1967) *On Becoming a Person: A Therapist's View of Psychotherapy*, London: Constable.

Rose, S. (1997) 'Transforming the World: An Examination of the Roles Played by Spirituality and Healing in the New Age Movement', Unpublished Ph.D. thesis, Lancaster University.

Ross, W. D. (ed.) (1928) *The Works of Aristotle*, vol. 8, 2nd edn, Oxford: The Clarendon Press.

Rowland, S. (1999) *C. G. Jung and Literary Theory*, London: Macmillan.

Rowland, S. (2002) *Jung: A Feminist Revision*, Cambridge: Polity Press.

Rubin, L. and Honorton, C. (1971) 'Separating the Yins from the Yangs: An Experiment with the *I Ching*', *Journal of Parapsychology* 35: 313–14.

Samuels, A. (1985) *Jung and the Post-Jungians*, London: Routledge.

Samuels, A. (1993) *The Political Psyche*, London and New York: Routledge.

Samuels, A. (2001) *Politics on the Couch: Citizenship and the Internal Life*, London: Profile Books.

Samuels, A., Shorter, B. and Plaut, F. (1986) *A Critical Dictionary of Jungian Analysis*, London and New York: Routledge & Kegan Paul.

Sandner, D. and Wong, S. (eds) (1997) *The Sacred Heritage: The Influence of Shamanism on Analytical Psychology*, London and New York: Routledge.

Schlamm, L. (2000) 'C. G. Jung, Mystical Experience and Inflation', *Harvest: Journal for Jungian Studies* 46, no. 2: 108–28.

Schlamm, L. (2001) 'Ken Wilber's Spectrum Model: Identifying Alternative Soteriological perspectives', *Religion* 31, no. 1: 19–39.

Segal, R. (1999a) 'Rationalist and Romantic Approaches to Religion and Modernity', *Journal of Analytical Psychology*, vol. 44, 547–60.

Segal, R. (1999b) *Theorizing about Myth*, Amherst: University of Massachusetts Press.

Segal, R. A. (ed.) (1992) *The Gnostic Jung*, Princeton, N.J.: Princeton University Press; London: Routledge.

Shamdasani, S. (1990) 'A Woman Called Frank', *Spring: Journal of Archetype and Culture* 50: 26–56.

Shamdasani, S. (1993) 'Automatic Writing and the Discovery of the Unconscious', *Spring: Journal of Archetype and Culture* 54: 100–31.

Shamdasani, S. (1994) 'Encountering Hélène: Théodore Flournoy and the Genesis of Subliminal Psychology', Introduction to T. Flournoy, *From India to the Planet Mars: A Case of Multiple Personality with Imaginary Languages* (1899), ed. S. Shamdasani, with foreword by C. G. Jung and commentary by Mireille Cifali, trans. D. Vermilye, Princeton, N.J.: Princeton University Press.

Shamdasani, S. (1995) 'Memories, Dreams, Omissions', *Spring: Journal of Archetype and Culture* 57: 115–37.

Shamdasani, S. (1998) *Cult Fictions: C. G. Jung and the Founding of Analytical Psychology*, London and New York: Routledge.

Shamdasani, S. (2003) *Jung and the Making of Modern Psychology: The Dream of a Science*, Cambridge: Cambridge University Press.

Shamdasani, S. (ed.) (1996) 'Introduction' to C. G. Jung, *The Psychology of Kundalini Yoga: Notes of the Seminar given in 1932*, Princeton, N.J.: Princeton University Press; London: Routledge.

Sheldrake, R. (1981) *A New Science of Life: The Hypothesis of Formative Causation*, London: Blond & Briggs.

Shorter, B. (1996) *Susceptible to the Sacred: The Psychological Experience of Ritual*, London and New York: Routledge.

Silverman, D. (ed.) (1997) *Qualitative Research: Theory, Method and Practice*, London: Sage.

Smart, R. N. (1997) *Dimensions of the Sacred*, London: Fontana.

Smith, M. (1997) *Jung and Shamanism in Dialogue: Retrieving the Soul/Retrieving the Sacred*, New York: Paulist Press.

Stanton, M. (1992) 'Otto Gross's Case Histories: Jung, Stekel, and the Pathologization of Protest', in R. K. Papadopoulos (ed.) *Carl Gustav Jung: Critical Assessments*, vol. 1, *Jung and His Method in Context*, London and New York: Routledge.

Starhawk [Miriam Simos] (1979) *The Spiral Dance: A Rebirth of the Ancient Religion of the Great Goddess*, New York: HarperCollins.

Stein, M. (1985) *Jung's Treatment of Christianity: The Psychology of a Religious Tradition*, Wilmette, Ill.: Chiron.

Stewart, I. (1990) *Does God Play Dice? The New Mathematics of Chaos*, London: Penguin.

Tacey, D. (1997a) 'Jung in the Academy: Devotions and Resistances', *Journal of Analytical Psychology* 42, no. 2: 269–83.

Tacey, D. (1997b) 'Reply to Responses', *Journal of Analytical Psychology* 42, no. 2: 313–16.

Tacey, D. (1999) 'Why Jung Would Doubt the New Age', in S. Greenberg (ed.) *Therapy on the Couch: A Shrinking Future*, London: Camden Press.

Tacey, D. (2001) *Jung and the New Age*, Hove and Philadelphia (Pa.): Brunner-Routledge.

Tacey, D. (2003) *The Spirituality Revolution: The Emergence of Contemporary Spirituality*, Sydney: HarperCollins.

Tambiah, S. (1990) *Magic, Science, Religion, and the Scope of Rationality*, Cambridge: Cambridge University Press.

Teilhard de Chardin, P. (1959) *The Phenomenon of Man*, New York: Harper & Row.

Thalbourne, M. A., Delin, P. S., Barlow, J. A. and Steen, D. M. (1992–3) 'A Further Attempt to Separate the Yins from the Yangs: A Replication of the Rubin–Honorton Experiment with the *I CHING*', *European Journal of Parapsychology* 9: 12–23.

Ulanov, A. (1997) 'Teaching Jung in a Theological Seminary and a Graduate School of Religion: A Response to David Tacey', *Journal of Analytical Psychology* 42, no. 2: 303–11.

Vaughan, A. (1979) *Incredible Coincidence: The Baffling World of Synchronicity*, New York: Harper & Row; Ballantine, 1989.

von Franz, M.-L. (1974) *Number and Time: Reflections Leading Towards a Unification of Psychology and Physics*, trans. A. Dykes, London: Rider & Company.

von Franz, M.-L. (1980) *On Divination and Synchronicity: The Psychology of Meaningful Chance*, Toronto: Inner City Books.

von Franz, M.-L. (1987) *On Dreams and Death: A Jungian Interpretation*, trans. E. X. Kennedy and V. Brooks, Boston and London: Shambhala.

von Franz, M.-L. (1992) *Psyche and Matter*, Boston and London: Shambhala.

Voogd, S. de (1984) 'Fantasy versus Fiction: Jung's Kantianism Appraised', in R. K. Papadopoulos and G. S. Saayman (eds) *Jung in Modern Perspective*, Hounslow: Wildwood House.

Watt, C. (1990–1) 'Psychology and Coincidences', *European Journal of Parapsychology* 8: 66–84.

Wehr, D. (1987) *Jung and Feminism: Liberating Archetypes*, Boston, Mass.: Beacon.

Weinstein, F. and Platt, G. (1973) *The Wish To Be Free*, Berkeley, Calif.: University of California Press.

Wharton, B. (1986) 'Deintegration and Two Synchronistic Events', *Journal of Analytical Psychology* 31, no. 3: 281–5.

White, A. D. (1895) *A History of the Warfare of Science with Theology in Christendom*, New York: D. Appleton.

Wilber, K. (1998) *The Marriage of Sense and Soul: Integrating Science and Religion*, New York: Random House.

Wilhelm, R. (trans.) (1950) *The I Ching or Book of Changes*, rendered into English by C. F. Baynes, New York: Bollingen; London: Routledge & Kegan Paul, 1951.

Williams, M. (1957) 'An Example of Synchronicity', *Journal of Analytical Psychology* 2, no. 1: 93–5.

Williams, M. (1963a) 'The Indivisibility of the Personal and Collective Unconscious', *Journal of Analytical Psychology* 8, no. 1: 45–50.

Williams, M. (1963b) 'The Poltergeist Man', *Journal of Analytical Psychology* 8, no. 2: 123–44.

Wuthnow, R. (1985) 'The Cultural Context of Contemporary Religious Movements', in T. Robbins, W. Shepherd and J. McBride (eds) *Cults, Culture, and the Law*, Chico, Calif.: Scholars Press.

York, M. (1995) *The Emerging Network: A Sociology of the New Age and Neo-pagan Movements*, Lanham, Md.: Rowman & Littlefield Publishers Inc.

Young-Eisendrath, P. (1997) 'Gender and Contrasexuality: Jung's Contribution and Beyond', in P. Young-Eisendrath and T. Dawson (eds) *The Cambridge Companion to Jung*, Cambridge: Cambridge University Press.

Young-Eisendrath, P. and Dawson, T. (eds) (1997) *The Cambridge Companion to Jung*, Cambridge: Cambridge University Press.

Young-Eisendrath, P. and Miller, M. (eds) (2000) *The Psychology of Mature Spirituality: Integrity, Wisdom, Transcendence*, London and Philadelphia (Pa.): Routledge.

Zabriskie, B. (1995) 'Jung and Pauli: A Subtle Asymmetry', *Journal of Analytical Psychology* 40, no. 4: 531–53.

Zumstein-Preiswerk, S. (1975) *C. G. Jungs Medium: Die Geschichte der Helly Preiswerk*, München: Kindler.

Zusne, L. and Jones, W. H. (1989) *Anomalistic Psychology: A Study of Magical Thinking*, 2nd edn, Hillsdale N.J.: Lawrence Erlbaum Associates.

Index